Going Ballistic!

Going Ballistic!

Inverness Caledonian Thistle FC:
the first decade, 1994-5 to 2003-4

Ian S Broadfoot

Published by Inverness Thistle and Caledonian F.C. plc, Caledonian Stadium, Stadium Road, East Longman, Inverness IV1 1FF

A catalogue record for this book is available from the British Library.

ISBN 0-9531240-1-0

Edited and designed by Sport and Leisure Books Limited

Cover design Zoran Jevtic

Printed by Highland Printers, Inverness

CONTENTS

ACKNOWLEDGEMENTS

Many people have contributed directly or indirectly to this book, and grateful thanks are due to them all. Three people top the list – club football secretary Jim Falconer, programme editor Bryan Munro and Radio Highland journalist Charles Bannerman. Jim has been a constant source of information and has always been at the end of the telephone when required. He also took time to read an early draft for glaring errors. Bryan and I have worked closely over the years and he assisted with many aspects of the book, particularly the assembly of photographs. Charles has been of immense help since the project started – by his early encouragement and later with advice on the final drafts. His experience and advice arising from *Against All Odds* helped avoid numerous pitfalls. Thanks also to Peter MacCallum, who has been my computer guru for many years and constant companion at matches all over Scotland. Charlie Christie also assisted by checking sections of the book. Brian Wingrove carefully read the whole book and corrected a number of facts using his own records and knowledge – quite a feat for a Belgian based in deepest England!

I was greatly helped in the assembly of information by the newspaper cuttings collected by Alan Stewart, George MacRae, Gordon Williams and Trevor Larkin. Trevor was also of major assistance with facts from the pre-merger days. Former *Inverness Courier* Sports Editor David Beck has always been keen to assist, particularly by making available the *Courier* archives. Similarly, Paul Chalk of the *Highland News* has been a source of encouragement and help. Direct club involvement has centred on chairman Ken Mackie and director Ian MacDonald. The business end of the project was handled by them, which left me to concentrate on writing. Thanks also to the Club's office staff – particularly Liz Duncan and Lisa MacKenzie who shared with me the task of preparing and distributing the team lines on match days. Morven Reid has also been a great help with the latter stages of the book's production and the preparations for its launch and sale.

I am immensely grateful to photographers Gordon Gillespie, Trevor Martin and Ken MacPherson for their major contribution to the book – all gave me free rein to use their work and provided valuable advice. Thanks also for photographic help to Sandy McCook and Joanna Fraser of the *Press & Journal* and to Brian Stewart, Phil Downie and Clive Grewcock.

The photograph of Sergei Baltacha is reproduced by kind permission of The Coca-Cola Company. Authors who have kindly allowed me to quote from their work are Bob Crampsey, Bill McAllister and Alex Main. Thanks also to Emily Cooke of Orion Publishing and Ian Rankin for permission to quote from *The Falls*. Jan Murdoch, Ian Davidson and David Thomson of the SFL provided useful information, as did John Watson of the Schools FA. Thanks also to the many journalists who have given permission to quote from newspaper articles. The headline 'Super Caley Go Ballistic Celtic Are Atrocious' is taken from an article by Gary Ralston in *The Sun*, 9 February 2002 (copyright NI Syndication, London).

My wife Jess has put up with a great deal through my football involvement and I am grateful for her patience and support. Daughters Julie and Lesley have also supported the cause in different ways. Lesley follows the team closely and has joined me at many games. Julie has no interest in football, but did sit through one match at Hampden and has carefully read the final draft for spelling and grammatical errors. The other member of the 'punctuation police' was my brother Alan, who has shared many a football match with me in Britain and abroad, from the highest to the lowest levels. Thanks to them all for their help and interest in the project.

Despite all the checks I have no doubt that people have been omitted and errors will have crept in. I take full responsibility for any mistakes, and apologise in advance to those whose contribution to the club's history has not been recorded.

Ian S Broadfoot

ABOUT THE AUTHOR

Ian Broadfoot is a chartered surveyor who lives and works in Inverness. Ian's football interest started at a very early age when he was taken to watch Queen's Park and this sparked a lifelong love of the 'beautiful game'. After moving with his family to Inverness in 1984 he followed the fortunes of all local teams. When the Scottish League came to town, Ian became firmly attached to Caledonian Thistle. He has been a member of the club's management committee since June 1995 and was appointed official club historian in 1997.

PREFACE

In May 1995 director Dougie Riach invited me to join the club's Management Committee, I am grateful he asked and very glad I accepted. Dougie thus started a chain of events that led to this book. A programme collection was started on behalf of the club, then a report on each match was included in the programme binders. Recording players' appearances and goals followed, then increased computer literacy led to records becoming more extensive. Rather than relying on others, I started writing match reports and these became used by the website and Matchday Programme. All this led to the official role of club historian. For many years reports and records have been collated into a booklet for internal club circulation, with copies also going to Inverness Library and the press. A natural progression of this was to join it all together in a book at the end of the club's first remarkable decade.

After moving to Inverness in 1984 I followed local football but it proved impossible to support just one team. I opted to watch Thistle, Caledonian and Clach, but with no particular allegiance. When the unified club was formed, the problem was solved. I bought season ticket number six for 1994-5. After a year as a loyal supporter, I took a ringside seat and watched at close hand as the story unfolded. *Going Ballistic!* necessarily covers some of the events already chronicled in Charles Bannerman's 1997 book *Against All Odds*. It focussed on the detail of the amalgamation and took the story up to the end of 1996-7. *Going Ballistic!* looks at the story from a slightly different angle and takes it through to the end of 2003-4. The two books should be seen as complementary.

A word or two about facts and statistics. The 'Match Results' generally cover all senior games, local cup competitions, pre-season friendlies and other matches involving first-team players. 'Appearances and Goals' totals only include matches in the Scottish League, Scottish Cup, League Cup and Challenge Cup. Attendances are a source of many problems and potential inaccuracies. In most cases the total quoted is the one announced on the day or noted in the newspapers. Figures published in the annual *Scottish League Reviews* can vary from the original figures, but normally the differences are minor. Two Celtic Park matches illustrate the problem. After the CIS Cup tie in October 2002 a crowd of 34,592 was reported but Scottish League officials kindly traced Celtic's official return for the match, and it gave 32,122. I have adopted this figure. The *Scottish Football League Review* records the February 2000 Scottish Cup tie total as 40,018 but 34,389 was announced on the night. Neither the SFA nor Celtic can solve this puzzle, but it is thought that the higher total was for tickets sold prior to the earlier postponed match rather than the actual attendance. The lower figure has been adopted and is still a club record.

This is first and foremost a football book but it is also a tale of travel and adventure. Travel throughout Scotland and Scottish Cup adventures which sent the club name reverberating around the world. In the early days of Third Division fare, future events were unthinkable – beating Celtic twice, reaching two Scottish Cup semi-finals and achieving the dizzy heights of the SPL were the stuff of only the most optimistic dreams. It all really did happen, and Inverness is now firmly on the national football map. The story of the decade should have finished on 15 May 2004 when the First Division title was won on a day of great excitement; but the drama was not over. The team had earned promotion to the SPL but it took weeks of move and counter-move, partly behind the scenes but mainly amidst a blaze of publicity, before promotion was achieved. The SPL machinations delayed the completion of this book but it was essential to await the end of the saga.

I hope that this book will be a platform for future club historians to continue the work and that generations to come will be as lucky as we have been.

Ian S Broadfoot

FOREWORD

It seems incredible that it is only ten years since the birth of Inverness Caledonian Thistle FC. I, of course, was not a part of the organisation until some six years after its formation and can only look back at the birthing pains from a distance and from second hand. From all I have read and heard, these were difficult times and much credit is due to those who brought the club into existence.

It, perhaps, is best not to look back on the problems but to celebrate the successes, of which there have been many. The club is still a small player in Scottish Football and has a short history when compared with many of the leading Scottish clubs. It has, however, in its short history achieved three promotions moving from the Scottish Football League Third Division to the Bank of Scotland Premierleague, won the Bell's Challenge Cup and reached the semi-finals of the Tennent's Scottish Cup in successive years. Many longer-standing clubs in Scotland would be proud to have such a record. It could be said that the club punches above its weight and I am sure Celtic and other clubs would testify to this. From this, it should be clear to Scotland that football of the highest order exists in the Highlands.

Ian Broadfoot has kept meticulous records of the Club's achievements, successes, failures and problems, and he has to be congratulated on turning his hard work and record-keeping into this volume, which sets out the highs and lows of ten years of progress. I know that journalists and others frequently turn to Ian when they require information on the club's record and he never fails them. Well done, Ian, and thank you for all your efforts.

Here's to the next ten years of Inverness Caledonian Thistle FC successes.

Ken Mackie
Chairman of Inverness Caledonian Thistle FC

CHAPTER I

THREE TIMES AROUND THE WORLD

(photo: the author)

The far-travelled Inverness Caledonian Thistle FC team coach and Rapsons' Tony Fraser who has driven it for ten years.

Ten seasons, 100 squad players, four chairmen, three managers, three promotions, two championships, two Tennent's Scottish Cup semi-final appearances, one Bell's Cup win, two Scottish Cup wins over Celtic and 76,000 miles of travel, the equivalent of three circuits of the world. The first ten years of Inverness Caledonian Thistle saw more headlines, more travel, more achievements and more action than many other clubs can boast in decades. Beating Celtic 3-1 at Celtic Park on 8 February 2000 put the club firmly on the world football map and this, along with more giant killing in 2002, 2003 and 2004, earned a fearsome cup reputation. From the Highland League to the top of the Scottish Football League in ten years is the stuff of fairytales, but this one came true. John Robertson's team beat St Johnstone 3-1 on the last day of 2003-4 to clinch the First Division championship and win the right to join the Scottish Premier League. The SPL's stadium criteria could only be met by a groundshare agreement with Aberdeen but even this did not guarantee promotion. It took two ballots, three weeks of chaos and a national backlash against the SPL before it was finally achieved.

The birth of Caledonian Thistle FC (Inverness was added at the start of 1996-7) was a painful one. The merger of Inverness Thistle and Caledonian, and a 1993 joint application for Scottish Football League membership, made perfect sense on paper but the human dimension led to almost insurmountable problems. The trials and tribulations of the amalgamation process should be studied by any clubs considering the same route. They may quickly decide that the pain is not worth the gain. In the case of Inverness it has certainly been worth it, but it took a while before matters completely settled down. Even after ten years there are some disaffected former Thistle and Caledonian fans who have no interest in the unified club, but they are the exception. The vast majority of their fellow Caley and Jags fans have embraced the reality and been rewarded with success beyond their wildest dreams. At this point it should be noted that to understand Scottish football you have to be a man or woman of letters. Scottish Football League is usually shortened to SFL, the Scottish Premier League to SPL and the Scottish Football Association to SFA. When Caley Thistle joined the SFL it ran all the leagues and the SFA governed Scottish football. In August 1998 the SPL came along to add another league tier. This did not change the role of the SFA, but it made the league set-up rather more complicated.

Four chairmen steered the club through its first decade. Former Inverness Thistle supremo John 'Jock' McDonald was invited at an early stage to be chairman-designate and he duly took office once the way forward was secure. His contacts in the Scottish game and long experience helped to smooth the path to the big time, but he had a tough start. Strong opposition to the merger had to be overcome and former rivals drawn together. He weathered many a storm, saw the club through to the end of its first season, then passed the baton to director Dougie McGilvray. McGilvray was already deeply involved with the challenge of building a new stadium and this was the prime focus as he began his term of office. With planning permission in place, it was all about finance – the realisation of assets and the attraction of grants. The package fell into place after much anguish: the opening of Caledonian Stadium in November 1996 was a tribute to McGilvray's drive and determination.

When McGilvray handed over to Tulloch PLC chairman David Sutherland in January 2000, the club had reached the First Division but there was a major economic problem to solve. The much-publicised Scottish Cup run of 1999-2000 saved the club from bankruptcy and Sutherland set out to stabilise finances for the future. He masterminded the creation of a charitable trust which took ownership of the stadium and, at a stroke, wiped out the escalating debt, by then in the region of £2.6m. At his side, during these financial trials and tribulations, was finance director Ken Mackie, who succeeded to the office of chairman at the start of 2002-3. His first challenge was to steer through a £500,000 investment package which resulted in Sutherland's company Tulloch taking a major share in the club. Mackie's steady hand ensured careful control of finances to the end of the decade, helped by runs to the Scottish Cup semi-final in successive seasons. The momentous capture of the First Division championship in May 2004 led to a dilemma of massive proportions. It ended with a formal application to join the SPL and a ground-share agreement with Aberdeen.

When the first manager Sergei Baltacha sent out his team to play East Stirling on 9 August 1994, it was very much a pioneering mission. It was impossible to tell how things would develop on and off the park and there was still a great deal of bitterness in the air. The merger between Inverness Thistle and Caledonian was a reality, and the team was on the park, but challenges against the transfer of the assets of both clubs threatened the whole basis of the venture. By the time Steve Paterson took over on 24 May 1995 planning permission had been granted for the new Caledonian Stadium, most issues had been resolved and the atmosphere had improved dramatically. Increased investment gave Paterson a better chance of progress than his predecessor. His budget was still low by the standards of top teams, but he bought well and took the team steadily up to the First Division. Despite his successes in the league, he will be remembered more for Scottish Cup giant-killing exploits against Celtic and Hearts, with the February 2000 Celtic win particularly proving to be a watershed. The long name of Inverness Caledonian Thistle had been the subject of much debate and criticism, but overnight it became a world-recognised brand. When John Robertson succeeded to the managerial hot-seat on Boxing Day 2002 he faced a difficult task – instead of replacing a sacked manager and inheriting a side needing a boost, Robertson had to keep the momentum of success rolling. With Donald Park at his side, the partnership took things to an even higher level. In 17 months they achieved back-to-back Scottish Cup semi-final appearances, won the Bell's Cup, then crowned it all by beating Clyde to the First Division championship in a dramatic 2003-4 finale. To take the club into the SPL in its tenth anniversary year was quite simply amazing.

It had taken ten years for the unified club to reach the top flight – but the story really started in 1885.

CHAPTER 2

INVERNESS FOOTBALL

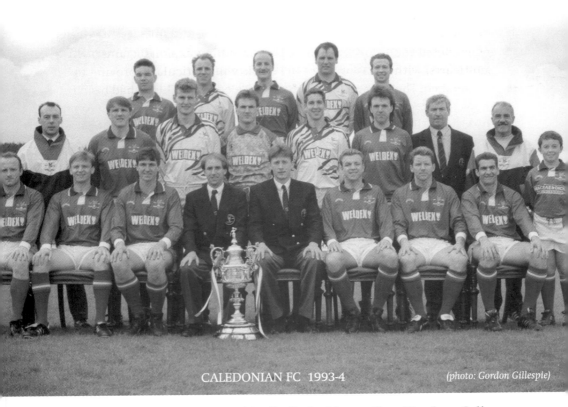

CALEDONIAN FC 1993-4   *(photo: Gordon Gillespie)*

(*Back*) Dave Brennan, David Caldwell, Kevin Mann, Alan Hercher, Colin Mitchell

(*Middle*) John King (physio), Mike Noble, Colin Sinclair, Robin Gray, Allan Smart, Billy Skinner, Tommy Cumming (kit man), Alex Young (trainer)

(*Front*) Wilson Robertson, Danny MacDonald, Mike Andrew (captain), Neil MacKintosh (assistant manager), Sergei Baltacha (manager), Mark McAllister, Charlie Christie, Martin Lisle, (ball boy) Kevin McLeod

Football in Inverness changed out of all recognition in 1994. For over 100 years it revolved around the Highland League, local rivalries and occasional giant-killing in the Scottish Cup. The elevation of Caledonian Thistle to the Scottish League moved it to a different level. Allegiances were sorely tested as Thistle and Caledonian followers either walked away or, in most cases, adopted the new club with its promise of regular national football. Clach fans watched from the sidelines as the drama of amalgamation unfolded and their team took on the new role of Inverness's sole representative in the Highland League.

Inverness Thistle and Caledonian played their first games in 1885 and were followed a year later by Clachnacuddin and Citadel. These clubs were founder members of the Highland League in 1893, along with Union, Ross County, Forres Mechanics and a team representing the Cameron Highlanders. There is evidence of a Crown team playing football in the mid-1870s, but it may have concentrated on the oval ball with the round ball as a sideline. A team called Northern Counties also existed in 1884, but details are sketchy. What we know for certain is that only three sides survived through to the latter part of the twentieth century and a fourth, Citadel, lasted until 1937.

When the Great War stopped play, the Highland League comprised nine teams and by World War Two it had grown to 15. For the four immediate post-war years the number increased to 16 but then went down again to 15. Brora Rangers brought it back to an even 16 in 1963-4 and there it stood until Fort William (1985-6) and Cove Rangers (1986-7) took the league to its peak of 18. The departure of Caledonian, Thistle and Ross County to the Scottish League in 1994-5 was a blow from which the Highland League has never fully recovered. The problem grew worse when Peterhead and Elgin City decamped to the senior ranks in 2000. Two of the gaps have been filled by Wick Academy and Inverurie Locos and the league now comprises a rather uneven 15 teams. This odd number led Caley Thistle to come up with a novel way to keep their reserves active in 2003-4 by arranging to play a friendly each week against the 'free' side.

The formation of the Highland League in 1893 provided regular competition for northern teams but a prime target has always been the Scottish Cup. The four teams that reach the semi-final stage of the North Qualifying Cup automatically enter the first round draw of the national competition. The dream is to reach the third round, when the big boys join the fray. The Scottish Cup has always held out the hope of a financial bonanza and, until 1994, it was the only chance for Inverness fans to watch Scottish League sides in competitive action on their home turf. It is not always a money-spinner, as Clach discovered to their cost in 2000-1. An away trip to Stranraer in the second round (after a bye in the first round) led to a 520-mile round trip, an expensive overnight stay and a 1-0 defeat. Splitting the proceeds of a 351 gate did little to dent the total bill, but the Clachnacuddin Supporters' Club came up trumps and funded both the team's travel and accommodation costs. The upside of the cup is a rare away draw against a top team and a good payday. When Thistle drew Celtic away in 1984-5 they earned enough to carry out urgent repairs to the boundary wall at Kingsmills Park – something they were struggling to afford. A home match against a Premier side is clearly also a major event even if less of a payday – Caley's 1983-4 home match with Rangers certainly caused great excitement in Inverness and drew a capacity crowd. Heavy defeats for the local sides in both these games were merely minor irritations!

Clachnacuddin

Although Thistle won the inaugural championship in 1893-4, Clach soon dominated the Inverness scene with a run of four titles from 1902-3 to 1905-6. In total they won 10 of the 21 championships prior to the 1914 break. The 1920s were a golden period for Clach as they again repeated the feat of four successive league titles (1920-1 to 1923-4) as well as clinching the North Cup three times and the Inverness Cup five times. Rod Clyne's Clach centenary book *The Lilywhites* compares the early 1920s side with the one he first watched in the late 1940s. The 1920s side is described as the 'Kings of the North' and a 1948 correspondent to the *Football Times & Highland News*, 'Threepenny Man', stated that few of the players of the 'present' would be able to hold their own with the team from the1920s – a cry heard by fans of each succeeding generation, misty-eyed with nostalgia.

Clach's 'grand old man of football', George B Rodgers, was team manager in 1947-8 when they swept the board – they won the League Championship,

League Cup, North Qualifying Cup and the Inverness Charity Cup. Rodgers (perhaps a little biased) hailed his side as 'the finest team ever witnessed in North football.' Rod Clyne agreed but 'Threepenny Man' clearly did not. The spell between 1946-7 and 1953-4 did not quite reach the heights of the 1920s for Clach (apart from the purple patch in 1947-8) but it did bring one league title, five North Cup victories and two each in the League Cup and the Inverness Cup.

The last fifty years have been lean ones for Clach, punctuated by occasional highlights such as the 1974-5 successes in the League and Qualifying Cup. The closing years of the twentieth century were to prove hard: bankruptcy was a distinct possibility. One bright spot was the 1981-2 clinching of the League Cup for the first time in thirty years. Brora were beaten 2-1, with both goals coming from Clach's most famous player in the modern era – Duncan Shearer. Fort William-born Shearer won seven Scottish caps during a successful top-level career which included spells at Chelsea, Huddersfield, Swindon, Blackburn and Aberdeen, where he achieved legendary status. In September 1997 he joined Inverness Caledonian Thistle as a player and eventually became assistant to manager Steve Paterson. 1990 was a year of trauma for Clach and it nearly ended in liquidation. Economic disaster was prevented at the eleventh hour by the intervention of a local consortium and the club was reconstituted as Clachnacuddin (1990) Ltd. Clach were originally part of the Inverness amalgamation discussions in 1993 but decided to retain their independence. Many of the polarisation difficulties could possibly have been avoided if Clach had remained part of the merger, but this can only be speculation. The unified club might well have been seen as more of a well-rounded Inverness venture rather than a straight amalgamation. It might also have been acceptable to adopt the name Inverness FC and avoid the wrangling that led to the current tongue-twister.

Economic difficulties were, however, not over and in 1996 Clach nearly decamped to Dingwall and a ground-share arrangement with Ross County. Caley Thistle chairman Dougie McGilvray popped up at the last minute to save the day and keep Clach in Inverness. A Caley Thistle-led group purchased Grant Street Park in November 1996 and leased it back to Clach. In December 2000 ownership passed to the Inverness Common Good Fund and Clach's future was secured when they signed a 21-year lease. Close ties with Caley Thistle developed following the 1996 purchase. The aim was to see players move in both directions but in reality it was all one-way. Young players went on loan to Clach and released players joined permanently. 2003-4 saw a resurgence in Clach's fortunes on the park with the clinching of the Highland League Championship after a 2-year gap and the capture of the Highland League Cup. As he celebrated these successes, chairman David Dowling was glad that Clach had withdrawn from the merger that produced Caledonian Thistle: 'Clach would have been a very small part of a merger and ultimately would have been forgotten.'

Citadel

The name of Citadel is largely unknown to current fans, but Inverness Citadel FC was a strong force in North football for most of its 50-year existence. Nothing remains of this club except memories and the preserved clock tower on the site of Cromwell's fort in the Harbour area of Inverness which gave the club its name. Citadel were known politely as the Maroons, but their ground's proximity to the slaughterhouse led to the less complimentary 'Sheep Bags'. Achievements were few but they did have an excellent 1931-2 when the North Cup, Qualifying Cup and Inverness Cup were all captured. That season Citadel also came third in the league, two points behind winners Elgin City. The Qualifying Cup success was particularly significant as it was the first time it had been played as North and South sections – previously it was an all-Scotland affair. The 4-1 victory came at Edinburgh's Easter Road on 12 December 1931 in the second replay against Murrayfield Amateurs, after two drawn games. Citadel complained bitterly about the Edinburgh location of the third match and had argued for a truly neutral ground. This was all forgotten as they proudly carried the trophy back to Inverness.

Citadel's one and only league triumph was in 1908-9 when they also won the North Cup. They took part in the Scottish Cup six times in the 1920s and early 1930s with limited success. The best run was in 1921-2 when they beat Clackmannan 5-3 away in the first round, then were drawn at home against Queen of the South. This tie, on 11 February 1922, marked the official opening of Shore Street Park. Citadel achieved a 2-2 draw in front of 3000 spectators; Queens won the replay 2-1.

George Campbell's 1990 book *Inverness Citadel Football Club* puts the club's eventual demise down to increased travel costs after World War One, when teams from the east joined the league, and the 1920s growth in Inverness housing around the grounds of the other clubs. Citadel withdrew from the Highland League in 1935, but continued for two more seasons, playing friendlies and taking part in local cups. In a last flurry they beat Thistle 2-0 to take the Inverness Charity Cup in 1936-7, then two months later the club was no more. The ground was absorbed into the expanding Longman Aerodrome and is now lost in an industrial estate.

Inverness Thistle

The first 100 years of Inverness Thistle were chronicled in the club publication *The Hub of the Hill*, which was distributed to those attending the centenary dinner in November 1985. Thistle were founded in 1885 by a Diriebught miller, Mr Smith, four of whose sons played in the first team. Rival Inverness club Crown was quickly absorbed and Thistle won the inaugural Highland League Championship in 1893-4. Further championship wins were thin on the ground with only four more up to World War Two. This included 1935-6 which was part of a good 1930s spell – three North Cup wins, five in the Inverness Cup and the 1932-3 Qualifying Cup.

In 1955-6 Thistle won the Scottish North Cup and the star of the era was prolific goalscorer Andy 'Joopie' Mitchell, who netted 52 league and 25 cup goals that season. This included four in an 11-0 win over Nairn on 18 February 1956 – a record score at the time. The 1960s proved to be a lean decade but there was a memorable trip in January 1964 to play Bobby Flavell's Ayr United in the Scottish Cup. Memories of a home defeat to Caley in 1954-5 caused Ayr to be wary and, although it was close, Ayr eventually won 3-2. In 1972-3 Thistle went back to Ayr, now managed by future Scotland manager Ally McLeod, but it ended in a 3-0 defeat. Thistle were going through a purple patch at this time, with back-to-back league championships in 1971-2 and 1972-3. The early 1970s exploits led to an unsuccessful application to join the Scottish League.

Thistle celebrated their 1984-5 centenary year with a famous Scottish Cup run. It started with a home second round tie against Edinburgh's Spartans on 5 January and a 1-1 draw. The replay took place a week later but, despite the loss of home advantage, Thistle won 2-1. This brought top-flight Kilmarnock to Kingsmills on 9 February and an historic match in front of a 2000 crowd. Goals from Dave Milroy, Gordon Hay and Brian

Fraser ensured an emphatic 3-0 victory, which set off a storm of anger in the Killie travelling support directed at manager Eddie Morrison. Thistle's reward was a visit to Parkhead a week later, a good pay day, a football lesson and a 6-0 defeat. Despite the scoreline, it was a day to remember for the club. Three of the Thistle travelling squad were to become major players with Caley Thistle – goalkeeper Les Fridge, forward (turned goalkeeper) Jim Calder and recently-signed midfielder Charlie Christie, who was ineligible to play.

There was further success in the 1980s – what proved to be the club's final league championship in 1986-7 then, in 1987-8, the North Cup, League Cup and Inverness Cup were all won. Thistle also captured the North Qualifying Cup in 1988-9 by beating Caledonian 3-0 in a replay. By the time amalgamation took place Thistle's finances were precarious, but they did hold the major asset of Kingsmills Park. Its location in a prime residential area proved vital in the gathering of cash for the new stadium in 1996, although initially it was thought that Thistle were merely tenants of the Church of Scotland.

Caledonian

Caledonian's centenary history was recorded in Alex Main's 1986 publication *Caley All The Way* but the author correctly points out that a team under the Caledonian banner played a friendly match on 9 December 1885, a 1-0 victory over 'Rovers'. Their first competitive match took place towards the end of 1886, a 3-1 defeat at the hands of the Cameron Highlanders in the Inverness Charity Cup. Prior to World War One, Caledonian were flying high and won both the Highland League championship and the North of Scotland Cup seven times. They also won the Inverness Cup ten times. Between the wars there was some success in the North Cup (in particular four wins in the 1920s) and the Inverness Cup, but only two league titles. In 1920 the 2.8 acre site of Telford Street Park was purchased for £275 – a shrewd financial move which paid dividends some 75 years later. In the same era there were many Scottish Cup appearances, but very little was achieved.

The immediate post-war period included three successive Qualifying Cup triumphs (1948-9 to 1950-1) and in 1950-1 and 1951-2 both the League Championship and North Cup were won. In 1950 the stand at Telford Street Park was destroyed by fire and with it went irreplaceable records and memorabilia. The 1950s was a decade of numerous Scottish Cup matches against southern opposition and a growing national reputation. A trip to Aberdeen on 27 January 1951 ended in a 6-1 defeat but things improved the following season. In 1951-2 Caley drew 3-3 with Dundee United in round one at home but lost the replay 4-0. An amazing record was set by Andy 'Joopie' Mitchell in a Qualifying Cup match against Fraserburgh in 1952-3. Mitchell's 1955-6 record with Thistle is recorded above but before that he was a scoring machine for Caley. On 6 September 1952 Caley beat Fraserburgh 10-3 in a Qualifying Cup-tie, and 'Joopie' scored all ten goals. His partnership with Donnie 'Ginger' Mackenzie dominated Caley's goalscoring in this era.

In 1954-5 Caley reached the sixth round of the Scottish Cup after an epic run of seven matches, including two replays, but they went down 7-0 at home to Falkirk. 1956-7 saw another great run – this time to round five. Tarff Rovers, Babcock and Wilcox, St Cuthbert Wanderers and Cowdenbeath were all beaten before Raith Rovers came to town and won 3-2. Caley's hero was 'Ginger' MacKenzie who scored 10 goals in the cup run. With Elgin dominating north football in the 1960s, Caledonian managed just one league title but they did win the Qualifying Cup four times. Scottish Cup exploits in the 1960s included a 3-0 win over East Stirling in the 1961-2 second round which earned an away tie against Third Lanark. Thirds comprehensively won 6-1. In 1964-5 a 2-1 win against Raith Rovers in the preliminary round resulted in Third Lanark coming north. This time Thirds won 5-1.

The 1970s were more successful with two league championships and three wins each in the North Cup and Highland League Cup. There was one Qualifying Cup win – a 4-2 defeat of Elgin in 1971-2. The hero of this match was 16-year-old Donald Park who scored twice. Park went on to a very successful senior career including two spells at Hearts and one with Partick Thistle before moving into a coaching role. The wheel turned full circle when he came to Caley Thistle in January 2003 as number two to John Robertson. A 1978-9 pre-season friendly against Rangers at Telford Street led to the loss of star striker Billy Urquhart. Urquhart was named 'Man of the Match' and an hour after the match he was signed by Rangers' new manager John Greig. 'The Legend' spent three years at Ibrox before a spell at Wigan then a return to Caley. In 1994-5 he would make a temporary return to senior football with Caledonian Thistle.

The period from 1981-2 to 1983-4 was an excellent one, with a trio each of League flags and Qualifying Cup wins. There was also the very successful Scottish Cup run in 1983-4. Albion Rovers, Gala Fairydean and Stirling Albion were all defeated before the fourth round draw brought the mighty Rangers to town. Inverness buzzed with anticipation and long queues formed to buy tickets. There was to be no happy ending except for the club treasurer – Rangers won 6-0. In 1984-5 the score was repeated away to Hearts in the third round after beating Berwick 3-0 in a second replay. Caley won the league title for the last time in 1987-8 and also took the Q Cup. The 1989-90 Scottish Cup led to a dramatic third round win over Airdrie – 5-4 on penalties after two tied games – then a 6-2 defeat to Stirling Albion.

Caley's final Q Cup success was in 1991-2 and this led to another memorable run in the Scottish Cup. Stenhousemuir were beaten 4-1 and Clyde 3-1, then St Johnstone were drawn in the third round. Saints were 2-0 ahead at Telford Street but goals from Alan Hercher (a penalty) and Iain Polworth earned a replay in Perth. Well over 3000 fans travelled south and sent a clear message to the rest of Scotland – Inverness deserves to have a team in the Scottish League. St Johnstone's McDiarmid Park was packed and many Caley fans missed out on seeing their team go down 3-0. Caley celebrated their final season with a North Cup win, but future Caley Thistle manager Steve Paterson's Huntly won the league and would retain the title for the next four seasons.

The managers

Both Caley and Thistle attracted high-profile managers in the 1990s. In February 1991 former Dunfermline manager Jim Leishman was appointed to the Thistle post amidst a blaze of publicity. It all started well when Leishman masterminded a 13-game unbeaten run, but results in early 1991-2 were poor and he was soon under pressure. The flamboyant Fifer stayed amidst much media attention until Hogmanay 1991 when he left for Montrose: 'I had good times at Inverness before being head-hunted by Montrose.' Leishman was to become a familiar figure in Caley Thistle's travels. He took over as Livingston manager in 1995 and the inter-club rivalry was fierce until Livingston won the First Division title to reach the SPL in 2000-1.

While it was a surprise to most people that a manager of Jim Leishman's calibre should come to Inverness, the arrival of Sergei Baltacha at Caledonian in 1993 was even more of a shock. Ukraine-born Baltacha was a Soviet internationalist who had come to the UK and Ipswich Town in December 1988 before moving to St Johnstone in May 1990. Why did he choose to make the unlikely move north? 'I felt with my experience it was time to move into the coaching side of things and I was informed that Caledonian FC were looking for a manager. I knew they were held in high regard and were very ambitious so I decided to apply.' After a season in charge, the merger happened. He was the obvious man to take the unified club into the Scottish League.

Peterhead's 1988-9 league title marked a distinct shift of focus to the east, although Bobby Wilson's Ross County brought the title to Dingwall in 1990-1 and 1991-2. For a side that took the wooden spoon as recently as 1986-7, this was a dramatic upturn in fortunes. County's turn for the better would lead them to a place in the Scottish League from 1994-5.

The birth of the Highland League on 4 August 1893 had brought cohesion to North football and determined the pattern of the Inverness game. On 27 May 1993 a vote by the Scottish League to admit two additional teams would lead to a new football era in the town.

CHAPTER 3

THE ROAD TO THE SCOTTISH LEAGUE

INVERNESS THISTLE FC 1993-4   *(photo: Ken MacPherson)*

(*Back*) Robert Farquhar, Steven MacDonald, Darren MacLachlan, Jim Calder, Tommy MacDonald, Iain Polworth

(*Middle*) Sandy Rose (trainer), Scott MacLeod, Ian MacLean, Billy Wilson, Allan MacDonald, Steven Bremner, Gary Watt, Ian Manning (physio)

(*Front*) Calum MacLean, Colin MacLean, Dave Milroy (captain), Henrick Madej (manager), Kevin Sweeney, Martin Murphy, Martin Bell

GOING BALLISTIC!

The lack of Scottish League football in the Highlands had long been a source of justifiable paranoia for northern fans. Scottish Cup exploits had alerted southern clubs to the quality of the Highland League but geography, road conditions and weather were all used as excuses to avoid admitting a North club. The potential support in Inverness was clear to all and, when SFL membership was finally achieved, the number of Caledonian Thistle supporters was well in excess of those at other Third Division venues, with the notable exception of Dingwall.

The Scottish League was constituted in 1890 and over the years there have been a remarkable number of changes to the set-up. Despite this, no Highland team could find a way to join the exclusive club. There was a high measure of stability up to World War Two but since then any one of numerous reconstructions could have led to the admission of a North club. It took a long time to happen.

The aftermath of World War Two saw the league split into Divisions A, B and C with a number of reserve teams making up the 1946-7 total of 40 clubs. This total increased to 44 by 1948-9 and stayed largely intact until the first post-war reconstruction in 1955-6. Many clubs had found it difficult to field reserve sides and had given notice of their intention to abandon this luxury. To accommodate the smaller clubs a rather mathematically-challenging arrangement was put in place – a Division A of 18 and a Division B of 19 clubs. These were renamed Divisions 1 and 2 the following year. This remained the set-up for 20 years until the Premier Division (later the SPL) came along. In June 1960 the Scottish League considered inviting Clachnacuddin to join the Second Division. It is not possible to discover more of the background to this as it is not mentioned in the Clachnacuddin centenary history and the Scottish League minutes are not available. There is only a passing reference to it by Bob Crampsey in his centenary history of the Scottish Football League *The First 100 Years* where the author describes this as a chance missed by the Scottish League. He also makes the telling point that there were not many towns in Scotland with a population of 30,000 and a hinterland of nearly 80,000 looking for a chance to play in the national league. Over forty years on, Bob Crampsey recalls this as a suggestion mooted in Scottish League circles to take the Second Division up to an even 20 clubs, but it came to nothing.

THE ROAD TO THE SCOTTISH LEAGUE

In December 1964 the League Management Committee had proposed a reorganisation to take effect from 1965-6. The aim was to address the perennial problem of falling attendances and a three-division 14/12/12 arrangement was suggested. The formation was to be based on attendances and would have meant the introduction of a new club to make up the total of 38. In the event, the proposal was rejected and the unwieldy two-division grouping continued until the introduction of the Premier Division in 1975-6.

An 18/20 arrangement was in place for 1966-7, but it arrived in rather bizarre circumstances. East Stirlingshire amalgamated with junior club Clydebank in the spring of 1964, and for 1964-5 only played as East Stirlingshire (usually shortened to ES) Clydebank at Kilbowie Park, Clydebank. It is interesting to note that, at 26 characters, this long name matches exactly the much-criticised Inverness Caledonian Thistle. After one season (and legal proceedings) East Stirlingshire decamped back to Falkirk under their original name and, after a gap year in the junior ranks, Clydebank gained entry to the league as a separate entity. The end result was an 18/20 league arrangement in 1966-7 but it only lasted for one season. The mathematical purists were soon to be disappointed, as this proved to be Third Lanark's last year in existence. They disappeared under a cloud of economic scandal and it was back to the uneven 18/19 set-up.

1974 brought a real chance for Inverness to gain Scottish League representation. It was decided that the 19-club Division 2 would be increased back to its 1966-7 level of 20 and applications were invited. These came from Inverness Thistle, Ross County, Forres Mechanics, Elgin City, Gateshead United, Hawick Royal Albert and Edinburgh works team Ferranti Thistle. In March 1974 Ferranti Thistle were elected just one vote ahead of Inverness Thistle, despite Thistle chairman John 'Jock' McDonald having held pledges before the vote that should have ensured success. Ferranti Thistle were renamed Meadowbank Thistle to avoid commercialism – a rather dirty word in the days before financial realities led to sponsorship deals and TV money. Meadowbank Thistle moved in 1995 and adopted the name of its new locality Livingston. They were to become arch rivals of Inverness Caledonian Thistle.

Thistle's failure to be elected was mainly based on the distance teams would have to travel to Inverness and the single-lane status of the A9.

There would also, of course, have been the problem of Thistle travelling to away games every fortnight. Clubs from the south would have faced one or two trips north each season, but Thistle would have had the economic challenge of regular overnight stays in the south without large home gates to compensate. The nature of Kingsmills Park and the lack of car parking would always have been limiting factors and Thistle might have been forced to a frugal lower division existence or perhaps, as Charles Bannerman suggested in his 1997 book *Against All Odds*, a merger would eventually have become an economic necessity. Alternatively, they could have attracted the best of the local talent and thrived. Perhaps they would have moved to a modern stadium, but finance would have been a major stumbling block.

Meadowbank's place in the 18/20 arrangement only lasted one season before the first of many three-division combinations came to pass. The Premier Division was created from the start of 1975-6 and this led to a 10/14/14 split, which survived for 11 years. A rethink produced 12/12/14 for two seasons from 1986-7, then 10/14/14 from 1988-9. In 1986 there had been a proposal for a breakaway league and this could have led to an opportunity for new clubs to join. In the event this came to nothing. Remarkably the 'new' arrangement lasted just three seasons before 12/12/14 was reinstated from 1991-2 – the reason given was that this was an effort to make matches more entertaining. At this time Scottish League officials were well aware that Inverness clubs were interested in membership and, with the A9 now vastly improved, one major reason for past rejections had disappeared. Many felt that it was only a matter of time.

The early 1990s saw Berwick Rangers struggling to survive. The Inverness sides watched every move before Berwick solved their problems. A proposed breakaway Superleague in 1992 led to applications to join from all three Inverness clubs and even talk of amalgamation. It took until 1993 before the league door was opened to newcomers and there was a real chance of Scottish League football in Inverness. The Scottish League AGM on 27 May 1993 voted to bring in four divisions of ten from 1994-5 and to invite applications from clubs to fill the two vacant slots. The motion was passed by a two-thirds majority, but this was only achieved when Raith Rovers director Bob Paxton cast four votes in favour, allegedly against the wishes of his club.

Merger talks begin

When the possibility of reorganisation was first suggested, all three Inverness clubs expressed an interest and immediately the risk of a split vote became apparent. Inverness was the clear favourite, but opposition was expected from other Highland League teams, as well as Borders' sides such as Gala Fairydean and Gretna. Bill McAllister's Highland League centenary book *Highland Hundred* records talk of a united team as far back as 1935-6. Highland League President James Sinclair of Clach, backed by Caley's James Riggs, mooted a Clach and Caley merger to form Inverness Celtic – primarily to solve both clubs' financial problems. This would have left Inverness with two clubs – Celtic and Thistle. Peterhead's Magnus Gibson suggested one could join the Scottish League and the other remain in the Highland League. A similar suggestion materialised 60 years later when Caley Thistle wanted their reserve team to join the Highland League, but registration problems ensured that this idea never materialised.

Variations on the merger theme had been debated over many years, but the 1993 opportunity galvanised minds. A week before the vital Scottish League vote, Inverness and Nairn Enterprise stepped in and announced the possible brokering of a deal. INE chairman Norman Cordiner was convinced that amalgamation was the answer and he was keen to ensure an Inverness team entered the national league. He also saw the economic potential for the area: 'Scottish League football would bring a "feel good" factor to Inverness, boosting morale in the town and raising its profile to attract more businesses.' INE had the foresight to see the benefits of national league membership to Inverness as a whole. Amalgamation would also make economic sense, as potential sponsors would not be weighed down by past backing of any one of the existing clubs and a united club would be in a strong position to obtain public funding. INE persuaded former Thistle chairman Jock McDonald to come out of football retirement and assist with the league bid. His 21 years as an SFA councillor and his standing in Scottish football circles were to be major assets in the months ahead.

The way was now clear for Highland League teams to make every effort to secure one, if not both, of the slots. Clach's involvement only lasted until 12 August, when they announced that the Grant Street club was pulling out of the proposed merger and would continue in the Highland League. Clach's decision left Thistle and Caledonian to persuade their members and fans that unification was in the interests of all and to work towards a joint Scottish League bid. To many, it seemed ironic that the capital of the Highlands should be forced to go down this road when other clubs could retain their individual identity and still apply. In the event, Ross County stayed independent and succeeded. Elgin City also submitted a solo bid but it was unsuccessful – they eventually joined Division Three in 2000-1 after a further reorganisation. At this point the reader is referred to Charles Bannerman's 1997 book *Against All Odds* for a full account of the meetings, motions, counter-motions and general mayhem which eventually led to the creation of Caledonian Thistle FC. What follows is merely a snapshot of events.

The first target date was 1 October – the closing date for league membership applications. The aim was to conclude a merger deal before then, but this was to prove very hard. If it had been a straight union of equal partners then perhaps things would have been simpler, but this was not the case. Caley had more members, greater fund-raising capacity and more assets – they owned Telford Street Park – and Thistle, it was wrongly thought, only leased Kingsmills Park. The varying strengths led to major problems over the balance of the board, the name of the new club and team colours.

Both clubs were to consider the issue on 9 September – less than a month after Clach's withdrawal changed the whole balance and only three weeks before the deadline. Some of the difficulties that arose can be put down to the short timescale, as supporters were being asked to shift a lifetime's allegiance in a matter of months. Caley members met in the Muirtown Motel and Thistle members at the Rannoch Lodge Hotel. The same six-page paper was put to both meetings. This set out the discussions with Inverness and Nairn Enterprise, proposed a 5 Caley/3 Thistle/3 INE board structure, suggested two separate trusts to hold each club's shares in the joint venture and detailed arrangements for the building of a new stadium by August 1995. The Caley meeting ended with a 55-50 vote in favour but the anti-merger members vowed to continue the fight. The Thistle meeting ended in a 33-12 vote in favour. The handling of both meetings, the exact motions on the table and the margins of victory would all be scrutinised minutely in the coming months but, for the moment, the merger was on. This major step allowed a formal application to be made to the Scottish League before the 1 October deadline, but the issue of asset transfer from the Caley side was soon to be a major stumbling block.

THE ROAD TO THE SCOTTISH LEAGUE

The 'Caley Rebels' came together at a meeting on 12 September and began a concerted campaign of opposition. Their trump card was the revelation that the club could only be wound up by a members' vote with a two-thirds majority. The 55-50 result at the 9 September meeting now looked very vulnerable. This turn of events did not stop the league application being submitted on time, but it did undermine the confidence of the participants. The dissidents forced a Special General Meeting which, after many delays, finally took place at Rose Street Hall on 1 December – just 15 days before the Scottish League presentation. By this time the official membership of Caley had swollen rapidly after spirited recruiting. 476 members attended the meeting and a second merger vote went 250-226 in favour. The rebels argued that a two-thirds majority was required but this was rejected. There was no doubt that such a majority was required for liquidation, but a simple majority would suffice for the transfer of assets. This distinction was to prove vital.

The next crucial date was Thursday 16 December 1993 – the formal presentation of the Inverness case to the Scottish League. It was clear that a united club would be almost certain of victory. Norman Cordiner stated that 'the Scottish Football League have got the final vote but all the feedback we have been getting says if we get this business sorted out we're pretty well assured of a place.' Queen's Park secretary Jim Rutherford gave an insight into the attitude of other clubs: 'South clubs are talking about how long it would take to get to Inverness rather than whether there would be an Inverness team in the league. We feel next season we will be travelling to Inverness, come hell or high water.' Raith Rovers' Peter Campsie summed up the situation neatly: 'If the two Inverness clubs are definitely getting together they must be strong favourites. If not they have a problem.'

Norman Cordiner and INE chief executive Fiona Larg were doing their best to solve the problem. Caley's second positive merger vote seemed to resolve the immediate issues and allow the presentation to go ahead, but it was not quite as simple as that. Cordiner sought peace and he met both the Caley committee and the rebels on 8 December to try to find common ground. The emerging proposal to call the team Caledonian and play in blue was flatly rejected by Thistle. Cordiner met the Thistle contingent on 11 December and was left in no doubt that, although they had been relatively quiet so far, they also had issues to be resolved. Three days before the presentation INE's shuttle diplomacy finally paid off. On 13 December two separate meetings were held – first with the Caley anti-merger group, then with Thistle officials. The revised proposals were recommended for acceptance. The team would be called Caledonian Thistle FC, the colours would be 'predominantly blue' and Telford Street Park would be used for the first season. Originally it was to be Kingsmills Park, but upgrading at reasonable cost was impossible and Caledonian's ground was the only real choice. The anti-merger group met the next night and the principle of the new club was accepted. Over the next year there would still be major threats to the union, but for the moment the club's representatives could present Caledonian Thistle's case in Glasgow.

The Inverness delegation comprised Norman Cordiner, Inverness Thistle chairman Charlie Cuthbert, Caledonian vice-chairman Ally MacKenzie, chairman designate of the unified club John 'Jock' McDonald and architect Bruce Hare. Four other clubs made presentations that day – Elgin City, Ross County, Gala Fairydean and Gretna. Ross County's excellent Scottish Cup run came just at the right time to put them in the public eye. Five days before the presentation they demolished St Cuthbert Wanderers 11-0 in the first round then, four days before the League vote on 12 January 1994, they beat Forfar Athletic 4-0 in the second. To their credit, Forfar seconded County on the day.

The secret vote took place in Glasgow's Royal Scottish Automobile Club: it was all over in 30 minutes and one ballot. It proved to be a landslide for Inverness – 68 votes out of a possible 86, 24 ahead of the number required to ensure success. Ross County took second spot with 57 votes, Gala polled 35 votes, Elgin ten and Gretna just two. Elgin eventually joined the Scottish League in 2000-1 and Gretna replaced Airdrieonians in 2002-3.

Jock McDonald was relieved at the voting result: 'I was confident but still had butterflies in my stomach. After all, I had more than sufficient pledges for Thistle in 1974 but we lost out. That was an agony I did not want to go through again.' Duncan McPherson, Highland Regional Council convener, hailed this as tremendous news for the Highlands: 'As one of the fastest-growing towns in Scotland, Inverness thoroughly deserves to have a side playing on the national stage.'

The preparations for 1994-5 could now start in earnest. The Caledonian

Thistle board first met officially in Balnain House on 24 February 1994 and comprised 11 members. Inverness and Nairn Enterprise nominees were Jock McDonald, Norman Cordiner and Ken Matheson. Thistle's inaugural board members were Scott Byrnes, Craig Maclean and Ian Gordon. Caledonian were represented by Norman Miller (who became vice-chairman), Ally Mackenzie, John Price, David MacDonald and Dougie McGilvray. During the first season Ken Matheson, Norman Cordiner and Scott Byrnes left and were replaced by Roy McLennan, Ken Thomson and Dougie Riach. David MacDonald left at the end of 1994-5. By the end of the first decade the board would be reduced to six. A slimmed-down board was always seen as the way forward but it took several years to achieve. At the first board meeting, Tomatin Distillery chairman and former Inverness Thistle supremo Jock McDonald was officially elected chairman of the unified club. This was only a formality, as he had been destined for the post since the early days of the merger negotiations.

Baltacha appointed manager

With Caledonian Thistle now set to join the Scottish League, it was time to put off-field arguments to one side and look to the creation of a team. The football story of Caledonian Thistle began on 10 March 1994 with the appointment of Sergei Baltacha as player/manager. His pedigree was impeccable, with 47 full USSR international caps and a club record which began at Dynamo Kiev, then continued in Britain with Ipswich Town and St Johnstone. Baltacha's only management experience was one season at Caledonian, but the new board were impressed by his top-flight background. Baltacha was unsuccessful in persuading Thistle manager Henrick Madej to be his assistant. Madej's other business commitments took precedence and Baltacha turned to his Caledonian colleague Neil Mackintosh. Mackintosh took the job in April but left in May – he claimed Baltacha had 'edged him out' but the manager insisted that it was Mackintosh's decision. Most posts were filled in early June. Dave Milroy was appointed a coach and Danny MacDonald player/coach. There was to be no official assistant manager, but MacDonald effectively filled this role with Milroy looking after the reserves. The backroom staff was completed by Alex Young (trainer), Tommy Cumming (kit), John King (physio) and youth coaches John Beaton and Jackie Sutherland. John MacAskill took on the role of club doctor. The first groundsman was Duncan Gillies.

Thistle and Caley still had to complete the 1993-4 Highland League season, although neither side was in the frame for the league title. Both did take something from the final season – Thistle beat Clach 1-0 to win the Inverness Cup and Caley beat Forres Mechanics 1-0 to secure the North Cup. The last Thistle and Caley derby match took place, amidst much nostalgia, on 11 May 1994 at Telford Street Park. Caley won 1-0 thanks to a Billy Urquhart goal. 'The Legend' had retired a season before but was included as a gesture to mark the importance of the day. The £200 fine for fielding an unregistered player was expected and paid immediately. Despite the merger now being a reality, the usual derogatory chants were heard from both sides. It was clear to the neutral observer that hostilities were not completely over.

Three days later, both teams played their last matches in the Highland League. Caley drew 1-1 away to Steve Paterson's Huntly, Wilson Robertson scoring what was to be the club's final goal. Thistle went down 2-0 to Lossiemouth at Kingsmills Park. With no Thistle goals in the last two games, the honour of scoring their final goal went to Steve Bremner who had netted in the 2-1 defeat at Keith on 7 May. Many a tear was shed at Kingsmills Park and Huntly as two fine teams passed into history. Both names were to live on with the unified club but nobody pretended that things would ever be the same again.

CHAPTER 4

INTO THE SCOTTISH LEAGUE
1994-5

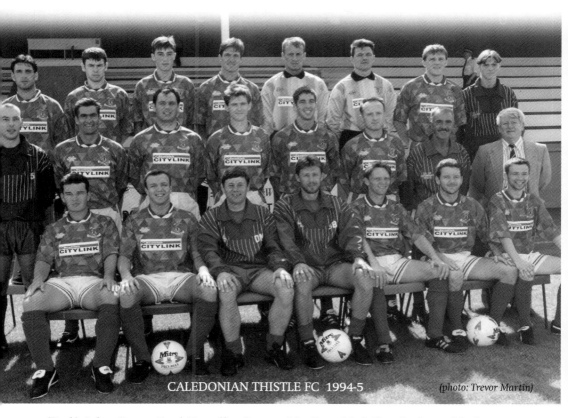

CALEDONIAN THISTLE FC 1994-5

(photo: Trevor Martin)

(*Back*) John Scott, Paul Presslie, Steven MacDonald, Mike Andrew, Mark McRitchie, Jim Calder, Mike Noble, Richard Hastings

(*Middle*) John King (physio), Martin Lisle, Alan Hercher (captain), Peter Hardie, Allan Smart, Wilson Robertson, Alex Young (trainer), John MacAskill (doctor)

(*Front*) Dave Brennan, Mark McAllister, Dave Milroy (coach), Sergei Baltacha (player/manager), Danny MacDonald (player/coach), Charlie Christie, Colin Mitchell

GOING BALLISTIC!

At last it was time to put the amalgamation problems to one side and concentrate on what it was all about – football. Sergei Baltacha had to assemble a new team in a short space of time and he relied heavily on the former Caledonian squad. Twenty-nine players were used in 1994-5, and 15 came from Caledonian, including Baltacha himself. Jim Calder, Steven MacDonald, Gary Watt and Kevin Sweeney came from Inverness Thistle and other former Kingsmills' players appeared in the reserve side. Had the merger happened in a different era, when Thistle's football star was burning brighter, there would no doubt have been a more even distribution. There were some new faces, including Paul McKenzie from Burnley, John Scott recently released by Liverpool, 'S' form signing Richard Hastings and Norman MacMillan from Nairn County.

Baltacha had played football at the highest level, and most of his players had cup-tie experience against top sides, but this was still a season of discovery for all. There were pressure games every week, long-distance travel every other Saturday, Scottish League standards to be met in every department, and everybody at the club had to learn as they went along. Baltacha was criticised for his cautious tactics in the first season but the reality was that, on a limited budget, his team was breaking new ground and trying to survive at a high level against strong, physical, well-organised teams. Steve Paterson would inherit an organisation where many of the teething troubles had been resolved and more money for players was available.

As the new team took the field there were still many important issues to be resolved. The lease of a site at East Longman for the new stadium had been agreed with the Council, but planning permission was still required, and there was the major problem of finance. The Caledonian Thistle board was firmly in place. However, the transfer of assets from the constituent teams had still to be approved, and Thistle's assets were the subject of an interim interdict brought by teenager Martin Ross.

Sponsorship deals with Citylink and Olympus Sports were announced prior to the start of the season. Citylink became the inaugural shirt sponsors and provided two buses to take the team and supporters to away matches. Olympus supplied boots through their Inverness shop Pro Performance Shoes.

The paper team finally became a reality on 20 July, but it was at RAF Kinloss, far from the gaze of the Inverness public. This friendly goes down in history as the first-ever Caledonian Thistle match. Captain Alan Hercher scored the first goal in the 2-0 win and Peter Hardie the second. Representing the club were Mark McRitchie, Billy Skinner, Mike Andrew, Mark McAllister, Danny MacDonald, Colin Mitchell, Mike Noble, Richard Hastings, Steve Murray, Alan Hercher and Peter Hardie plus five substitutes – Jim Calder, Steve MacDonald, Neal Sinclair, Chris Stone and Innes Simpson. Another friendly was played two days later – a 5-1 win at Golspie.

850 spectators turned out on Saturday 30 July 1994 for the official unveiling of the new side – a friendly at Telford Street Park against St Mirren. In the souvenir programme chairman Jock McDonald signalled the start of a new era and stated the board's determination 'to flourish in due course to be a fitting legacy of the coming together of two splendid old clubs'. The new manager stated: 'I took this job because I believed Inverness has the talent and the potential support to do justice to the national scene. With everyone pulling together we can make the most of this wonderful opportunity.' Over the next decade the optimism of both men would prove to be well-placed as far as the football was concerned but, while attendances started off well, they did not grow significantly as the team climbed up the league ladder. Saints' 3-0 winning margin in the opening game was unimportant. Caledonian Thistle had arrived on the public scene as a football team.

An important feature of this match was the presence of 'new' Inverness supporters – disaffected fans of Caledonian and Thistle were fading into the background, but they were more than replaced by former neutrals. Over the next ten years the level of local support would be strongly criticised, but for the moment this was a big step forward. Baltacha's team for the St Mirren game was Mark McRitchie, Dave Brennan, Mark McAllister, Mike Andrew, John Scott, Mike Noble, Danny MacDonald, Martin Lisle, Alan Hercher, Paul Presslie and Wilson Robertson. Five substitutes were used – Jim Calder, Steve MacDonald, Peter Hardie, Colin Mitchell and Allan Smart. In the event, Paul Presslie and Peter Hardie did not sign for the new club and never played competitively. Another match across town that day included players who were to have a significant influence in years to come. Clach were beaten 5-0 by Hearts in a friendly and Graeme Bennett made his farewell appearance for the Lilywhites. Future Inverness Caledonian Thistle manager John Robertson scored from the penalty spot for Hearts.

GOING BALLISTIC!

On Wednesday 3 August Bruce Rioch brought a strong Bolton side to Inverness as part of a northern tour. Bolton had to work hard for their 2-0 win, although their team included future Celtic player Alan Stubbs, Scottish Internationalist John McGinlay and the Republic of Ireland's Jason McAteer. They had thumped Ross County 7-0 two days earlier, so 2-0 was a good result. A newspaper report at the time commented on the defensive approach by the home side and stated that this would not be popular with fans. This complaint was to be heard often in the coming months. There was one more home friendly the following Saturday before the real business could start. Opponents Brechin City were a Second Division side at the time, and they gave a better indication of the quality of future league opposition than did St Mirren or Bolton. This match marked the debut of Graeme Bennett and ended 0-0, although CT trialist Craig Stewart had a goal chalked off.

The long-awaited opening competitive game came on the evening of Tuesday 9 August when Alan Hercher led the team out at East Stirling. This was a Coca-Cola first-round tie and the first of many long trips down the A9 for players, officials and supporters. The team for the St Mirren game proved to be very close to Sergei Baltacha's starting line-up. Baltacha was injured, and former Thistle, Caledonian and Celtic midfielder Charlie Christie was still recovering from a hernia operation. The debut team was Mark McRitchie, Dave Brennan, Mark McAllister, Alan Hercher, John Scott, Mike Andrew, Danny MacDonald, Paul McKenzie, Mike Noble, Graeme Bennett and Wilson Robertson. Allan Smart came on for Paul MacKenzie but the other substitutes, Jim Calder and Martin Lisle, stayed on the bench.

The result was a triumph as the visitors won 2-0 and earned a second round tie at Dundee. Home keeper Jim Moffat denied both Alan Hercher and Mark McAllister, before Wilson Robertson broke the deadlock. He played a one-two with Paul McKenzie before writing his name in the history books with the club's first competitive goal. Just on half-time Caley Thistle went two ahead – Alan Hercher distracted Iain Lee and a John Scott corner ricocheted into the net. Hercher was officially credited with the goal although some records show it as an own goal. In the second half the result was never in doubt. Both Danny MacDonald and Alan Hercher came close to increasing the visitors' lead. In the last minute a Michael Geraghty shot nearly gave East Stirling a consolation goal, but it came off the bar.

INTO THE SCOTTISH LEAGUE

At last: the Scottish League

On Saturday 13 August Scottish League football at long last came to Inverness. Caledonian Thistle played Arbroath in the new Third Division in front of a massive 1700 spectators. The new team put up a magnificent performance to win 5-2 and Alan Hercher made his mark in a big way with a hat-trick. In 13 minutes Hercher rose high to head home Graeme Bennett's free kick and record the club's first league goal. On 31 minutes he hit through a ruck of players for his second. The hat-trick was completed two minutes later with another header. Arbroath pulled back two in the second half before Paul McKenzie and Wilson Robertson scored the fourth and fifth goals. The 5-2 scoreline was the biggest win of the season: it was over a year before five goals were again scored in a senior match. 'Man of the Match' Hercher was delighted: 'There was so much hype that there was a fear we would fall flat on our faces. Conditions were perfect and it was an incredible feeling to win so comfortably. It was great to score one goal but a hat-trick was fantastic.'

There was an air of confidence around Telford Street with these early victories, but the following mid-week everyone came back to earth. The Coca-Cola Cup run ended abruptly with a 3-0 away defeat at the hands of First Division Dundee. The crowd of 3112 was the highest attendance for a cup match all season. Whilst the Dundee defeat was not too much of a surprise, there was great disappointment the following Saturday when Queen's Park came north and convincingly won 4-0. The visitors' coach Eddie Hunter performed a forward roll on the track to express his delight! This match marked the debut of Richard Hastings at only 17 years and 94 days – his record as the club's youngest player still stands.

27 August saw the start of a new tradition of local derbies with a league encounter against Ross County. This took place at Dingwall in front of 3157 fans, which turned out to be the highest of the season for an away league match. The size of the crowd sent out a clear message to the rest of Scotland that the decision to admit both clubs to the league was the right one and that strong Highland support existed. The match was won by the visitors 3-1 but marred by nine yellow and two red cards. The winning margin included own goals by Sandy MacLeod and Chris Somerville – Wilson Robertson scored the third and County's consolation came courtesy of an Andy MacLeod penalty. This result put Caley Thistle into fourth place in the Third Division.

GOING BALLISTIC!

September was a good month in the league and Sergei Baltacha was named 'Manager of the Month'. A narrow 1-0 away victory against Albion Rovers on the third was significant, in that it marked the debut of Charlie Christie after his return to full fitness. He was to prove the most influential player of the club's first decade and would make a record number of appearances. A 3-1 home victory against Forfar the following week was enough to secure top place and smash Forfar's 100% record.

A 1-1 draw at Alloa was sandwiched between a home friendly against a Celtic XI and a B&Q Cup second-round tie against Dundee. The Dundee match on the 28th drew a 2000 crowd and was the first of many exciting home cup-ties over the years. Danny MacDonald gave the home side the lead after just two minutes, and it took until the 69th minute before Morten Wieghorst equalised. With no goals in extra time, the visitors narrowly won the penalty shoot-out 4-3. However, it was a very creditable performance against First Division opponents. A Dundee substitute that night was Mike Teasdale, who joined the Inverness side in December 1995 and went on to become a major player at the club.

On 1 October East Stirling came to Inverness in the league and, after an exciting comeback, Caley Thistle snatched a 3-3 draw. Mike Noble gave the home side a 19th-minute lead with a penalty but a Mark McAllister own goal a minute later cancelled it out. By the 66th minute it was 3-1 to the visitors, but the home cause was helped when David Watt was red-carded. With a minute left, McAllister made amends for his earlier mishap by scoring a headed goal at the right end. He quickly picked the ball out of the net and raced to the halfway line to ensure a speedy restart. Immediately, Caley Thistle regained possession and Wilson Robertson ran through to score with a superb angled drive right on the whistle. The stunned East Stirling players trooped off the pitch, shaking their heads in disbelief. Losses to Cowdenbeath and Montrose led to a slip to sixth place. On the 22nd Arbroath were defeated 2-1 away thanks to a double from trialist Bruce McCraw – the winning goal coming two minutes into injury time. A week later, Inverness hosted the second derby, an exciting match but no goals. County's Andy MacLeod missed a penalty – the ball hit the post and rebounded into the arms of a very relieved Mark McRitchie. There was a minor improvement to fifth place by the end of October.

There were mixed fortunes in the league during November – two wins, one defeat and a draw. Playing Queen's Park on the hallowed Hampden turf for the first time on the 5th realised an ambition for manager Baltacha: 'I'm not going to play for my mother country again so this may be my last chance to play at Hampden. All the players are excited about it.' They were inspired to a 2-0 victory and revenge for the 0-4 score in August. There was the first chance of silverware on the 9th in the final of the Inverness Cup at Telford Street, but Caley Thistle were defeated 1-0 by Brora. A 2-1 away defeat at the hands of table-toppers Forfar was followed by a 2-1 home win against Albion Rovers. Charlie Christie came off the bench to score both goals, and the following week Christie opened the scoring at home to Alloa. The visitors hit back with two goals and it took an 86th minute Mike Andrew penalty to earn a draw.

Scott Byrnes resigned from his post as football secretary in November to move south, after important work behind the scenes over the first crucial months. Byrnes had been a full-time employee of the club, combining the secretary's position with the role of treasurer. He was replaced on a part-time basis by Jim Falconer. Director Craig Maclean took over as treasurer. The bulk of the football administration work falls to the football secretary and, having been secretary of Caledonian since 1986, Jim Falconer brought long experience to the club. His quiet professionalism continues to ensure that all football-related tasks are carried out efficiently. The football secretary has a wide remit, particularly in relation to matches – he contacts opposing clubs, liaises with officials and arranges transport and meals for away games. The secretary is the club's contact with the Scottish Football Association, Scottish Football League and the North of Scotland Football Association. He is also responsible for players' contracts, together with the payment of bonuses and expenses. Physio John King left the club in November 1994, to be replaced by the experienced Ian Manning, formerly of Hibs and Inverness Thistle. 'Healing Hands' Manning was to give valuable service until the end of 2001-2.

The defeat at Forfar on 12 November was the final game in Allan Smart's short Caley Thistle career. Smart left for Preston, then Carlisle and Watford. He was part of the Watford team that won promotion to the Premiership in 1998-9 and the highlight of his English career was scoring the winning goal in the Premiership play-offs. The agreement with Preston was that Caley Thistle would receive a cut of any future transfer fee, but rumoured big-money deals fell through and no further cash was ever paid.

League status meant automatic entry into the Scottish Cup instead of the customary strain of the North Qualifying Cup. The debut match was on 17 December at home to Queen of the South – postponed from the previous week because of bad weather. There was no hint of future cup glories as Queens outplayed their hosts and won more easily than the 2-1 score suggests. The tie was lost by conceding two goals in identical circumstances – direct shots from free kicks just outside the area. Mark McAllister scored a consolation goal in the final minute. There were only two league games played in December due to the rescheduled cup-tie and the postponement of the Montrose match due to be played on Hogmanay. The first was at East Stirling on the 3rd and the home side easily won 2-0. The other game to survive was the Boxing Day visit to Cowdenbeath – for an hour Caley Thistle were one down but Mike Andrew gained a point with a 70th minute penalty goal.

After the attendance figures for the Third Division up to the end of December had been analysed, Scottish League secretary Peter Donald paid tribute to the club: 'Averaging about 1500 spectators for home games, the Inverness side have more than justified their admission into the Scottish League and we can only hope they maintain this high level.'

Ross County hosted the first New Year derby on 2 January but the match only went ahead after a major snow-clearing exercise by 40 volunteers. The County fans were rewarded for their efforts with a 3-1 win, despite Mike Andrew once more converting a penalty to give the visitors a 20th minute lead. The rest of January was little better. A 1-1 home draw against Arbroath was only earned by Dave Brennan's 89th minute header, then it was back to Hampden and a resounding 4-1 defeat. It was a poor performance, but the cause was not helped by the red card shown to Paul McKenzie. With goals hard to come by, Baltacha was striving to sign a proven striker, and he turned to former Scottish internationalist John MacDonald – he played as a trialist at Hampden and scored Caley Thistle's only goal. After one more appearance, signing terms were offered but south-based MacDonald was not keen to travel to Inverness on a regular basis. Baltacha was still not ruling out the possibility of promotion, despite lying seventh at the end of January. The squad was bolstered by the signing of former Caledonian favourite Billy Urquhart. He came out of retirement to play reserve football but eventually made three appearances for the senior side in the closing weeks of the season.

February started with a visit by Forfar and a 1-1 draw then a 2-1 away victory against Albion Rovers. The winning goal against the Coatbridge side came five minutes from time and was scored by Caledonian veteran Martin Lisle – this was to be his only competitive goal for the first team. On the following Tuesday a much-postponed match against Montrose was finally played at Telford Street. A second-half goal blitz from the visitors effectively ended any chance of promotion, but Baltacha had not given up hope. Even after a 1-0 defeat at Alloa the following week, he was upbeat: 'There is still an outside chance of us gaining a promotion place, it only takes a run of good results.' A 3-3 draw at home to East Stirling in February's last game put an end to all talk of promotion. The score matched that of the previous October, but this time there was no last-minute scramble. Caley Thistle were in the lead three times but three times East Stirling fought back. There had been a drop to seventh place at the turn of the year and there was no improvement by the end of February.

By March, Baltacha was resigned to another season in the Third Division, and his future plans began with transfer-listing five players. Postponement of the Albion Rovers home game on the 25th left only three matches during the month. An excellent 3-1 home win against Cowdenbeath was followed by a last gasp win away to Montrose – Wilson Robertson's 89th minute curling shot broke the deadlock. Montrose defender Kevin Tindal's boot came off, flew into the away dug-out and struck Baltacha around his right eye. He suffered cuts and bruises and came out in the second half wearing an eye patch. Eventual champions Forfar won decisively 4-1 on the 18th thanks to a hat-trick by David Bingham and a goal by Bobby Mann – both future Inverness players. The two March wins were enough to secure a small rise to sixth place.

April was catch-up time, but it was a disaster – five defeats from six league matches. Billy Urquhart made a surprise first-team debut on the 1st in the 1-0 away defeat at East Stirling. The score was repeated at home against Alloa then, on a cold Tuesday night, bottom club Albion Rovers came to Inverness and recorded a 2-0 win – only their fifth of the season. One bright spot was beating Cowdenbeath 3-1 at Central Park on the 15th. It was a bad-tempered match, in front of only 220 spectators, and the home side finished with nine players. The crowd was the lowest of the season – a record that stood until 1999 as the all-time worst. Defeats by Montrose and Arbroath gave little cause for optimism. One April success was the capture of the *Inverness Courier* Challenge Cup on Monday 17th, defeating Clach 3-1 after extra time. In mid-April Danny MacDonald resigned as first team coach to concentrate on his own return to fitness after cruciate ligament damage. The reserve team played in the North Caledonian League and won both the championship and the Chic Allan Cup. The Chic Allan Cup Final was against Bunillidh Thistle at the beginning of April. Caley Thistle came from behind to win 3-2. The North Caledonian League championship was sewn up at the end of the month with a 9-0 demolition of Bonar Bridge.

Baltacha resigns

Once it was clear that promotion was impossible, Baltacha decided to blood youngsters and thus used a high number of players – 31 squad players, with 29 actually taking the field. On 24 April Baltacha denied a national newspaper report that he would resign if the merger turmoil was not resolved and spoke of his plans for 1995-6: 'It has been a good season for us – a good learning process. I would hope to bring in some new faces for next season.' In the end, he did decide to go. Baltacha was living in an Inverness flat but his main home was still in Perth. Family reasons were cited for his resignation on 3 May despite two years of a three-year contract remaining. It had clearly been a hard task to take the new club into the Scottish League, not helped by a succession of injuries and confusion behind the scenes: 'I will leave a piece of my heart at the club. I am sure that the club will be in a better position in the near future and will eventually be able to mark the progress it deserves to a higher position.' Baltacha's defensive football style was not popular with fans, but players and officials still talk about him with great affection. He left behind the nucleus of an organisation which future managers would take forward to great success. Vice-chairman Norman Miller paid tribute to the man he had brought to Inverness: 'It has not been easy for the manager of this club in all the circumstances and we greatly appreciate the commitment Sergei has shown in laying the basis for the future.'

There were two games to go, including the final derby at Telford Street on 6 May. County were thumped 3-0 but played for most of the match with 10 men after Andy MacLeod's dismissal. The visitors had still been in the promotion race but defeat ended their chances. The crowd of 3562 was the highest of the season. Baltacha bowed out after a 1-1 home draw with Queen's Park on the last day of the season. Billy Urquhart ended his short

Caley Thistle career in this match at the age of 38 years 172 days, but his record as the oldest player was to be well beaten by Jim Calder.

Captain Alan Hercher netted the equalising goal against the Spiders and therefore scored the first and last league goals of the season. Hercher summed up the season: 'There was a great buzz at the club when we joined the Scottish League and the start was tremendous. We knew it would be difficult to sustain and it was made worse by injuries to key players. Teams in the league were well organised and powerful so you were punished for your mistakes. Our form dropped off but things improved and we finished well.'

The first league campaign ended in sixth place with a total of 45 points. Top goalscorer was Alan Hercher with seven, three of these from the first league match in August. Over a total of 40 league and cup matches, the team scored 52 goals and conceded 67. The scoring credits went to a total of 16 players plus two own goals from Ross County players. Mark McAllister came close to appearing in all 40 games but missed the away league match at Alloa on 18 February – he still finished the season with by far the most appearances. The nearest contender was Mark McRitchie with 33. Three substitutes were allowed this season but one had to be a goalkeeper. This resulted in Jim Calder sitting on the bench for 27 games and playing only seven times.

Distance, road conditions and weather had been the main reasons put forward over the years to exclude a north team from the SFL, but a visit to Inverness twice a season pales into insignificance compared with the number of trips required down the A9 by Caley Thistle. Travel throughout the Highlands had been the norm, apart from occasional cup forays south, but from August 1994 the A9 was to become very familiar. A routine was quickly established to ensure that the team reaches its destination as refreshed as possible, the main ingredients being a comfortable bus and a good driver. Rapsons' Tony Fraser filled the role admirably throughout the club's first decade, with his son Alan taking over when Tony was off on other duties. Their devotion to the cause and high professionalism have ensured that the drudgery is kept to a minimum.

The routine for away matches, which has been followed since joining the SFL, starts with a 9.30 am departure from Inverness and a lunch stop around noon – in Perth, Cumbernauld or somewhere else convenient, depending on the final destination. South-based players normally meet up with the rest of the team for lunch and the full party continues from there at around 12.30 to 1 pm. The aim is always to arrive around 2 pm as this gives time to stretch the legs, inspect the pitch and fully prepare for the match. Long journeys to places like Ayr or Dumfries may involve overnight stops, particularly in mid-winter, and the routine obviously has to change for evening games in midweek. Local derbies are a welcome break from the trips south, and even playing St Johnstone in Perth is regarded as a short run.

In June 1994 Sergei Baltacha asked Caledonian's youth coaches John Beaton and Jackie Sutherland to continue their work with the unified club. They started with just two teams at under-14 and under-16 level, with players drawn from the Inverness Street League. The organisation was to expand greatly with entry to the Moray Firth League, the enthusiastic leadership from February 1996 of director Jim Jarvie and the work of Danny MacDonald and his team from the summer of 2003.

The matchday programme has been edited since August 1994 by Bryan Munro. He took over after the first three 1994-5 issues, and by May 2004 had been responsible for 228 home programmes. Bryan is assisted by a number of contributors and photographers but the main burden falls on his shoulders. Timetables are sometimes very tight and cup-ties can create many headaches. A classic example was when the 1997 Scottish Cup-tie at Stranraer was delayed and eventually took place on Monday 13 January. The match was drawn and a programme for the Wednesday replay was produced in less than two days, thanks to the burning of much midnight oil. The job of editor also involves the provision of information to other clubs for away programmes.

The management committee was created in 1994-5 from those former Caledonian and Thistle committee members who did not join the board. From Thistle came John Falconer, Ian MacKenzie and Renatto Turriani. Original members from Caledonian were Sheddie Carr, John Cumming, John Douglas, David Jessiman, Roy Lobban, Brian MacKenzie, George Macrae and Mike Shewan. The author joined in June 1995 from a neutral background. The committee remained largely unchanged over most of the club's first decade except for the death in May 1997 of Roy Lobban and the addition of Peter MacCallum. In 2003-4 gaps were filled, and the committee expanded, by the inclusion of Irene Maclean, Dot Urquhart, Gordon Munro, Ally Mackenzie, Ken Davidson, Brian Marshall and Myles Soane. Ian MacKenzie is chairman and he liaises directly with the board. There was no respite from off-the-field politics throughout 1994-5. Team colours were a bone of contention with the Thistle faction. The promised 'predominantly blue' first team strip turned out to be blue and white. This gave ammunition to the Thistle fans who claimed it was a takeover and not a merger. Black and red were incorporated from the second season but this was one problem that could easily have been avoided.

A major part of the original application to the Scottish League was a promise to provide a new stadium by August 1995 – a date that was to prove unrealistic. In June 1994 East Longman became the preferred site and in the same month Inverness District Council approved in principle the lease of 9.03 acres for a stadium and car parking. One original plan showed the proposed facility as 'Moray Stadium' but the council wanted 'Longman Stadium'. The site area would eventually be increased to 12.88 acres and be leased for 99 years at a starting rent of £12500 per annum. The eventual name of 'Caledonian Stadium' was part of the agreement between the constituent clubs brokered by Inverness and Nairn Enterprise in December 1994. The Council wanted the club 'to use its best endeavours' to include Inverness in its title, but this did not happen until 1996-7.

Doubts were expressed in certain quarters regarding the choice of East Longman. The *Courier* quoted Citadel players who remembered the Shore Street ground in the 1930s as an inhospitable place. Citadel outside left Jock Paterson recalled the atrocious cold and windy conditions that greeted the team: 'The elements coming off the seas, the wind and the rain meant that we didn't get many spectators. I don't know what they are going there for at all. It is a terrible place.' Citadel forward Murdo Shand agreed that it was cold but pointed out that 'it's cold anywhere in the north in winter time. Even Clach Park or Caley Park is cold in winter.' Provost Bill Fraser was quoted as having deep concerns about road safety in the vicinity of the stadium and the potential for accidents on the adjacent A9: 'There is no law to prevent people crossing a dual-carriageway. There is no guarantee that fans won't take a shortcut across the road.'

Disputes over assets in August had led to a warning from Scottish League secretary Peter Donald that league status was being placed in danger. When Thistle failed to meet a deadline for asset transfer, it was suggested that, even at this late stage, Caley could 'go it alone.' Donald rejected this and stated that the League acceptance was on the basis of a joint bid:

'If there were to be a material change in the structure of the club it is obviously something that the League would be interested in, and if it were to be effectively a one-club entity that may well place the membership in jeopardy.' Chairman Jock McDonald was in no doubt that matters would proceed as planned: 'We have got a team, we have been accepted and the team will go ahead.' An exasperated Norman Cordiner said that over the last 12 months more heat than light had been generated: 'These negotiations are not about one side or the other coming out on top... they are about finding a settlement which is agreeable to all and reflects the principle behind the merger that no one club should be allowed to dominate.'

At the end of the season, chairman Jock McDonald moved to the honorary post of life president and was replaced by stadium director Dougie McGilvray. McGilvray's drive and enthusiasm were to prove crucial in the years ahead. McDonald had seen the club through its difficult debut year with the continuing rebellions and asset transfer problems. While most of the 1994-5 team and management came from a Caledonian background, the Chairman was very much a Thistle man. To his great amusement he was abused by Caley fans and during the heat of the merger negotiations, he was the target of an unusual protest at Telford Street. Forty dissidents dropped their trousers and 'mooned' in McDonald's direction. As he made a tactical withdrawal at the insistence of the police he noted that 'I didn't recognise any of them'.

When Caledonian Thistle were elected to the league, Gala Fairydean came third in the voting and took advantage of the continuing internal strife to threaten court action. In a letter to the Scottish League they claimed that the Inverness side was playing under a 'nom de plume' and claimed it was 'ludicrous that a 'non-club' should continue to fill a position in the Scottish League. Their application is now void as they are unable to fulfil the criteria for Scottish League membership.' Gala's protests came to nothing, but it took until December 1994 before Thistle and Caledonian supporters' meetings effectively cleared the way for the final transfer of assets to the unified club. An interim interdict granted to teenage Thistle member Martin Ross on 24 June 1994, regarding alleged voting defects in the transfer of the club's assets, prolonged the agony. This threat to the union ended with a judgement against Ross by Sheriff James Fraser on 4 May 1995. The way forward for the unified club was becoming clearer. The next steps were the appointment of a new manager, strengthening the team, and the no small matter of providing the promised new stadium.

CHAPTER 5

THE ARRIVAL OF STEVE PATERSON
1995-6

CALEDONIAN THISTLE FC 1995-6 *(photo: Ken MacPherson)*

(*Back*) Martin Lisle, Alan Hercher, Danny MacDonald, John Scott, Iain MacArthur, Paul McKenzie, Mark McAllister

(*Middle*) Norman MacMillan, Davie Ross, Mike Noble (captain), Mark McRitchie, Jim Calder, Graeme Bennett, Dave McGinlay, Dougie Green

(*Front*) Alex Caldwell (assistant manager), Colin Mitchell, Iain Stewart, Robbie Benson, Dave Brennan, Charlie Christie, Richard Hastings, Steve Paterson (manager)

The ink on Sergei Baltacha's resignation was not even dry before speculation began about his successor. Various high-profile names were put forward, including ex-Blackburn Rovers manager Donald Mackay, but Huntly's Steve Paterson was always the favourite. On 9 May Caley Thistle played a Highland League Select (managed by Paterson) at Christie Park and, prior to the game, the Huntly committee met to consider a request to speak to their manager. Reluctantly, permission was granted and two weeks later the deal was done. Paterson's appointment was officially announced at a press conference on 24 May. He initially signed a three-year part-time contract but was eventually to go full-time and stay for seven and a half years.

'Wednesday May 24 1995 will probably go down as the day Caledonian Thistle Football Club finally came of age.' These were the words of Dougie McGilvray as he reflected on the appointment of Steve Paterson as manager, the granting of planning approval for the new stadium and cessation of hostilities regarding the transfer of assets. At the press conference to introduce Paterson, McGilvray also announced that Highland Regional Council's planning committee had voted 13-10 in favour of the new stadium at East Longman. The work was to start in July 1995 and be completed by August 1996. These dates proved optimistic, but things were certainly on the move. The new manager said that the job presented him with the biggest challenge of his managerial career: 'When the initial approach was made I felt I had to speak to the directors to get their side of the story and once I had done that my decision was virtually made. I had to accept the opportunity that was offered.' Most of the players he was inheriting were well known from their days in the Highland League and he was clearly not impressed: 'Using Huntly as a yardstick I don't think there is that many out of the present squad that I would have signed.' Fans were happy to hear Paterson's pledge that the team's defensive days were over: 'There's no doubt that at Caledonian Thistle the emphasis will be on attack.'

Thirty-seven-year-old Steve 'Pele' Paterson started his career as a schoolboy with Nairn County before being signed by Tommy Docherty at Manchester United. After five years he moved to Sheffield United, but his time there was cut short by an ankle injury. On regaining fitness he became a global traveller, moving to Hong Kong Rangers, Sydney Olympic and Japan's Yomiuri Tokyo before returning to the Highland League with Forres Mechanics in 1986. He joined Elgin City as player/manager in 1988 then moved to Huntly in 1990, first as a player then as manager. Paterson guided the Christie Park club to two league titles, two Qualifying Cup victories and two League Cup successes. This strong background was to set him up well for the challenge of the Scottish League.

Martin Ross's failed legal bid to halt the transfer of Inverness Thistle's assets was the last major shot in the long unification battle. With this now settled, Thistle members met the night before the 24 May press conference and instructed their legal advisers to set the wheels in motion for the transfer. The timing could not have been better, as it allowed Paterson to start work in an atmosphere far removed from that which his predecessor had endured. It was also announced that a new strip would be introduced for 1995-6, incorporating blue, red and black.

Stadium director Dougie McGilvray was elected chairman to succeed Jock McDonald on 29 May and Norman Miller remained vice-chairman. McDonald became life president and always remained available to lend his experience and wisdom to the board. McGilvray was seen as the ideal man to drive the club forward and ensure that the promised new stadium was built in a reasonable time scale. He came from a strong business background as managing director of crane hire firm Weldex (International) Offshore Ltd, and was a Caledonian nominee to the board. He had also been a Thistle season ticket holder and thus had connections with both sides of the merger. Before taking over the chairmanship he was instrumental in persuading Huntly to part with their manager and for convincing Steve Paterson that his future lay in Inverness. The fruitful McGilvray/Paterson partnership would last for four and a half years.

After taking office, McGilvray continued with the immense task of providing Inverness with a stadium that satisfied the promise made to the SFL. There have been criticisms made of the stadium design, its location and the financial legacy, but in the period from 1995 to 1996 the priority was to meet the stadium obligation. The club's league place would otherwise have been in serious jeopardy.

On 16 June a four-figure sponsorship package by the *Inverness Courier* was announced. This strengthened the already strong ties between the club and the local, twice-weekly newspaper. On 29 June the inaugural AGM of the Caledonian Thistle members' club was held, with McGilvray in the chair. The members' club was set up as part of the unification agreement to preserve the interests of the members of both Thistle and Caledonian. From the start it held a 51% controlling interest in the football club, but on 12 June 1997 the club's interest was reduced to 49% in advance of the first share issue. Similarly, it was reduced to 20% at an EGM on 5 March 1998. The members subsequently agreed to reduce the percentage by one point for every £100,000 of further investment, and in 2002-3 the interest was reduced to 14%. As the decade closed, serious consideration was being given by both the supporters' and members' clubs to the formation of a supporters' trust.

The football management team was completed in early June with the appointment of former St Johnstone and Dundee defender Alex Caldwell as assistant manager. Edinburgh-born Caldwell was based in Inverness and he brought vast experience to the partnership, from eight years at Dundee and captaining St Johnstone to the First Division title in 1982-3 through to spells in the Highland League with Elgin City, Lossiemouth, Rothes and Clachnacuddin. Paterson and Caldwell set in motion a major clear-out of players (in the end, eight left) and made a number of key summer signings – Iain Stewart from Lossiemouth, Iain MacArthur from Elgin and Brora Rangers' Davie Ross. Sergei Baltacha had tried to lure Stewart to Inverness a year earlier, but had failed. Paterson's success in signing the proven goalscorer led to an SFA tribunal hearing in August and a fee determination of £30,000. This was thought high at the time, but five years and 82 goals later it was clearly a bargain. Other new faces were Robbie Benson from Clach, Dougie Green from New Elgin Juniors and Huntly's Dave McGinlay. Benson's career was to be restricted to just five appearances due to a cruciate ligament injury. Green made only 13 appearances and McGinlay played for one season. Throughout his long tenure as manager, Paterson applied the same basic principles with his squad – each year, a small number of players would leave and be replaced with carefully-chosen recruits. As the team moved up the divisions, he would consider how players adjusted to the higher levels and buy or sell accordingly.

In July there were five pre-season matches, with mixed results, and an open day. A narrow defeat at Lossiemouth was seen by the locals as sweet revenge for 'stealing' their star striker Iain Stewart. Then Buckie Thistle were beaten convincingly. The best result came in a home match when Motherwell were beaten 2-0 on the 28th in Inverness. Inverurie Locos were to host the Rhys Bendall Memorial Tournament over the next two days, but the SFA had reservations about the Locos pitch and it was cancelled.

Instead, the four teams played friendlies on a local authority playing field and Caley Thistle suffered defeats at the hands of the hosts and Huntly. The substitutes rule was changed from the start of 1995-6 to allow a total of three with no restriction on playing position – previously, one had to be a goalkeeper. Kingsmills Park went on the market on 7 July with planning permission for residential use and, in a sad twist, the stand was destroyed by fire on the 30th with vandalism suspected.

Merchandising of club-branded souvenirs started on 22 July at the first Open Day. It became a regular, and financially successful, feature at home matches. It progressed from a table at the terracing entrance to an adapted metal container which remained on the Telford Street Park terracing until the move to Caledonian Stadium. The operation was based at the stadium in a dedicated shop until its closure in June 2002. The *Inverness Courier* then took a franchise to sell from its offices at New Century House, Bank Lane and via the internet. There was clearly still demand for an outlet at the stadium and a matchday portakabin was opened on 26 August 2003. On the day of the 2003 Bell's Cup Final a temporary shop was erected outside McDiarmid Park, with around £5000 of ticket and merchandise business taking place prior to the match. As the club's first decade came to a close, sales began from an outlet in Debenham's Inverness city-centre shop. The club's kit supplier for the first season was Matchwinner, but sales of replica items by the club did not start until the summer of 1995, when the brand had changed to Le Coq Sportif. There was a supplier change to Errea of Italy in 1999-2000.

Paterson's senior managerial debut involved a marathon trip to England – a Coca-Cola Cup-tie at Berwick on 5 August with the prize of a second-round home match against Premier side Partick Thistle. An own goal by Tom Graham gave Caley Thistle the lead but Neil Clegg equalised. It stayed at 1-1 after extra time and the Inverness side went out 5-3 on penalties. The following week Paterson's first league match should have been at the new home of Livingston – the renamed, and relocated, Meadowbank Thistle. With late completion, the alternative would have been the Commonwealth Stadium in Edinburgh but it was unavailable and the match was switched to Inverness. The programme contained Paterson's first message to the fans: 'I would like to express my delight at becoming part of the Telford Street set-up. My achievements at Forres, Elgin and Huntly are in the past and count for nothing from now on. I am starting with an empty blackboard, new faces and a great deal of hope for the future of football in Inverness.' Over the next seven and a half seasons this optimism would prove to be amply justified, but the ninety minutes against Livingston were a lesson on how hard it would be. Jim Leishman's side were well worth their 3-0 win and Paterson recognised that: 'Coming up against Livingston so early in the season may yet prove to be a blessing in disguise as far as providing an excellent guide to the standards we have to achieve to progress at this level.' This was the start of a long rivalry between the sides. A home 2-1 league defeat by Brechin City and exit from the League Challenge Trophy at the hands of Alloa (also 2-1) by the end of August did not augur well. The only upside of the Brechin game was Iain Stewart's debut goal. Caley Thistle propped up the league at the end of August.

On 22 August Inverness District Council met to vote on the possible grant of £900,000 towards the stadium development. Chairman Dougie McGilvray addressed the meeting: 'We can fund the stadium. The main problem we have is the infrastructure, the access roads and car park. We are opening up an area that has not been opened up before.' Councillor (later MP) David Stewart proposed the motion that led to a 14-11 vote in favour but there were many twists and turns before the money was eventually paid. The District Councillors were not truly masters of their own destiny at this time, as the new Highland Council was due to take office in April 1996. Legal advice had to be sought to ensure that they were within their rights in making the grant.

The first league win looked on the cards away to Albion Rovers on 2 September, thanks to two Alan Hercher goals, but it ended 2-2. Jim Calder displaced Mark McRitchie in goal for this game – he had made only seven appearances the previous season but now took his chance and never looked back. Spectators were amused to see a Jaguar drive round the track and park behind the visitors' goal. The driver was clearly bored with proceedings as he took out golf clubs and began practising his swing!

First League win

The elusive first win came the following week with a home 3-1 score against Queen's Park. An Iain Stewart penalty gave a 25th-minute lead but the Spiders equalised in 71 minutes. Late goals from Dougie Green (his only goal for the club in 13 appearances) and Alan Hercher gained the welcome victory. After the game, Steve Paterson commented on the sense of relief and delight on the faces of the players: 'With the slow start to the season we've had, following great expectations over the summer, the relief was not surprising. Hopefully we can build on this win and get our season going.' Things continued to improve and, despite a 2-1 away defeat at Arbroath, there was a climb up the league to sixth by the end of September. This was helped by a crushing 5-0 win at Alloa on the 23rd, including a Charlie Christie hat-trick and a brace from Iain Stewart. Traditionally at Recreation Park the 'Man of the Match' title goes to an Alloa player, but Christie took the award and the match ball.

The first Ross County derby of the season took place the following Saturday in Inverness in front of over 3600 supporters. It was a bad-tempered 1-1 draw, with Alan Hercher's strike cancelled out by Jamie McPherson. The game was marred by seven yellow and three red cards – Graeme Bennett and Charlie Christie of the home side and County's Jamie McPherson were all sent for an early shower.

Work on the new stadium finally started on 3 October when Provost William Fraser cut the first ceremonial turf. Local firms shared the work – McGregor Construction (Highlands) built the stadium and Morrison Construction were awarded the infrastructure contract. The chairman was clearly relieved that things were on the move: 'This marks a very important milestone in the club's short history.' The Provost took the opportunity to make a plea for Inverness to be included in the club name: 'I would hope that by next year when the new stadium opens for business the name of the town appears somewhere.' On 11 October the £900,000 grant moved a step closer when Councillors heard Queen's Counsel's advice that they were within their rights to make the payment, but recommended the seeking of additional information, primarily a detailed business plan.

League fortunes improved in October with ten points from four games and a climb up to third place. October also heralded the first of Steve Paterson's fifteen 'Manager of the Month' awards. The wins included 5-0 away to East Stirling and 6-1 at home to Albion Rovers. At the interval the Albion score was 6-0 and the visitors were down to ten men. The manager was furious that his team had eased up and lost the second half 1-0! His fear was that goal difference could make all the difference at the end of the season, but in the event this was not an issue. Three of the six goals were scored by Iain Stewart, who was now proving to be a prolific marksman. Before the Albion Rovers game, the club held a poll about a name change – 95% of the fans were in favour of Inverness being included and this led eventually to the adoption of the rather lengthy Inverness Caledonian Thistle. The 3-2 win on the 14th at home to Cowdenbeath was only achieved by an Iain Stewart winner three minutes into injury time. The final game of the month was a 0-0 away draw at Brechin on the 28th – no goals but an exciting match dubbed by the press as 'a tale of two keepers.' One lady Brechin fan will certainly remember it. On the journey south, Supporters' Club Chair Ann Nicoll suffered back spasms and physio Ian Manning came to her rescue with massage. The treatment took place in the ladies' toilet at Glebe Park and the home fan who interrupted them departed with great haste and a story to tell!

The Centenary Club started life as the Caledonian Lottery but was renamed and relaunched in 1985-6 as the Caledonian Centenary Club. In October 1995 it became the Centenary Club, and it continues to be a major source of revenue for the football club under its committee and the management of Charlie Christie. Daily, weekly and special prizes are on offer, and members eagerly await that letter, telephone call or visit from Charlie which means that the electronic board has flashed up one of their numbers. In common with many fundraisers, the club suffered badly when the National Lottery was introduced in November 1994. Membership dropped, but it survived that scare and by the end of 2003-4 had 2500 subscribers. Over ten years, it has contributed in excess of £700,000 to the football club.

In early November the successes continued with wins against Arbroath 5-1 at home and Queen's Park 3-0 away. Both scores included braces from Iain Stewart. An eight-game unbeaten run was ended at the season's second local derby on the 18th. This time, the venue was Victoria Park in front of a 4288 crowd and it was a much more placid affair than in September. County won 2-0 thanks to a Jamie MacPherson double. November's fixtures were completed with a disappointing 1-1 home draw with Alloa. Caley Thistle now lay fourth.

In late November, Inverness and Nairn Enterprise offered £655,000 for land renewal to establish an access road via the harbour to the new stadium. This grant was dependent on the Council confirming its £900,000 and the Harbour Trust also contributing. INE correctly realised that the project was not just about a football stadium – the East Longman area would be opened up for development and this would ease the severe shortage of building land. In time, the road was to become a popular (and vital) route via the harbour area to the A9 and would eventually service prime development land.

There were only two league games played in December. A home 1-1 draw with East Stirling and a goalless away draw at Cowdenbeath led to a minor slip to fourth by the year end. The biggest event of December took place on 9 December with the Highland Office Equipment-sponsored Inverness Cup Final against Ross County at Grant Street Park. On the day before this match Steve Paterson made two important signings when Mike Teasdale arrived from Dundee and Brian Thomson from Huntly. Paterson noted with delight that: 'We have got two quality players for less than we paid for Iain Stewart.' Chairman Dougie McGilvray optimistically hailed the signings as 'our first big step towards the Premier Division.' Both made their debut in the final. Teasdale scored the fourth goal in the 5-2 win. Iain Stewart scored a hat-trick and Charlie Christie netted one. Teasdale had been close to signing in October, after terms had been agreed between the clubs, but he wanted to remain full time. Eventually he had a change of heart and moved to Inverness.

December 1995 also saw the mooting of controversial proposals to change the league set-up to 16/12/12 from the start of 1996-7. The instigators were the leading First Division clubs who, of course, had the most to gain. Both Caledonian Thistle and Ross County were unhappy, as they would have nothing to play for over the rest of 1995-6. Neither had a vote as they were only associate members of the Scottish League for the first five years. In the event, reconstruction did not happen.

On 18 December the Council ratified the £900,000 grant after a motion introduced by David Stewart was passed 14-12. The grant would be paid 'subject to Objective One and INE funding being payable'. The exact wording was to prove a major problem, but all three payments were now agreed and inter-dependent.

Remarkable Cup run

A major snow clearance operation took place at Telford Street between Christmas and New Year in an abortive attempt to save the derby match on 2 January. Attention then turned to the Scottish Cup-tie against Livingston the following Saturday. The snow removal revealed deep ice – then a sudden thaw caused a flood and necessitated the use of a water pump. It all proved worthwhile, as the pitch was declared playable and the second-round match went ahead. It was to herald the start of a remarkable Cup run. The home side were ahead 2-0 in 24 minutes through Davie Ross and

Mike Teasdale but Livingston pulled two goals back in 67 and 76 minutes. From the restart Iain MacArthur set up Alan Hercher who slid the ball past Rab Douglas for the winner.

There was a footnote to the match when the Caley Club received a letter from Duncan Bennett, secretary of the official Livingston FC Supporters' Club: 'On behalf of the membership of Livingston FC Supporters' Club I wish to take this opportunity to thank you for the excellent welcome we received prior to the Scottish Cup fixture on 6 January and would ask that you also convey our thanks to your own staff and membership for their warmth of hospitality. We did however note that a few of your rather misguided membership actually wanted their team to *win* the fixture; I do hope you will discourage this unreasonable behaviour in future.'

Interest was growing in 18-year-old full back Richard Hastings. The former Scottish schoolboy international was watched by Celtic, Dundee United and Manchester United (amongst others) in November, but by January the front runners were Hibs. In the event, no transfer took place and Hastings was the first player to turn full-time with the club in the summer of 1997.

The team went through January undefeated in the league, climbed to second place and Steve Paterson was named 'Manager of the Month' for the second time. January's triumphs included a 5-1 win at East Stirling on the 20th with another hat-trick from Iain Stewart and an important milestone when Mark McAllister became the first player to reach 50 appearances. The New Year home derby was finally played on the 23rd and attracted a season league record crowd of 4931 – quite an achievement considering it was a Tuesday night in January. The match ended 1-1.

East Fife were drawn at home in the third round of the Scottish Cup and the match took place at the end of January. Once more, snow had to be removed to allow the game to go ahead. Iain Stewart gave the home side the lead in 11 minutes but a spectacular late equaliser from Trinidad international Arnold Dwarika took the tie to a replay. This was at Methil on 12 February and it was a quite a match. East Fife thought it was all over when they took the lead in 75 minutes, then held on to the last minute. With three minutes left, player/manager Steve Archibald substituted himself, then replaced Richard Gibb with seconds to go. This all took place in slow motion and the time wasting was to prove decisive. The whistle was looming when Iain

MacArthur sent a long throw goalwards and it finished up in the net. Alan Hercher was credited with the last touch and extra time was needed with East Fife having dispensed with, arguably, their best players. There were no more goals and it was on to a dreaded penalty shoot-out. Caley Thistle won 3-1 and the right to an away match at Stenhousemuir only five days later.

Sandwiched between the East Fife games was an away league match at Cowdenbeath. This was scheduled for Telford Street but was switched to Cowdenbeath on the Friday because of a frozen pitch. Central Park was not much better and, despite taking an early lead through Charlie Christie, Caley Thistle lost 2-1. The crowd was a pitiful 229 – only fractionally more than the record-low of a year earlier.

There was high demand for places on the supporters' buses to Stenhousemuir for the cup-tie on 17 February. Many more travelled by car. The 500 or so travellers were rewarded with a narrow victory, but it was a long time coming. Second Division Stenhousemuir had a formidable cup reputation, having defeated St Johnstone and Aberdeen the previous season, and they had beaten Falkirk 2-0 in the third round. The Warriors' record made them pre-match favourites, particularly with home advantage, and they made a good start by piling on first-half pressure. The tide began to turn in the second half and Caley Thistle's efforts paid off in 75 minutes. Brian Thomson latched onto a cross from Mike Teasdale, steadied himself, then scored with a rocket. This would be his most valuable goal for the club. It was enough to settle the tie, although Stenhousemuir had a disallowed effort in the last minute. Charlie Christie was named 'Man of the Match'.

The 'Gers in Dundee

The quarter-final draw brought the biggest cheer of the day. Scotland manager Craig Brown pulled out Caledonian Thistle and one of his predecessors, Ally MacLeod, drew the mighty Rangers. Spirits were deservedly high on the bus home – so high that Perth was passed without dropping off the Aberdeen contingent who had left their cars at McDiarmid Park. A quick about-turn at Dunkeld was necessary, but it was not a day for complaining about a few extra miles. The unified club's first taste of real cup fever started immediately, but there were three more league matches to be played in February – home victories against Arbroath and Albion Rovers and a dismal 1-0 home defeat at the hands of Brechin. The Brechin game attracted 2514 spectators and the kick-off was delayed for ten minutes, but not all were there for the football. Vouchers were being given out for cup tickets and the queue ran the length of Telford Street. February's successes resulted in Steve Paterson winning his third 'Manager of the Month' award.

Difficulties surfaced over the District Council's £900,000 grant, with doubts over the meaning of the word 'payable' in the motion approved on 18 December. Counsel's opinion was that this meant the money had to actually have been paid by the other bodies before the Council could release the £900,000. A District Council meeting on 26 February just failed to pass a motion to pay the money immediately. Seventeen out of 26 members voted 'Yes' but the requisite two-thirds majority was not quite achieved. This put the responsibility for the final decision on the incoming Highland Council which was due to take over the former Highland Regional Council area in April.

In February reserve team coach Dave Milroy left to become manager of Forres Mechanics and the same month saw the possibility mooted of Clach ground-sharing at Caledonian Stadium because of their financial difficulties. On 15 February the members' club agreed a change of name to Inverness Caledonian Thistle from the start of 1996-7, the inclusion of Inverness in the title being a condition of the £900,000 grant. The club had agreed in June 1995 that a change was necessary and this was the formal adoption of the new name.

March was dominated by the Rangers cup-tie on the ninth, but first there were two league matches – a satisfying 2-2 away draw against a strong Livingston side, then 1-1 at home to Queen's Park. This result was a major blow to the still-live promotion chances and the Rangers' game was certainly a distraction. Canadian national Under-20 team manager Bruce Twamley travelled with the team en route to the away match at Livingston to run the rule over British Columbia-born Richard Hastings. He selected Hastings for Canada's World Cup qualifying campaign. This was the start of a very successful international career and much transatlantic travel.

Within minutes of the quarter-final draw the chairman insisted that the Rangers tie would take place in Inverness, but the local police expressed doubts over safety. Superintendent Donald Finlayson, Area Commander for Inverness and Nairn, explained the position of the police: 'My concerns were based on a variety of issues, both inside and outside the ground. One of the major problems within the ground was the possibility of opposing fans mixing. That, and no aisles on the terracing, would have made crowd-control very difficult....I know I'm not the most popular man at the moment but public safety is paramount.' There were also worries over traffic management and crowd control problems in Telford Street. SFA security adviser Bill McDougall came to Inverness and, after consulting with the police, recommended that the tie be moved south. The SFA chose Dundee United's Tannadice with its 12,600 capacity, although the club's preferences were Hampden or Perth's McDiarmid Park. Despite the revised location, demand was very high when tickets went on sale in the Caledonian Social Club on 27 February.

The road to Dundee was packed with Caley Thistle supporters on 9 March – 5500 fans travelled in 30 buses and a cavalcade of cars. There was a carnival atmosphere, but Rangers were always firm favourites. The players enjoyed a touch of luxury the night before at Dunblane Hydro, and a classic team talk from Paterson and Caldwell – one fondly remembered by all the players. Gone were complicated tactics, to be replaced by a light-hearted approach. This helped the players not to be too over-awed by the occasion and to go out in a positive frame of mind.

Midfielder John Scott, a Celtic fan, had an extra reason for relishing the match as on the day he was to celebrate a special birthday: 'One way or another I'm never going to forget my 21st birthday but I'm sorry we're not playing Celtic.' Scott's special target – apart from winning the match – was to swap shirts with Rangers' legend Paul Gascoigne and, having agreed the deal at the warm-up, he achieved this at the final whistle. The underdogs put up a good show but Rangers never looked like losing. After surviving the first 15 minutes, things began to go wrong. A long clearance from Andy Goram set Peter van Vossen on a run and, as he attempted to find Brian Laudrup, the pass was intercepted by Brian Thomson. By a cruel twist of fate the ball broke the wrong way and flew past Jim Calder to give Rangers the lead. It was all effectively over in 35 minutes when Gascoigne made it 2-0 with a classic goal. He side-stepped Iain MacArthur's challenge and flighted the ball into the top corner from 20 yards. Seven minutes into the second half Gascoigne made it 3-0 when he headed home from the back post after a perfect Laudrup cross. In the build-up, Gascoigne elbowed Ally McCoist who needed treatment before continuing. Caley Thistle fought on and they did have chances. The best came when Brian Thomson and Charlie Christie combined to set up Iain Stewart – Stewart beat David Robertson and in trying to bend the ball past

Goram he put it wide. Mike Teasdale and John Scott brought out saves from Andy Goram and the consolation goal was not to be. In the end, Rangers were clear winners but the Inverness side went home with their pride intact. Shirt-swapping followed the final whistle and the Caley Thistle players took home souvenirs as well as memories. A respectable result, the bank manager was happy, a good day out was had by all and it was back to the league. Not surprisingly, the crowd of 11,296 was a season record for the club.

The manager's biggest fear had been a heavy defeat, particularly a repeat of Rangers' 10-1 thrashing of Keith in the third round, but in the end he was happy: 'It's not often I could say after a 3-0 defeat that I'm delighted. We set out to keep our self-respect and the reaction of the crowd at the end proved we succeeded in that. The support was out of this world and I'm sure they all enjoyed the day as well.' Defender Graeme Bennett described the Rangers' match as 'Undoubtedly my most memorable moment in football. Particularly the excitement and hype it created for the week beforehand and also how well we coped on the day.' Goalkeeper Jim Calder describes his most memorable moments in football up to then as the discovery that Rangers had been drawn in the cup and the match itself – not surprising, as he was named 'Man of the Match'.

Substitute Dave McGinlay arranged a ticket for his brother, Scotland international John, but the Celtic fan found himself at the Rangers end. He was recognised very quickly and had to endure a great deal of friendly banter throughout the match. At the final whistle Dave negotiated with the security officials and brought John along the track to the players' entrance – much to the amusement of the Rangers' contingent in the main stand who 'gave me absolute pelters.'

Paterson had hoped that the cup excitement would spur his team on in the league but it did not happen. Three days after the Tannadice trip, promotion hopes took a major dent with a goalless home draw against Alloa. The strain of the cup run was clearly telling on the part-time players and it was not any better the following Saturday when the final derby match went County's way 2-1 in Dingwall. County were really up for the match and were always on top. Caley Thistle's only consolation was a late goal from substitute Mark McAllister.

March was completed with four points from two games. Before the Rangers game, Livingston were in pole position, with Brechin second. Caley Thistle were five points adrift in third place but with a game in hand. At the end of March there was a slip to fourth, nine points behind joint leaders Brechin and Livingston. Ross County were one point ahead in third place. The chase for promotion was effectively (if not mathematically) over for another season and the management team began to turn their attention to the future. The first priority would be to decide which players were to be discarded and who could be brought in to strengthen the squad.

The complicated web of grants was unravelled on the new Council's first day in office – April Fool's Day. The shadow Highland Council had met prior to that date and all indications were that it would refuse to honour its predecessor's commitment. Chief Executive Arthur McCourt masterminded an eleventh-hour deal that won the support of members and avoided the threat of legal action. McCourt recommended that the town's Common Good Fund be used, as its 1996-7 income was largely uncommitted. This won the day and it was agreed that the payment would be split over two years. The other inter-dependent grants from the European Objective One Fund and Inverness and Nairn Enterprise were confirmed. Chairman Dougie McGilvray was relieved that the saga was over: 'We will now be working along with the Council to develop the Longman for the good of the people of Inverness.'

Going into April there was still a tiny glimmer of promotion hope, but a 3-0 home defeat by East Stirling on the 6th was a major setback. Paterson was disappointed at the lack of passion and declared that confidence in the dressing room was at rock bottom – a far cry from the heady days of Tannadice a month earlier. On 13 April Cowdenbeath were beaten 2-0 at home but promotion became mathematically impossible the following week with a 1-1 home draw against Albion Rovers. A 1-0 away win at Brechin on the 27th was academic to Caley Thistle, but it did end the newly-promoted side's championship challenge. The season finished on 4 May with a visit from champions-elect Livingston. The Livi Lions won 2-1: Steve Paterson's first league campaign started and ended with defeats by Jim Leishman's side.

Third in the League

In the end, Caledonian Thistle finished third with 57 points. Ross County were one place and four points behind. In 43 league and cup matches, a total of 72 goals were scored and 48 conceded. Iain Stewart was top scorer in the division with 24, well ahead of anyone else at the club. Alan Hercher and Charlie Christie were the closest on 12 each. The goals were shared by a total of 13 players with an additional two own goals. Captain Mike Noble achieved a 100% appearance record with 43; Iain Stewart was one behind on 42. By the end of the season six more players had joined Mark McAllister in passing the 50 career-appearance milestone. The reserve side finished the season third in the North Caledonian League with 33 points from 24 games. The 'Player of the Year' awards were presented at a dinner in the Caledonian Hotel after the final match. At the dinner Chairman Dougie McGilvray reminded everyone that he had fulfilled two of the promises made on taking office – he had taken the club a long way (Berwick) and made it a big name in Scottish football (Inverness Caledonian Thistle)!

As the season came to a close the promised player clearout started. Eventually seven left – Mark McRitchie, Dave Brennan, Martin Lisle, Dave McGinlay, Colin Mitchell, Doug Green and Paul McKenzie. Bruce McCraw and Mark Holmes – both on loan to Clach – were also released. Richard Hastings was linked with a move to Ipswich Town in early May and a trial was arranged. Ipswich manager George Burley had been tipped off about the youngster's potential by his former team-mate Canadian coach Bruce Twamley. As with previous high-level interest in the player, it came to nothing.

There was one more competitive game on 8 May when Clach were beaten 3-1 in the *Inverness Courier* Challenge Cup. On the same day the club appointed Bruce Graham as its first general manager. In other off-the-field events the club announced a share issue to the value of £700,000 and, on 14 May, it was also confirmed that Telford Street Park had been sold to Ladbroke Group Properties for £1 million. Ladbroke were the successors to Texas Homecare who had been watching events and waiting patiently to purchase the site. Kingsmills Park had raised £486,000 and its site was to be used for a private nursing home and houses. There was one change to the board during the season. The existing nine members were augmented in February 1996 by the addition of Jim Jarvie, who took on the responsibility of youth development.

Work on the new stadium was now well under way: pitch contractor Sports Grounds Ltd started turf-laying on 24 April. It was, however, clear that it could not be ready for the start of 1996-7. The Scottish League agreed that Telford Street could be used until completion and they also approved the new club name. Steve Paterson's first season had been a success and all now looked forward to more of the same and the move to Caledonian Stadium.

CHAPTER 6

DIVISION THREE CHAMPIONS
1996-7

INVERNESS CALEDONIAN THISTLE FC 1996-7   *(photo: Ken MacPherson)*

(*Back*) Robbie Benson, Scott McLean, Mike Teasdale, Davie Ross, Iain MacArthur, Neal Sinclair

(*Middle*) John MacAskill (doctor), Tommy Cumming (kit), Paul Cherry, Don MacMillan, Jim Calder, Alan Hercher, Ian Manning (physio)

(*Front*) Steve Paterson (manager), Charlie Christie, Barry Wilson, Mike Noble (captain), Richard Hastings, Graeme Bennett, Alex Caldwell (assistant manager)

GOING BALLISTIC!

Euro 96 ensured that fans were not starved of football during the close season and the club prepared for what turned out to be a red-letter season – a change of name to Inverness Caledonian Thistle, a new stadium and promotion. On 27 July the club held an open day at East Longman to allow fans to see what all the fuss had been about. Almost 1000 turned up and the verdict on the stadium's progress was very positive. The chairman was enthusiastic: 'There's not a team in the third or second division with a facility with the potential of this. The response today is absolutely fantastic and everybody is amazed by the size of the park and the size of the stand.' The players posed for photographs then played a bounce game on the new pitch.

Following an open meeting, and encouragement from the board, an official supporters' club was formed at the Greig Street Social Club on 30 July. Ann Nicoll was elected to the chair with George Macrae vice-chairman, Iain Kennedy secretary and Gordon Munro treasurer. The new committee held its inaugural meeting on 12 August and the club was welcomed as a new member at the AGM of the Scottish Federation of Football Supporters Clubs in Edinburgh. Ann Nicoll remained in office until mid 2000-1: she officially resigned at the AGM on 14 June 2001. Vice-chairman George Macrae took charge temporarily until the AGM when secretary Mairi Maclean was elected to the chair. The main activity of the official supporter's club over the years has been the organisation of travel to away games. For seven years George Macrae organised the supporters' buses with great success; this was continued by Kath 'Lady' Fraser when she succeeded to the post at the beginning of 2001-2. Peter MacCallum is the only original committee member to remain in post at the end of 2003-4. Other supporters' clubs have come and gone over the years but the official one remains the lynchpin of the local supporters' movement. It is augmented by the website's 'Internutters' who are all members and who spread the word worldwide. The 'Internutters Supporters Club' came together on the website's message forums and includes members from China, Australia and North America as well as all over the UK. It has always been affiliated to the official supporters' club, and in 2003-4 was fully integrated. There is a Smithton and Culloden supporters' club and other groups travel regularly to matches from the Social Club in Greig Street, Fairways Leisure, the Thistle Bar and a variety of other hostelries.

Injury had curtailed Danny MacDonald's first team career. In July he was appointed the club's full-time community and development officer to add to his role of reserve team manager. He did not rule out a return to top-level football, but was now to become deeply involved in all aspects of the game in the local community. MacDonald was confident that the long-term benefits for the club would be enormous: 'By raising the profile of Inverness Caledonian Thistle within the schools and the local community I hope to encourage more and more people to take an interest in their own football club.'

As well as the planned player clearout there was one unexpected departure – promising midfielder John Scott decided to take up a soccer scholarship in New York. Steve Paterson strengthened the squad with a number of signings. Former Hearts and Cowdenbeath defender Paul Cherry came from St Johnstone, despite a number of other opportunities: 'I had offers from First Division clubs and two Irish league outfits. Initially I wanted to stay at the highest level possible but decided on Caledonian Thistle. I was impressed with the plans for the club and the enthusiasm of Dougie McGilvray and Steve Paterson. They had a 5-year plan to get into the First Division and I wanted to play a part in helping them achieve it.'

On Cherry's recommendation Paterson also signed Scott McLean from St Johnstone. Ex-Ross County favourite Barry Wilson came from Raith Rovers, after playing a trial match with St Johnstone. Saints invited him back for a second time but Wilson was anxious to make a choice and accepted an offer to come to Inverness: 'It was a big decision and I think I made the right one. After speaking with the chairman and having a tour of the new stadium I was impressed with the whole set-up.' Seventeen-year-old Ross Tokely signed from Huntly and Burghead youngster Wayne Addicoat joined from junior side Deveronside. After the season had started Paterson went back to his old club Huntly for a third time and signed Marco De-Barros. Neal Sinclair was recalled from loan at Nairn County.

The goalkeeping situation proved complicated. Mark McRitchie left for Lossiemouth and attempts to sign Les Fridge or Barry Thomson failed. Former Inverness Thistle player Fridge was available on a free transfer from Raith Rovers, but he wanted to stay full-time. He eventually went to Dundalk in Ireland and came to Inverness in May 1997. Thomson had been released by Dundee and looked set to join. He turned down the move and the club were left with no understudy to Jim Calder. The post was filled by former Brora Rangers and Ross County goalkeeper Don MacMillan. He joined in the knowledge that Calder was number one choice and played all season with the reserves, apart from one first-team appearance.

GOING BALLISTIC!

After pounding the sand at Lossiemouth in pre-season training, real football started with the Buchan Cup at Peterhead on 20 to 21 July. A 3-2 win against Fraserburgh on the Saturday earned a final place against St Johnstone the next day. Saints narrowly won 1-0. In home friendlies the following Friday and Monday, Queen of the South were beaten 2-0 and Hamilton held to a goalless draw.

Saturday 3 August saw the first game under the new name – an away Coca-Cola Cup-tie against Clyde. There was added pressure: the winners would play Celtic at home. A decision on the venue had to be made in advance and an agreement was reached to use St Johnstone's McDiarmid Park. Press officer Ken Thomson compared the tie with the Rangers one and anticipated the same crowd control problems: 'While Rangers may be the biggest crowd-pullers in Scotland the game with Celtic would still be a sell-out. We are desperately disappointed that the game cannot be played at Telford Street but we felt we had to make arrangements as soon as possible to move the match.' En route to Broadwood, tickets for the Celtic match were collected in Perth but they were not required. Despite the hype and incentive, the game was a drab affair and a major disappointment. A goal from Eddie Annand six minutes into extra time gave Clyde a 1-0 victory.

A week later Livingston were knocked out of the League Challenge Cup at Almondvale. Brian Thomson gave Caley Thistle the lead in nine minutes and it lasted until a Jason Young equaliser in 71 minutes. With 15 seconds to go, it remained 1-1 but a powerful Paul Cherry header from a Brian Thomson cross brought victory. This match marked the last appearance of full back Mark McAllister before he moved to London and a new career.

Every Caley Thistle fan remembers 1996-7 as the Third Division championship season, but many will have forgotten that things did not start well. The league campaign began on 17 August with a 3-1 home defeat by Cowdenbeath. Iain Stewart missed a penalty at 0-0 and Brian Thomson scored from a second award to make it 1-1. At 1-3, with three minutes left, Charlie Christie was brought down and a third penalty was initially given. The award was reversed and Paul Cherry red-carded for an off-the-ball incident. There was a similar score at Forfar a week later. Then it was down to Stirling in midweek for the second round of the Challenge Cup. The 3-1 score in favour of the home side did not tell the full story. All the goals came in the second half and Stirling were 2-0 up after 74 minutes. With nine minutes left, Iain Stewart pulled one back and Caley Thistle chased the equaliser. The tie was settled when Alex Bone scored Stirling's third a minute from time.

The league tide turned on 31 August at home against Alloa – but only at the last minute. It looked like ending 0-0 when defender Mike Teasdale popped up to head the winner. Paterson praised his team's display: 'Getting a win at last is a fantastic relief – but we should have had the game won before we did. We played really well and after Mike Teasdale's header landed in the back of the net you could feel the sense of relief around the ground.' This still left Caley Thistle in a lowly eighth place.

The first win set up a good September with two wins and two draws. A goalless draw away to Albion Rovers on 7 September was followed by a 2-0 home win against East Stirling. Alan Hercher and Mike Noble scored the goals in a match dominated by Caley Thistle. There was a disappointing 2-2 draw at home to Queen's Park on the 21st. Goals from Iain Stewart and Charlie Christie had made it 2-1, with pressure for a third goal. The points looked safe but Queen's broke away and equalised with nine minutes left. The month ended with the first derby of the season at Dingwall. Two Iain Stewart goals and a last-minute strike from Brian Thomson ensured a 3-1 victory. The game was marred by a coin-throwing incident at the County end, in which a County player was hit and the game stopped for several minutes. By the end of September there was a major improvement in the league with a climb to fourth.

The 2-0 victory against Arbroath on 5 October was the last competitive match at Telford Street, and then it was four matches on the road to allow the completion of Caledonian Stadium. The first goal against Arbroath was scored by Brian Thomson and the historic second by Iain Stewart, the last competitive goal at the former Caledonian FC ground. The following week it was off to Montrose's Glebe Park and a 2-2 draw. Caley Thistle were in the lead twice through Iain Stewart and Davie Ross, but twice Montrose came back. It had looked as if Ross's 81st minute goal would secure a win and the home fans started to leave. With three minutes left, a Mark Craib header made it 2-2.

On 19 October it was down to Cowdenbeath and an exciting encounter which earned top place in Division Three. It was quite a match – or rather quite a finish. Brian Thomson gave Caley Thistle the lead in only four minutes but Cowdenbeath equalised then pulled ahead. By the 73rd minute the home side were 3-1 up but Alan Hercher made it 3-2 three minutes later. It still looked good for Cowdenbeath until five minutes into injury time, when Barry Wilson was brought down and Brian Thomson hammered in the penalty. From the restart a Ross Tokely cross fooled Cowdenbeath goalkeeper Neil Russell – he dived too early and Iain Stewart nipped in to score and take all three points. The 4-3 scoreline was the highest aggregate of the season. Edinburgh-based supporter Jim Rendall had a traumatic afternoon. Jim's cousin Craig Sinclair was playing for Cowdenbeath and had to be stretchered off with a serious knee injury – it was this that led to the lengthy spell of added time. The obvious steal of the points in these circumstances did not go down well with the rest of the family and Jim's celebrations were understandably muted.

Farewell to Telford Street

On Sunday 20 October the curtain came down officially on Telford Street Park. The first Telford Street pitch had come into use in 1889 and Caley moved to the site now being vacated in 1905. The final match was a friendly against a Highland League Select. The Select won 3-0 and the honour of scoring the last goal went to the Select's Gary Clark with a 90th-minute penalty. There were emotional scenes all round, and the bulldozers moved in shortly after to start work on a retail park. Souvenir hunters had their moment, with official sanction, and a number of gardens around Inverness can boast lawns created from the hallowed pitch. Programmes for the last match are still at a premium because of a short print run and high demand. October was completed by a 2-0 defeat at Forfar on the 26th and a slip back to fourth place.

A drab 0-0 draw at East Stirling on 2 November is best forgotten. It was time to move into the new home. Caledonian Stadium was opened by a low-key match against an Inverness Select on Wednesday 6 November. This was to allow everyone to find their way around the new ground. Caley Thistle beat the Select 6-2, including four from Scott McLean. The honour of scoring the first goal went to the Select's Norman Kellas.

Albion Rovers were the visitors for the official opening on 9 November and Provost Allan Sellar took the first kick. Prior to the match, chairman Dougie McGilvray was presented with a cheque for £500,000 from local

MPs Sir Russell Johnston and Charles Kennedy on behalf of the Football Trust – part of a total grant of £618,600 towards the stadium costs. The 1-1 draw did not live up to the expectations of the crowd of 3734, but it was an historic day despite that. Albion's Dave McKenzie scored the first league goal and Iain Stewart the equaliser. The chairman said that he could not have asked for a better day: 'It's been great. This stadium represents the dreams of everyone connected with the club. The only way is up.'

The following week Caledonian Stadium hosted its first derby and a crowd of 4562. This turned out to be a bad-tempered affair, with County's Sandy Ross seeing red and seven players receiving yellow cards. An Iain Stewart brace gave the home side a 2-0 victory but the game was marred by a bad injury to key goalscorer Brian Thomson. It would be March 1997 before Thomson could play again. Thomson's misfortune allowed Scott McLean to come in for an extended run in the team. A 3-2 win at Hampden against Queen's Park on 23 November sent Caley Thistle back to the top of Division Three. Scott McLean, Barry Wilson and Charlie Christie scored in the first 20 minutes but Queen's pulled a goal back just on half time. Steve Paterson described the scoring spell as 'arguably our best 20 minutes of the season'. In 61 minutes it was 3-2 and, despite continuous Spiders' pressure, victory was secured. Caley Thistle were to hold pole position almost continuously until the end of the season. It was now all about consistency: this was achieved with a string of five league wins from 16 November to 21 December, part of an undefeated run of 22 league games from 2 November 1996 to 19 April 1997. There is no doubt that moving to the new stadium, with its high-quality wide pitch, played a large part in maintaining this purple patch. Southern teams began to fear the trip north.

Tommy Cumming was appointed groundsman at the new stadium, adding to his duties as kitman. Tommy joined Caledonian in June 1972 and has been at the club ever since. He is a busy man in the lead up to matches, both home and away. In advance of a home match there is much preparation – the grass has to be cut in the growing season, watering is needed in dry spells, repairs may be required, the pitch has to be lined and goalposts and nets erected. Things become fraught in mid-winter, particularly when there is a snow or frost risk but, thanks partly to the Moray Firth location, few games have had to be cancelled. At times of heavy snow, teams of volunteers are called in to clear the pitch. When games are in doubt, a local referee will inspect the pitch and make an early decision to prevent unnecessary travel for away teams. In the close season, major repairs and re-seeding are carried out. Tommy's kitman duties involve ordering items in the correct sizes, arranging for kit to be washed and ensuring that all items are laid out in the dressing room ready for a match. Away matches mean the same kit routine but with the added tasks of packing and loading/unloading the team bus.

Clach's immediate future was resolved during November, with a consortium involving Caley Thistle taking ownership of Grant Street Park at a cost of £280,000 and leasing it back to the club. It looked for a while as if Clach would move to Dingwall, following an agreement with Ross County, but the decision was reversed at the eleventh hour. The aim was now to forge close links between the two Inverness clubs and this came to pass. A number of Caley Thistle youngsters were to spend loan periods with Clach to mutual advantage.

In December a David Balfe-produced club song featuring the golden tonsils of Mike Noble and Graeme Bennett was released on cassette. 'Bring It On Home' was not destined for the charts, but it earned popularity with the fans and was regularly aired over the tannoy. With no game on the 7th, top spot in the league was temporarily surrendered, only to be regained a week later when Montrose were defeated at home 2-0 with goals from Iain Stewart and Scott McLean. The number one position was to be held until the end of the season. Only one other match was played in December – a 2-1 home win against Cowdenbeath on the 21st with Iain Stewart continuing his remarkable run by scoring both goals.

There was disappointment on 28 December when an away match at Alloa was postponed 90 minutes before kick-off. The team bus reached the ground shortly after referee Kevin Toner deemed the pitch too hard and with the supporters' bus in Bridge of Allan. The postponement was hard to take, as everyone except the referee thought the pitch playable – indeed Alloa later played a bounce game on it. There was nothing for it but to head back up the A9. Alloa were embarrassed by the incident and chairman Pat Lawlor was very apologetic. Fans were compensated with free soup and pies.

January was dominated by a Scottish Cup saga involving a long away trip to Stranraer. The second round tie was initially scheduled for the fourth but was delayed a week due to the weather. The team and officials stayed overnight in Ayr before the rearranged match on the 11th but, prior to leaving for Stranraer, they heard that it had been postponed again. The supporters' bus was turned back at Stirling. A waterlogged pitch was blamed for the cancellation and frantic efforts were made to allow the fixture to be switched to the Sunday. This failed, everyone went home and the tie went ahead on the Monday. The evening kick-off meant Stranraer could be reached without another overnight stop – but the journey took its toll. Iain MacArthur took ill during the first half and had to be substituted. The match ended 1-1 with Scott McLean's 63rd minute goal being cancelled out 12 minutes later. It was now Stranraer's turn to make the 520-mile round trip two days later. The replay ended 0-0 but Caley Thistle won the penalty shoot-out 4-3, thanks mainly to two Jim Calder saves at critical moments.

There were two home league matches before the third round of the cup. Arbroath were soundly beaten 4-1 on 18 January, thanks partly to a double from Alan Hercher. It had been feared that the midweek travel and exertions against Stranraer would take their toll, but all proved to be well. On the following Wednesday, Queen's Park came north and were beaten 1-0. The only goal came from a disputed 80th-minute Iain Stewart penalty after Barry Wilson was tripped in the box. The Hampden officials were livid and referee Sandy Roy was not popular in Mount Florida for some time thereafter. A back injury forced Jim Calder to miss the game and Don MacMillan took his place between the posts. The 1-0 win ensured that MacMillan's only first-team match was a shut-out.

The third round of the Scottish Cup threw up a home tie against Second Division Hamilton on 25 January. Despite taking a 12th-minute lead, the match was eventually lost 3-1. A two-goal hero for Hamilton that day was Paul Ritchie who was to join the Inverness side in the summer of 2001 and score 63 goals in three seasons. The attendance of 3310 was the highest of the six cup matches played over the season.

There were five league games squeezed into February's 28 days, starting with a visit to Montrose on the 1st. Striker Scott McLean's drive to the match ended abruptly when his car ran out of petrol. He hitched a lift, arrived late and had to settle for a seat on the bench. Alan Hercher took his place but was injured after 22 minutes. McLean came on and scored the first goal. Iain Stewart clinched the points with an 89th-minute penalty after Chris Masson had handled in the box. The following Saturday, a gale-force wind at Caledonian Stadium could not prevent an exciting 3-2 win over East Stirling. Early goals from Iain

Stewart and Barry Wilson seemed to set up a comfortable afternoon, but two East Stirling strikes either side of the break made it 2-2. Scott McLean ensured that the title march kept on the right road with a 71st-minute winner. The following Wednesday, it was off to Dingwall and the derby match postponed from New Year's Day. In a 3-0 win, Scott McLean scored twice and Barry Wilson once, despite barracking from fans of his former club. Only heroics from County goalkeeper Steve Hutchison kept the score down. This match nudged the Third Division record attendance up to 5017 and saw Caley Thistle go ten points clear at the top of the table with a game in hand.

There were two other league games in February – 3-0 away to Albion Rovers and 1-1 at home to Forfar. The Coatbridge match was hard fought: 0-0 at half time. The Wee Rovers finally succumbed to three second-half goals. The Forfar game was a top-of-the-table clash played in high winds. Forfar took the lead through Bobby Mann, but Iain Stewart managed a late equaliser. There were chances at both ends before a hectic last few minutes. Forfar were awarded an indirect free kick on the six-yard line, but ten home players packed the goal line and Paul Cherry cleared the danger.

The lead at the top of Division Three was stretched by four straight victories in March, culminating in another 3-0 victory at home to Ross County. It started on the 1st with a 3-1 home win against Alloa in wet and windy conditions – Iain Stewart scored two and Davie Ross one. Then it was a stuttering 2-1 win at Hampden on 8 March. Queen's Park scored first in 72 minutes but Iain Stewart equalised just three minutes later. Ross Tokely scored the winner two minutes later – a fitting way to celebrate his 18th birthday. The club's 100th league game took place on the following Tuesday at Alloa and ended successfully in a 2-0 win. Mike Noble became the first player to reach the 100-appearance milestone and scored the second goal after Scott McLean had given Caley Thistle the lead. The home derby against County on the 15th ended 3-0 and contained the usual ingredients – a new record crowd of 5525, one red card (for County's Sandy Ross) and five yellow cards. Iain Stewart scored a brace and Brian Thomson scored the third on his return from long-term absence. He came on as a substitute for Scott McLean, who had sustained a bad leg injury. It would be a year before McLean returned to the side. The following week it was off to Arbroath, where victory would seal promotion. Hopes were high – but the reality was rather different. In a poor match, Arbroath held a nervous Inverness side to a 0-0 draw. The party had to be delayed – but the champagne was only kept on ice for another week.

On 5 April a 3-2 home victory over Montrose made promotion certain. The venue seemed the right one for the celebrations. It was also fitting that Iain Stewart should score all three goals. His sharpshooting skills were a major factor in the winning run and these goals pushed his tally for the season to 28. Stewart scored the first in 13 minutes but things deteriorated for a while as Montrose equalised from a penalty, defender Iain MacArthur went off injured, and Montrose took a 2-1 lead just before the interval. Two more strikes from Stewart in the second period eased the tension and secured promotion. His third goal was a trademark lob over Jim Butter nine minutes from time, and the normally subdued crowd could at last celebrate. The hat-trick hero was delighted: 'It was an amazing experience to clinch promotion with three goals in front of a large home crowd and the TV cameras.'

Chairman Dougie McGilvray looked forward: 'This is a great day for the town but we have to continue planning and keep the momentum going for the good of the club. I believe we have no option but to turn full-time.' A relieved and proud Steve Paterson praised his players: 'The performance in turning the game around showed the character and determination that separates champions from the also-rans.' Caley Thistle just pipped St Johnstone as the first team promoted for the season.

Third Division triumph

A 4-1 home victory on 12 April against Albion Rovers clinched the Division Three title in style. Brian Thomson's early goal paved the way, but Rovers equalised. Thomson scored his second just before half time and there was no way back for the visitors. Barry Wilson and Marco De-Barros added numbers three and four in the second half, and it was all over. The goal from De-Barros was a great solo effort and his only strike in 25 appearances. 'We are the Champions' came over the tannoy and the champagne flowed. An emotionally-drained Dougie McGilvray was 'delighted, absolutely delighted'. Steve Paterson described this as 'the pinnacle of my career so far'. Brian Thomson described the manager's contribution: 'His presence in the dressing room is amazing. The boys have total respect for him – and when you have that for your manager then you go out and give him all you've got.'

The rest of the season was rather an anti-climax, and the target of 80 points was not quite reached. East Stirling were defeated 3-0 the following week at Firs Park and Charlie Christie became the second player to notch up 100 appearances. The unbeaten run was ended by a 2-1 away defeat at Cowdenbeath on 26 April. Paul Cherry scored Caley Thistle's only goal and had a header cleared off the line in the dying seconds. Cowdenbeath's Central Park once more earned the title of smallest crowd of the season – this time, only 282.

3 May was a proud day as the Division Three championship trophy was presented after the match against runners-up Forfar. A non-derby record league crowd of 3852 turned up, but Forfar spoiled the party by recording a thumping 4-0 victory – the biggest defeat of the season. Forfar's captain was Bobby Mann, who came to Inverness in February 1999 and took over the captaincy at the start of 2000-1. It was one of these days when nothing went right on the park, but all that was forgotten when Mike Noble accepted the trophy and the team took a lap of honour.

The final game of the season was another anti-climax, with a 1-0 away defeat at Alloa on 10 May. This was Graeme Bennett's last appearance and he was made captain for the day. He moved on to become player/manager at Clach, his first signing being Alan Hercher, whose Caley Thistle career had also come to a close. Bennett returned in early 2000 as director of football. There was one more match in 1996-7 when Aberdeen came to Inverness for a friendly on 14 May and were beaten 3-2. Iain Stewart scored all three goals and the Aberdeen team included three players who would eventually join Caley Thistle – Duncan Shearer, Nicky Walker and Russell Duncan. This game also marked the debuts of Les Fridge and trialist Norwegian defender Vetle Andersen.

In this title-winning season, a total of 76 league points were amassed. In 42 league and cup matches a total of 75 goals were scored and 46 conceded. Top goalscorer by a mile was Iain Stewart with 29 – he was also the Third Division's top scorer. The goals were shared amongst 13 players, but Stewart's dominance is illustrated by the fact that the second highest goalscorer, with 11, was Brian Thomson, who had missed four months of the season through injury. Stewart was also voted Third Division 'Player of the Year' by his fellow players. Mike Teasdale started all 42 matches and Iain Stewart appeared in 42. He started in 39 and came on three times as a substitute. Jim Calder was one behind, with 41 appearances.

DIVISION THREE CHAMPIONS

Steve Paterson won three 'Manager of the Month' Awards and was named 'Third Division Manager of the Year'. The ICT programme was voted 'Third Division Programme of the Year' in the Programme Monthly awards. In the North Caledonian League, the reserve side came second to Ross County with 32 points from 22 games, Ross Tokely won Scotland caps at Under-17 level against Belgium and Denmark in September 1996. Richard Hastings played for the Canadian Under-20 side.

Caledonian Stadium hosted two internationals in March 1997. On Thursday 6th Scotland Under-16s beat England 5-1 and two weeks later Scotland Under-15s beat Wales 2-1. Future Caley Thistle players were featured in both Scotland sides. Russell Duncan captained the Under-16s and Mark Brown was in the starting line-up for the Under-15s. Brown also came on as a substitute in the Under-16 match.

On 16 September 1996 a share issue was launched with a target of £900,000. Applications closed on 9 November 1996 (the date of the official opening of Caledonian Stadium) and £564,370 was raised. There was one board change during the season with the departure of John Price. As the season drew to a close, plans were being laid to go full-time from the start of 1997-8. The key to this was Steve Paterson. With a blossoming career in social work he had to make a difficult personal decision. After much deliberation, the challenge was too great to resist and he accepted a four-year contract. He confirmed that he had 'decided to match the ambitions of the club by turning full-time'. This was announced on 3 May, and three days later Richard Hastings became the first player to sign a full-time contract. Most of the squad would eventually do the same. Now it was onwards and upwards to the Second Division.

CHAPTER 7

DEBUT IN DIVISION TWO
1997-8

INVERNESS CALEDONIAN THISTLE FC 1997-8 *(photo: Trevor Martin)*

(*Back*) Marco De-Barros, Barry Wilson, Paul Cherry (joint captain), Mike Teasdale, Ross Tokely, Scott McLean, Mike Noble

(*Middle*) Vetle Andersen, Brian Thomson, Les Fridge, Jim Calder, Davie Ross, Alan Hercher

(*Front*) Iain MacArthur (joint captain), Charlie Christie, Alex Caldwell (assistant manager), Steve Paterson (manager), Richard Hastings, Iain Stewart

GOING BALLISTIC!

The Second Division at last – and the start of full-time football in Inverness. Steve Paterson and most of the first-team squad accepted full-time contracts but for some important players this 100% commitment to football was not practical. Paul Cherry, Jim Calder, Iain MacArthur, Iain Stewart and Mike Noble stayed part-time and remained at the heart of the club. It would be a further five years before all players were full-time. This was a time of high confidence around Caledonian Stadium – but most of the season was to be spent in the relegation zone. Les Fridge and Vetle Andersen became first-team regulars following their debut match against Aberdeen at the end of 1996-7 and there were several major signings through the season. Graeme Bennett left for the manager's job at Clach and took Alan Hercher and Robbie Benson with him. Fridge's arrival led to the end of Don MacMillan's single-season Inverness career. Richard Hastings had a very short close season as he spent most of June in Malaysia representing Canada at the World Youth Championships – he played against Australia, Argentina and Hungary. Former Caledonian manager John Docherty was appointed reserve team coach on 4 June. On 23 August the full story of the Thistle/Caledonian merger became available with the publication of Charles Bannerman's book *Against All Odds*.

The football started with the usual run of pre-season matches. Six games in seven days began with a visit to Wick on Sunday 19 July for the Norfrost Challenge Cup. The first goal in a 5-0 win was scored in a remarkable 32 seconds down the Harmsworth Park slope by Marco De-Barros. The next day Dunfermline came to Caledonian Stadium and won 3-1. Then it was across the Minch to Lewis for two matches against local select teams with 4-0 and 7-1 successes – one at Fivepenny, Ness and the other at Goathill Park, Stornoway. Most of the Western Isles travellers rested while a team composed mainly of youngsters drew 2-2 at Deveronvale. The week concluded with a 3-1 home win against a spirited Huntly side. The new season's strips were introduced at an open day on Saturday 26 July when all parts of the stadium were open for inspection. A large number of fans turned up and players were available for photographs and autographs.

The last pre-season match was Alan Hercher's testimonial on 28 July against St Johnstone. This was the club's first testimonial and 'Herchie' fully deserved the honour after seven totally-committed seasons with Caledonian and three with the unified club. The former club captain's August 1994 hat-trick against Arbroath and day job as a plumber inspired the tabloid comment that he was 'hell bent on keeping his place after flushing Arbroath down the pan'. St Johnstone won the testimonial 3-1: an unusual feature was the appearance of Les Fridge in the Saints' team as they had travelled north without a fit goalkeeper.

The opening competitive match of the season was a home Coca-Cola Cup-tie against Stenhousemuir on 2 August. Brian Thomson scored a hat-trick in the 5-1 win and was only denied a cash prize from the sponsors because one of the goals came from the penalty spot. The score rather flattered the home side as the Warriors fought hard. They took the lead in 13 minutes through James Henderson, but Charlie Christie equalised in 32 minutes after beating three men and playing a neat one-two with Iain Stewart. Thomson's 69th-minute penalty gave Caley Thistle the lead but the victory was only assured by three goals in the last ten minutes – one from Barry Wilson and two from Thomson. That evening, the club's achievement in winning the Third Division Championship was honoured at a civic reception in the Town House. Provost Allan Sellar welcomed players, directors and officials on behalf of the Inverness Area of Highland Council and Dougie McGilvray spoke in reply. The speeches highlighted the achievements made in just three seasons and looked forward to further success. The chairman sported a kilt in the new club tartan, as did director Dougie Riach.

The Second Division debut game on 6 August turned out to be a repeat of the manager's baptism in the Scottish League two years earlier against Livingston at home. The presentation of the Third Division Championship flag was followed by another tough encounter – but no disappointment this time. Livingston took the lead through a Tom Graham header just after the interval, but the home side gained a point thanks to a last minute goal from Brian Thomson. The crowd of 2232 was to prove to be the highest for a home league match all season.

Motherwell provided Premier opposition at Fir Park in the second round of the Coca-Cola Cup a week later. It was a big day out for everybody and, at 2-0 down after 22 minutes, things looked black. Motherwell were cruising until the referee awarded rather a soft penalty for a challenge on Charlie Christie. Brian Thomson hammered the spot kick past Stevie Woods in his customary style and Caley Thistle were back in the game. Teenager Wayne Addicoat had only just come on as a substitute when he achieved hero status with an 87th-minute equaliser. The home side had Brian Martin sent off in the first period of extra time: when Billy Davies protested at the decision he was also red-carded. Despite the lack of numbers Motherwell held on and easily won the dreaded penalty shoot-out 4-1. Under-pressure Motherwell manager Alex McLeish was a mighty relieved man as he came onto the team bus and congratulated Caley Thistle on their performance. Steve Paterson was upbeat: 'I cannot be too disappointed. I thought Charlie Christie ran the show in the second half. Things are looking good for the season, although we need players to bolster our squad.'

The exertions at Motherwell took their toll. Queen of the South benefitted the following midweek in round one of the League Challenge Cup. Thunder, lightning and heavy rain threatened postponement of this home match, but it went ahead in the continuous rain. The pitch stood up well to the soaking, but not so the home side. Queens deserved their 2-0 victory in a less than memorable match with seven bookings, mostly ill-timed tackles in the difficult conditions. It was back to the league and a visit to Brechin on the 16th. In a thrilling game Brechin took the lead twice, but Caley Thistle earned a draw with goals from Brian Thomson and Iain Stewart.

Paterson's squad was strengthened in mid-August by the signing of Mark McCulloch from Dunfermline on a three-year contract. Inverness-born McCulloch spent three years at Dunfermline after moving from Clach but fell out of favour: 'The manager Bert Paton told me I was not in his plans and when I heard that Caley were interested I thought there was no point in hanging about. Even though the club has only been full-time for a few months it is ambitious. If we can consolidate our position this season then maybe next year we can push for promotion.'

McCulloch made his debut on 23 August in a home match against East Fife but it was a disappointing 1-0 defeat. The only goal was Paul Cherry's header past his own 'keeper Les Fridge. The encounter at Stenhousemuir the following week was a little better, but the home side were always in the driving seat. The Warriors were 2-0 up at half-time, a Brian Thomson penalty made it 2-1 in 47 minutes then the game was effectively lost following a hotly disputed penalty three minutes later. The ball hit Iain MacArthur's shoulder and a spot-kick was awarded. David Roseburgh converted and, although Wayne Addicoat scored late in the game, it ended 3-2. The lack of a league win meant that August finished with the newly-promoted side struggling in eighth place.

DEBUT IN DIVISION TWO

Duncan Shearer arrives

The club pulled off a major coup in September with the signing of Scottish internationalist and Aberdeen legend Duncan Shearer. Shearer had other good offers, but Caley Thistle came up with the added incentive of combining playing with the post of community and development officer which had just been vacated by Danny MacDonald's departure to become youth development coach at Ross County. Shearer's reasons for choosing Inverness were both football and family ones: 'This is the area where I began my career and I also have family ties here and in Fort William. I have always wanted to get involved in coaching – I'm keen to become involved in that side of the game to put something back into the sport, but first and foremost my job will be to score goals.' Shearer made a dream start in his home debut against Stranraer on 13 September. He scored in only seven minutes, Stranraer went 2-1 ahead and a late Iain Stewart penalty saved a point.

A bad-tempered match at Dumfries the following week led to a 2-1 defeat, five yellow cards and two red – Queens' George Rowe and Caley Thistle's Charlie Christie. Paul Cherry had a bad afternoon as he scored another unfortunate own goal then was stretchered off with a head injury. Barry Wilson equalised with a neat lob over David Mathieson, but Tommy Bryce's immediate reply secured the three points. A 2-1 home defeat by Clyde on the 27th ensured that September finished with Caley Thistle propping up Division Two.

The 2-1 defeat at Forfar on 4 October was a bitter blow after the best first-half display seen all season. Barry Robson had just signed from Rangers and made his debut. Robson took some time to establish himself in the first team, but came through after a loan spell at Forfar from October 1999 to April 2000. He eventually matured into a valuable match-winning player before leaving for Dundee United in May 2003.

When Caley Thistle played Rangers in March 1996 chairman David Murray promised to bring a side north to officially open Caledonian Stadium. This finally happened on 7 October and a strong Rangers team narrowly won 4-3. A week later the 1996-7 final of the Inverness Cup was played at Caledonian Stadium against Ross County. This match was much delayed by the busy playing schedule of both clubs towards the end of the previous season. Paul Cherry and Duncan Shearer scored to retain the trophy by a 2-0 margin. A boring 0-0 draw at home against Clydebank on the 18th is best bypassed in order to focus on the long-awaited first league win on the 25th. High-flying East Fife were deservedly hammered 5-1 at Bayview with Iain Stewart netting a hat-trick. Steve Paterson praised his side's style and flair and was clearly relieved that his side had broken the league 'duck'. The victory did not result in any change to the tenth league position but it improved morale.

November started with a 0-0 draw at home to Brechin on the 1st. Despite general superiority, the killer touch was missing and frustration spilled beyond the final whistle. Norwegian defender Vetle Andersen was red-carded for remarks to an assistant referee en route to the dressing room. Paterson and Andersen were called into the referee's room and the manager was seething: 'This just capped an unhappy afternoon. This kind of behaviour will not be tolerated at the club – not as long as I'm there.' A few days later the Norwegian was placed on the transfer list but he was to stay until the end of the season.

Things improved on the 8th when Stenhousemuir were soundly beaten 4-1 at home in Steve Paterson's 100th game as manager. Duncan Shearer was taken to Raigmore Hospital for stitches in a head wound after 22 minutes and was replaced by Wayne Addicoat. Brian Thomson and Barry Wilson scored to make it 2-0, but Ian Little pulled one back just before the interval. The match was settled when Addicoat scored the third goal with a spectacular overhead kick while lying on his back. Iain Stewart added the fourth.

The following week there was a marathon round trip of 520 miles for the first league match at Stranraer. With Queen of the South and Stranraer both in Division Two, this meant four trips to the deep south in 1997-8 – a total of over 1500 miles for just six hours of football (and no points!). The first visit to Stair Park, Stranraer, resulted in a disappointing 2-1 defeat. *Scotland on Sunday* reporter Raymond Travers joined the supporters' bus and recorded it as a little chunk of football history: the longest trip ever undertaken for a Scottish League fixture.

On the 22nd travel was rather easier to Broadwood for an exciting match against Clyde. Clyde led 3-1 after only 23 minutes, with Brian Thomson scoring Caley Thistle's only goal. Paul Cherry scored just after the break to make it 3-2 then another goal was lost in 57 minutes. Iain Stewart brought it back to 4-3 in 71 minutes. The visitors pressed hard for a fourth to take a point but, despite a frantic last five minutes, Clyde held out. Caley Thistle finished November in tenth place despite a 2-1 home victory over Queen of the South on the 29th. Iain Stewart scored both goals and the game marked the first appearance of former Rangers and Dundee United player Sandy Robertson, who had signed on a short-term contract. Robertson's Tannadice career had ended with a three-month prison sentence for assault, and he was now trying to rebuild his football life: 'Caley Thistle are ambitious and are giving me the chance to play which is what I really need.' He was to stay until the end of March, then move on to Livingston.

In the programme for the Queens' game the manager spelled out the club's current situation at the foot of the Second Division: 'I hope my players accept the gravity of our current predicament and respond in a determined manner. We are all here for the good of this club and not vice-versa.' It would be January 1998 before his side climbed above ninth place.

The Scottish Cup

The Scottish Cup provided a welcome diversion from the relegation battle. The home first-round match against Whitehill Welfare on 6 December proved to be the start of a successful run. Two early Iain Stewart goals seemed to make things easy but a Whitehill penalty conversion gave them hope. With 10 minutes left Barry Wilson struck to end the contest. On the 13th it was back to the league and a first ever visit to Dumbarton's Boghead to play ground-sharing Clydebank. The match was memorable for little except the low attendance of 326 and the injury to referee Tom Brown. He was carried off after damaging his ankle in the 29th minute and was replaced by an assistant. Clydebank led 1-0 for most of the game but Davie Ross snatched an equaliser with two minutes left. On December 20 defender Paul Cherry scored both goals in the home 2-2 draw against Forfar. Victory was denied when Iain Stewart missed a penalty four minutes from time.

The year ended with a home 4-0 thrashing of East Fife. Paul Cherry scored the opener and Barry Robson made it 2-0 with his first goal for the club. Mike Teasdale added a third from 30 yards, then Barry Wilson ran the length of the Fifers half with the ball before rounding the 'keeper and netting number four. The year ended with a small, but psychologically important, climb to ninth place.

1998 opened with round two of the Scottish Cup and a first foot from Queen's Park. With storms sweeping Scotland, this was one of the few cup games to survive. Gales and rain dominated the first half and there was little good football. Things improved after the break and Caley Thistle took the tie with goals from Barry Robson and Iain Stewart. On 6 January the final of the 1997-8 Inverness Cup was played at Caledonian Stadium. Clach were narrowly beaten 2-1 and the cup retained.

Weather problems led to a break until a snowy January 17 when the Clyde team only just made it up the A9 and many of their fans had to turn back. Brian Thomson created a new competitive club record with a goal in 1 minute 22 seconds, setting up a resounding 5-1 victory. Iain Stewart scored two goals, Barry Wilson one and Sandy Robertson netted the fifth – the only goal of his 20-match spell with the club. The welcome points ensured a one-place climb to eighth spot. An optimistic Steve Paterson pointed out that 'we are only five points from third position'.

Paul Sheerin joins

Paul Sheerin made his debut as a trialist in the Clyde match after arriving via Sweden and a trial with Ross County. Sheerin was to become a major influence over four seasons – and a firm favourite with the fans. He eventually followed Steve Paterson to Aberdeen in 2003 via Ayr United. The third round Scottish Cup draw brought another East of Scotland League team, Annan Athletic, to Inverness on 24 January. Annan took a surprising 8th-minute lead but were finally demolished by a record 8-1 score. Annan did not go down gracefully and their bad-tempered tackling resulted in a red card for Stanley Leslie. It was not Leslie's day: earlier he had scored an own goal. The other seven goals were made up of two each for Barry Wilson and Brian Thomson, plus one apiece from Iain Stewart, Barry Robson and Duncan Shearer. A long, fruitless trip on league business to Dumfries completed January – a narrow 1-0 loss despite hard work and some good football. This result ended a run of eight league and cup games without defeat. It was back to ninth place with relegation still looming large.

On 7 February league leaders Clydebank came to Inverness and were beaten 3-2. The winning goals included two from Duncan Shearer and a Brian Thomson penalty. Clydebank manager Ian McCall vented his frustration with a kick at a container holding open one of the doors to the players' tunnel. It turned out to be a tin of paint and it created quite a mess – as well as a photo opportunity. The episode was well documented in the national papers, accompanied by a picture of management committee member Mike Shewan at the scene of the crime.

Dundee United Cup double

The following week it was the fourth round of the Scottish Cup and a lucrative game against Dundee United at Tannadice. A 2000-strong travelling army headed for Dundee and the crowd of 8770 was the highest of the season. The TV pundits noted kindly that 'it'll be a nice day out for the Inverness supporters' but it proved to be much more than that. It was a classic game and the visitors came close to producing a shock. Paul Sheerin's 15-yard shot into the roof of the net gave a 27th minute lead and Caley Thistle held it until nine minutes from time, thanks partly to a fine display from keeper Jim Calder. There was great disappointment for the travelling support when Kjell Olofsson earned United a replay with an 81st minute equaliser. Paterson thought his side were going to hold out: 'I think that at the end of the 90 minutes it was a fair result but with 80 minutes gone I thought we had weathered the storm. I felt frustrated not to get the victory.' Paterson singled out 'Man of the Match' Jim Calder for praise: 'It's a lucky ground for him. He's not done badly for a guy with a dodgy back.'

The return match took place the following Wednesday in front of a home record crowd of 5821. The atmosphere was electric and there was the massive prize of a home tie against Celtic in the next round. In years to come, the match would be over-shadowed by major cup wins against Celtic and Hearts, but for a long time this was the big one.

Caley Thistle fought like tigers, but it was Dundee United who took the lead through Olofsson in only seven minutes. Play raged on and Jim Calder kept the Inverness side in the game with a penalty save from Steven Pressley on the half hour-mark. When Gary McSwegan made it 2-0 in 84 minutes it seemed all over, but Brian Thomson headed a goal just one minute later. Mark McCulloch equalised 90 seconds into added time with a goal fit to grace any match. He set off on a run down the right, played it to Barry Wilson, who backheeled into his path, then McCulloch hit a glorious 20-yard angled volley past Sieb Dijkstra. As legs tired, it was United who grabbed the winner three minutes into the second period of extra time with a Lars Zetterlund drive from the edge of the box. Caley Thistle went out of the cup with heads held high. Dundee United manager Tommy McLean praised the Highland side: 'They did well and deserve all the credit. It's Caley Thistle's night – they showed the spirit, the attitude and the freshness in which cup-ties should be played.' Paterson acknowledged that the result was a credit to his side: 'We have played three games against Premier opposition and haven't been beaten in 90 minutes. It speaks volumes for the distance we have come from the Third Division.'

It was back to the relegation battle at home to Livingston the following Saturday and a 2-2 draw. Livingston took an early 2-0 lead, but were pegged back by half-time thanks to goals from Duncan Shearer and Mark McCulloch. Despite facing a strong wind and driving rain in the second half, Caley Thistle held out for a point. The expected cup hangover finally hit at Brechin the following midweek. This rearranged league match ended in a comprehensive 3-1 defeat despite Paul Cherry scoring the first goal. An unlucky own goal from Richard Hastings made it 1-1 and, at 1-2, Caley Thistle pressed hard but lost a third goal on the counter attack. Things were rather better on the 28th at Stenhousemuir. Snow on top of frost put the game in doubt, but it went ahead and Caley Thistle won 3-0. The highlight was Barry Robson's opening goal straight from a corner. 'Man of the Match' Robson insisted that it was no fluke and that he had tried to use the wind to get the ball over the keeper. Iain Stewart found that sitting on the bench could be dangerous. When Robson scored he jumped up to celebrate and hit his head on the dug-out roof. Stewart was then preparing to replace Robson when physio Ian Manning elbowed him on his way to treat an injury. Paterson reckoned that 'he was probably glad to get onto the field where he no doubt felt safer!' February ended with a small climb back out of the league danger zone to eighth place.

March was a busy month, catching up with postponed games. It started with a midweek trip to Livingston, where the January match finally went ahead after four cancellations. Barry Robson scored the opening goal in 19 minutes, but Graham Harvey equalised a minute later. In 37 minutes Jim Calder was sent off after a clash with Harvey, and Brian Thomson went into goal. His first action was to pick the ball out of the net as Harvey scored from the resultant penalty. The ten men held on well with Thomson making a fine one-handed save from a Tom Graham header to keep the game alive. With nine minutes left, Barry Wilson made it 2-2 and nearly snatched a winner in the last minute. The following Saturday Stranraer made the long trip north, just making it through the snow. They were rewarded with a 2-1 victory, following a poor display by the home side.

The midweek catch-up continued at Forfar and the club's first ever win at Station Park. Paul Sheerin's two first-half goals were enough to gain the points despite the loss of a late penalty goal. The result opened up a five-point gap over next opponents, second-bottom Clyde. Caley Thistle's record at Broadwood has never been good, but the visit on 14 March proved very successful. The resounding 6-1 win included two from Brian Thomson and equalled the league record for the club.

The topsy-turvy form continued with a 2-0 home defeat by Queen of the South the following week. The performance was slated by Paterson: 'That was by far our worst show this season. To plummet to such depths asks major questions about certain individuals in the team.' Then it was back to Dumbarton on the 28th and a strange match with Clydebank. There was a move afoot to resettle the troubled Clydebank in Ireland, and the small remaining band of fans objected. Irish flags were waved throughout the game and the 'supporters' slow-handclapped their own team. Despite the surreal atmosphere the 'home' side recorded a 1-0 win. This match marked the debut of former Ayr United captain Gregg Hood on loan. He played three matches before accumulated bookings earned a suspension and his brief Inverness career came to an end. The seven points gained in March were enough to retain eighth place. At the end of March, Davie Ross left for Ross County, initially on loan although he eventually signed for the Dingwall side.

The opening game of April on the 4th was a dismal 0-0 home draw with Forfar then, on the following Tuesday, a Celtic XI came to play in a testimonial for former Thistle, Celtic and Caledonian midfielder Charlie Christie. It looked all over when the young Celtic side took a 3-0 lead in 35 minutes, but three second-half goals – two from Iain Stewart and one from Paul Cherry – earned a 3-3 draw. It was an evening of nostalgia as former Caley Thistle favourites Graeme Bennett, Mike Noble and Alan Hercher all played. Light began to be seen at the end of the relegation tunnel when three valuable points were gained on 11 April at home to Stenhousemuir amidst heavy hail showers. Defender Mike Teasdale was the hero with two goals after Stenhousemuir had taken an early lead. Teasdale chased his hat-trick and came close in the dying seconds when he back-heeled the ball past the post from a Duncan Shearer pass. The following week is best forgotten – another long trip to Stranraer and a 3-1 defeat.

With relegation still a possibility, the 1-0 away win against East Fife on the 25th was vital. Brian Thomson's 9th-minute goal secured the points in a very close match. On the same day the reserve side played in the North Cup Final at Caledonian Stadium, losing 3-1 to Elgin City. April's seven points secured a climb to sixth and safety from relegation was in sight.

Division Two status retained

Division Two status was assured with a 2-1 home win against already-relegated Brechin on 2 May. In a stormy match, Caley Thistle took a 2-0 lead with goals from Brian Thomson and Iain Stewart late in the first half, then Brechin's Roddy Black scored close to the hour mark. There was a scare when Brechin were awarded a penalty but Jim Calder saved from his opposite number Stuart Garden. Thomson's red card in 78 minutes gave Brechin hope, but they could not capitalise on their numerical superiority.

There was only one competitive game left: an away match at Livingston on 9 May. This was to prove a traumatic affair for Livingston. They started the day at the top of Division Two and were seeking not just promotion but the championship. The kick-off was delayed to allow in the crowd of 2812 (the highest away league crowd of the season) and, when the game finally started, the pressure was all on the home side. They went behind in 34 minutes to Iain Stewart's 20th goal of the season then Tom Graham equalised just after half-time. In 75 minutes Paul Sheerin sent a 25-yard free kick into the top corner for what proved to be the winner. As other results came in, Livingston were stunned to discover that they had been leapfrogged by both Clydebank and Stranraer: no championship and no promotion. For Caley Thistle, the victory pushed them up to a very creditable fifth with 49 points. This was remarkable considering that most of the season had been spent in the bottom three.

Richard Hastings was top of the appearance chart in 1997-8 with 43 out of a possible 44. It was a good year for the young full back: he celebrated his 21st birthday with a full international debut for Canada on 18 May – a 1-0 defeat of Macedonia in a friendly. He was to spend part of the close season in Mexico with Canada's Olympic squad. Brian Thomson made 42 appearances and Barry Wilson 41. Richard Hastings, Iain Stewart, Jim Calder and Davie Ross all passed the 100 career-appearance barrier. With Mike Noble dropping out of the first team, Paul Cherry and Iain MacArthur shared the captaincy over the season. Joint top goal-scorers were Iain Stewart and Brian Thomson on 20. These totals were also the highest in the Second Division. This was Thomson's swansong as he reverted to part-time Highland League football with Fraserburgh at the end of the season. A total of 88 goals were scored and 62 conceded in 44 league and cup matches. The goal-scoring credits went to 14 players, with an own goal by Annan Athletic's Stanley Leslie. The reserve team won the North Caledonian League Championship with 34 points from 20 games.

Ross Tokely once more represented Scotland – this time at Under-18 level. In October 1997 chairman Dougie McGilvray was honoured by Inverness District Chamber of Commerce for his work with the club when he was named Inverness Citizen of the Year. The trophy was presented just before the Rangers match by Chamber chairman Thomas Prag. At the end of March Bruce Graham left his post as general manager to be replaced by John Sutherland.

Between 26 April and 8 May the European Under-16 Championships were held in Scotland: Caledonian Stadium was one of eight venues. The six matches in Group D (Russia, Israel, Croatia and Ukraine) were split between Dingwall and Inverness. One quarter-final match was also played in Inverness. On May 17 an ICT XI played a Chic Charnley Select in aid of Cerebral Palsy Action and on 23 May the stadium hosted the Women's UEFA Championship 1-1 draw between Scotland and the Czech Republic.

CHAPTER 8

PROMOTION TO DIVISION ONE
1998-9

INVERNESS CALEDONIAN THISTLE FC 1998-9 *(photo: Gordon Gillespie)*

(*Back*) Mike Newlands, Duncan Shearer, Jim Calder, Les Fridge, Martin Bavidge, Ross Tokely

(*Middle*) Steve Paterson (manager), Scott McLean, Charlie Christie, Paul Cherry, Wayne Addicoat, Paul Sheerin, Mike Teasdale, Alex Caldwell (assistant manager)

(*Front*) Iain MacArthur, Barry Wilson, Mark McCulloch (captain), Gary Farquhar, Barry Robson, Richard Hastings

GOING BALLISTIC!

After the relegation battle of 1997-8, 1998-9 was to be a relatively stress-free season, ending with a well-deserved step up to the First Division. Mark McCulloch was named captain and summer signings were Martin Bavidge, Gary Farquhar and Mike Newlands. The most successful of these was Bavidge, who made 122 appearances over four seasons despite spending most of 1998-9 on loan to Forres. Farquhar only made 14 appearances in three seasons and Newlands never played competitively for the first team as, after a season, he was forced to retire through injury. A number of youngsters were given their chance, including Grant Munro, Andrew Allan, David Hind, David Craig and Jordan MacDonald, but by early 2001 most had left. Munro remained to become a first-team regular, Allan went to Clach and the others to Elgin. Mike Noble started the season on the fringe of the first team but eventually signed for Forres; his last game after a long career with Caledonian, Thistle and the unified club was in an Inverness Cup-tie at Elgin on 27 October. Martin Glancy arrived from Dumbarton in January 1999, but the vital signing of the season was Bobby Mann, who came from Forfar in February 1999. He was to become captain after Mark McCulloch left for Livingston in the summer of 2000.

The pre-season friendlies kicked-off on 18 July with two away matches. One team played at Cove whilst another helped celebrate the centenary of Thurso Academicals with a challenge match. A home 2-2 draw with Aberdeen on Wednesday 22nd was the pre-season highlight, with goals from Scott McLean and a Paul Sheerin penalty. Future Caley Thistle players Russell Duncan and Darren Mackie made substitute appearances for the Dons. Hamilton came to Inverness the next Saturday and were beaten 2-0, with Scott McLean and Duncan Shearer the scorers. On the same day, Mike Noble lent his experience to a young Caley Thistle side as they won the Keyline tournament in Oban.

The League Cup first-round draw resulted in a trip to Dumfries on 1 August. Queen of the South were convincingly beaten 4-1 to earn a home tie against Aberdeen. The result was never in doubt after Paul Sheerin scored in the sixth minute and further goals came from Scott McLean, Duncan Shearer and Paul Cherry. Queens' only goal was a last-minute consolation, but at 2-0 they should have come back into it. They were denied by the latest in a long line of penalty saves by Jim Calder. Assistant

PROMOTION TO DIVISION ONE

Manager Alex Caldwell was happy with the result: 'It was good to get the season off to a bright start for a change.' 1 August was also the opening day of the first Scottish Premier League season following the ten-club breakaway from the Scottish Football League. The criteria for the step-up to this new 'exclusive club' were to be the subject of regular discussion in First Division circles over the next few years, dominating the headlines when ICT won the championship in 2003-4.

Barry Wilson scored the only goal in the opening league fixture of the season at Partick. This was the first meeting of the clubs and it was a good win against one of the promotion favourites. The Aberdeen League Cup match took place on 8 August after much hype and a build-up of excitement in the town. Much of the pre-match chatter surrounded Duncan Shearer meeting up with his old team. The 2-2 pre-season draw encouraged optimism. It evaporated in 17 seconds when Billy Dodds scored the first goal of a hat-trick. Aberdeen dominated and the match ended 3-0. The 5164 spectators brought in much-needed revenue and was the highest cup crowd of the season. Steve Paterson was disappointed: 'We left ourselves with a mountain to climb after being caught cold in the opening seconds of the match and from then on we were left to chase the game.' The suspension of the League Challenge Cup meant that this was the last cup match until January.

The rest of August brought two league wins and a draw. Livingston were narrowly beaten 2-1 at home on the 15th. Playing at number 9 for the visitors was recent recruit John Robertson. On Boxing Day 2002, the former Hearts and Scotland striker became Caley Thistle's third manager. A week later it was 1-1 at Alloa but a controversial decision robbed Caley Thistle of victory. Ross Tokely gave Caley Thistle a first-half lead, Alloa's Willie Irvine hit the post with a penalty early in the second half – then Alloa equalised. With ten minutes left, Mike Teasdale looked to have scored a winner. The referee at first awarded it, then changed his mind after spotting his assistant's raised flag. Ross Tokely was adjudged offside, despite seemingly not interfering with play.

The top score of the month was a 5-1 away victory at East Fife on the 29th but it was not as convincing as the final score would suggest. A Paul Sheerin penalty and a Duncan Shearer header made it 2-0 by half time, but East Fife pulled one back 15 minutes from the end. This goal and a red card for

Charlie Christie gave the visitors hope, but it evaporated when they lost three goals in the last nine minutes – Paul Cherry, Martin Bavidge and Mike Teasdale all scored. On the bus home, Barry Wilson claimed that his shot was in before Bavidge touched the ball over for the fourth goal, but he was over-ruled. The result took Caley Thistle to top spot in Division Two. They were to stay in the top two for the rest of the season.

Three wins in September

There were four league matches in September, with three victories and a defeat. The run started on 5 September with a 2-1 home win against Arbroath – although the margin should have been much greater. Duncan Shearer scored one goal and the other was self-inflicted. On the same day Scotland played a European Championship qualifying match in Lithuania, and the 0-0 draw highlighted once more that the international side needed someone to put the ball in the net. *Scotland on Sunday* noted the Arbroath goalscorer: 'Given the recent dusting down of creaky old international strikers, this sudden Duncan Shearer renaissance might just hold broader significance!' It was a similar story the following week, when Queen of the South were beaten 3-2 at home. Queens had taken the lead against the run of play in the 20th minute and it stood that way at half time. A dressing-down from the manager did the trick, and a flurry of goals made it 3-1, before the Doonhamers scored a second with five minutes left. On the 19th there was a first visit to Stirling's Forthbank Stadium and a 1-0 win thanks to Duncan Shearer. It was another day of superiority, but not enough to show for it.

Things went badly wrong the following week at Broadwood against Clyde. It started when Duncan Shearer was injured in the warm-up. Then Richard Hastings was stretchered off in the 27th minute. Hastings would not return to action until January. Clyde won 4-1, with all the goals scored in a 15-minute spell. Clyde made it 3-0 in a dramatic five-minute period just before half time then, in the 51st minute, Paul Cherry pulled one back. Clyde's fourth ended the comeback and the unbeaten run. The defeat resulted in a drop to second place on goal difference.

Hastings' injury led to the arrival of Hugh Robertson, on loan from Dundee, who made his debut in the 2-2 home draw with Forfar on 3 October. Scott McLean scored an early first goal, but Forfar equalised, then took the lead with nine minutes left. It only lasted two minutes, as Barry Wilson equalised direct from a free kick. On 10 October it was down to Almondvale and another fascinating encounter with Livingston. The home side dominated the first half and scored once, with what the *Sunday Post* called, 'a flash of John Robertson brilliance'. A Jim Calder penalty save from future Caley Thistle striker David Bingham restricted the damage. Caley Thistle piled on the pressure in the second half, but Livingston made it 2-0 on a rare break. The only consolation was a Scott McLean goal three minutes from time.

Sheerin sets record

The highlight of the 3-2 home win against Partick Thistle on 17 October was Paul Sheerin's opening goal in only one minute twenty seconds – a new record that was to stand for four years. Scott McLean scored the other two goals. Partick's second was scored three minutes from time and set up an anxious finish. Partick must have forgiven McLean, because they gave him a lift on the team bus to Glasgow after the game. Despite the scoreline the visiting supporters seemed to enjoy their day out and even started a conga on the terracing, probably to combat the cold!

On 24 October East Fife were beaten 4-2 at home but defensive lapses let the Fifers back into the game. Caley Thistle took the lead twice in the first half through Duncan Shearer and Charlie Christie, but this was squandered: at half-time the score was 2-2. Two second-half goals ensured victory. An away match at Arbroath on the last day of October saw the debut of teenager Andrew Allan and a narrow 1-0 victory. Paul Cherry secured the points with a 48th-minute header and claimed to have been spurred on by a piper on the terracing. This left Caley Thistle second, a point behind Livingston but seven points clear of third-placed Clyde. The pattern for the rest of the league season was to be a challenge for top spot with Livingston and anxious glances over the shoulder to watch the progress of a determined Clyde.

November started with a home match against Stirling Albion on the 7th – and another match in which superiority was not fully translated into goals. Scott McLean scored a goal in each half for 2-0, but Stirling's Alastair Graham made it 2-1. Barry Wilson scored two minutes from time to secure the win after a lob from Charlie Christie set him free on the halfway line. With no offside given, he ran the length of the Stirling half, rounded Gary Gow, stopped on the goal line to make sure all was well, then tapped into the empty net. A point was earned at Dumfries on the 14th but Queen of the South's battling performance belied their lowly league position. Paul Sheerin scored with a rare header and Scott McLean netted the other in the 2-2 draw.

Second played third in Inverness the next week, and this was Clyde's big chance to close the eight-point gap. Barry Wilson scored the opener in 25 minutes and Clyde equalised ten minutes from time through Ritchie McCusker. Late flurries at both ends came to nothing. Caley Thistle's second position was secure. Clyde gained some ground a week later when they won and Caley Thistle were held to a 2-2 draw at Forfar. The Station Park side only gained the point in the last minute when Andy Cargill scored his second goal after Duncan Shearer and Scott McLean had put the visitors ahead twice. Steve Paterson was disappointed to be 'outfought by a battling part-time side'. The gap between Caley Thistle and Clyde was now down to six points.

A Scottish Cup first-round bye meant the first scheduled December match was at home on the 12th to Alloa. It was postponed (the Wasps were involved in a Cup replay) and played the following Wednesday. On a very windy evening, Caley Thistle gained a tight victory. Hugh Robertson was credited with the 27th-minute opening goal, assisted by a deflection from Alloa's Mark Cowan. Alloa scored twice to take the lead, then Mark McCulloch made it 2-2 in 65 minutes. Scott McLean scored a minute from time to secure a 3-2 win.

The year ended with two disappointing away results. On the Saturday before Christmas, Partick won 2-1 at Firhill despite Caley Thistle having most of the play. Two fine first-half Partick goals and resolute defending won the day, despite a Barry Wilson penalty giving hope. The last game of the year on the 27th was the club's first ever Sunday fixture and a visit to re-homed East Fife at New Bayview Park, Methil. With the lights not yet installed, the kick-off was a strange 1.45 p.m. Despite dominance for most of the game, it was not translated into victory. The cause was not helped by Paul Cherry's 37th-minute dismissal. East Fife took the lead right on half time, but Mike Teasdale equalised with a header and then set up a headed goal for Scott McLean. The lead did not last long, but Caley Thistle still seemed the more likely to snatch a winner. They were devastated three minutes from time when John Martin earned the Fifers all three points with a headed goal. Results elsewhere meant that Caley Thistle turned the year in second place, six points behind Livingston and five ahead of Clyde.

PROMOTION TO DIVISION ONE

The respective league positions added an edge to the second-round Scottish Cup-tie against Livingston in Inverness on 2 January. With Hugh Robertson's loan period over, and Richard Hastings not quite fit to return, midfielder Paul Sheerin played as a stand-in left back. Livingston took the lead in nine minutes, surrendered it to an Alan McManus own goal just before half time, then grabbed a winner in 62 minutes. Dreams of cup glory were over, but at least there would be no distraction from the quest for promotion. The manager described it as 'the tamest performance I've seen from a side which I have managed'. The following Saturday in the league, Arbroath were defeated 2-0 at home. Paul Sheerin scored just after the half-hour mark, then Barry Wilson celebrated his 100th club appearance by adding the second goal two minutes later.

On the 16th it was touch and go whether the team would make it down to play Clyde at Broadwood, but the snow gates on the A9 closed behind them and they went on to draw 1-1 on a wet and windy afternoon. Steve Convery's opening goal in 41 minutes was cancelled out by Dumbarton on-loan striker Martin Glancy two minutes later. The wind was so strong that Mark McCulloch claimed they had to tie 'wee' Martin down but he still managed to score. There were few away fans at Broadwood as the Supporters' Club bus was stopped by the heavy snow. This was a particular disappointment for bus convener George Macrae: 'Since we joined the Scottish League I had managed to go to every match but this spoiled my record.' With the A9 shut, the team bus returned via Aberdeen and most of the travellers voted to take the train from Perth. The bus reached Inverness first! The last match of January was on the 30th at home to Forfar. Barry Wilson and Charlie Christie scored for a deserved 2-0 win, but Forfar nearly crept back into the game at 1-0 when they were awarded a soft penalty. Justice was done when Jim Calder continued his penalty record with a save from Andy Cargill. Livingston remained top and Caley Thistle second at the end of January.

Four wins out of four

The Caley Thistle promotion machine moved into top gear in February with four wins out of four. It started with a 5-1 away win at Stirling on the sixth, including two from Martin Glancy who signed for the club a fortnight later. Clyde had been beaten midweek and the other Saturday results proved helpful. The gap between ICT in second place and Clyde lying third was now a mighty 11 points.

A home win against Queen of the South on the 13th was rather more difficult, needing an own goal from player/co-caretaker manager George Rowe to break the deadlock. The high scoring resumed at Alloa on the 20th with a 4-1 win, including a brace from Duncan Shearer. February finished with an important home encounter against league leaders Livingston. Heavy rain and a blizzard put the match in severe doubt, but the pitch was declared playable at 2 pm. Mark McCormick scored first for Livi but goals from Scott McLean and Barry Wilson gave Caley Thistle a 2-1 lead at half time. In 70 minutes Duncan Shearer sealed it with a third goal, but there was more drama to come. Livi's Paul Deas was sent off for a last-man tackle on Wilson then, with five minutes left, Les Fridge also received a red card when he raced out of goal to tackle Brian McPhee. The contact was deemed illegal and Ross Tokely took over in goal. Tokely managed a shut-out and the 3-1 win reduced the gap between first and second to only four points. Despite Fridge's dismissal, he was named 'Man of the Match'. The crowd of 3279 was the highest of the season for a home league match. Paterson was jubilant: 'We had to win to keep the championship dream alive and in the end we were fairly comprehensive victors. We're in excellent form just now on a winning streak. There's a lot of confidence within the ranks and our unbeaten run has now been stretched to seventeen games.' Livingston manager Ray Stewart put a brave face in defeat: 'The championship race is still very much alive and it gives both teams something to aim for – but we're in front and they've got to catch us.' While not mathematically certain it was now clear that, barring disaster, Caley Thistle and Livingston would be promoted.

It was quite a different story at 'Fortress Gayfield' on 6 March, when relegation-threatened Arbroath won 3-1. Paul Cherry was sent off on his 99th appearance only three minutes after coming on as a substitute. Charlie Christie made his 150th appearance at home against East Fife on the 13th in a fine 4-0 win, despite Ross Tokely's red card in 70 minutes. Livingston surprisingly lost to Queen of the South, so Caley Thistle moved to within two points of the top. The 13th was unlucky for the reserve team when their bus had an accident en route to Thurso. They eventually made it, but the day's events took their toll and they lost their North Caledonian League match 5-0. Sandwiched between the Arbroath and East Fife games was a testimonial for the fans' favourite goalkeeper Jim Calder on 9 March. Hibs were the guests and Calder captained the side to a 2-1 victory. The former striker turned goalkeeper had been due a testimonial at Thistle but the merger got in the way. Mike Noble returned to the side to honour his former team-mate.

Scotland's match with Bosnia-Herzegovina on the 27th meant that the final league match of March took place on the 20th. Forfar were soundly beaten 3-0 at Station Park in front of a season-low crowd of 504. Scott McLean netted two goals and Paul Sheerin one. As other results filtered through, it was clear that top place in Division Two had been reached on goal difference. Promotion and possibly the championship were now in sight. There was one more match in March – a Ross Tokely goal earned a 1-0 victory in the Inverness Cup final against Ross County at Caledonian Stadium on the 26th.

The first league target was reached on 3 April at home to Clyde. An emphatic 3-0 win ensured promotion after only two seasons in Division Two. Barry Wilson's third-minute goal set up the win, with Paul Sheerin adding a penalty conversion and Duncan Shearer completing the scoreline. The main pressure was off and the championship was now the aim. Chairman Dougie McGilvray praised the team: 'It's a superb achievement for the club, its officials, its players, its fans and the business community of Inverness. We have achieved what we have in a remarkably short time without sacrificing our identity – most of our players are Highland League products with local roots.' Steve Paterson was also a happy man: 'It's an historic day for the club. We really couldn't have scripted it any better.' Defender Paul Cherry looked ahead: 'That's the first half of the job done. Now for the second half – the championship.'

Confidence was shaken when the next two games produced disappointing draws and sent Livingston back to the top. At home to Stirling on the 10th, high winds caused problems and the visitors took the lead in 49 minutes. Duncan Shearer equalised in 78 minutes, then scored what seemed to be the winner a minute from the end of normal time. After an amazing five minutes of added time, Stirling's Alex Bone headed home to make it 2-2. It was a similar story at Dumfries the following week. Barry Wilson made it 1-0 early in the first half but George Rowe equalised a minute from time. At the same moment a John Robertson strike earned a draw for Livingston at Arbroath and the two-point gap between the top pair remained. A hard-fought home match against Partick the following week resulted in a 3-2 win, a precious three points and a climb back to the top of the league. Partick took a 27th-minute lead, then a quickfire brace from Scott McLean made it 2-1. A headed goal from Willie Jamieson ensured an exciting finish and Mark McCulloch netted the winner for Caley Thistle five minutes from time.

GOING BALLISTIC!

'Decider' against Livingston

What was billed as the championship decider took place at Livingston on May Day. It was not as cut and dried as a 'decider' but the winners would be in pole position. It was an amazing match, which will be remembered for a long time by the record 6013 crowd. There is no doubt that cup exploits dominate fans' memories of the first decade, but this game is only a whisker behind. Livingston raced to a 4-0 lead after only 22 minutes as the Caley Thistle defence was posted missing and it looked like a rout. The 2500 away fans could have been forgiven for departing at that stage but strangely they set up a suicidal chant of 'we want five!' For supporters criticised at home for a lack of atmosphere, they made a tremendous noise which really lifted the team and helped spark a revival. It was not all one-way traffic for the first period, but Livingston took their chances. The fight-back started after the half-hour mark but not until Livi nearly scored a fifth. Mark McCulloch started the comeback in 37 minutes with a volleyed goal as the visitors began to dominate. Charlie Christie and Iain Stewart made it 4-3 by the 67th minute and set up a frantic last 20 minutes. Livi struggled as Caley Thistle fought in vain for an equaliser. As the minutes ticked away, the pressure on the home goal was relieved by substitute John Robertson whose up-field runs created danger and wasted precious time. With five minutes left he beat the defence and Les Fridge but his angled shot ran along the front of the goal. A fourth Caley Thistle goal would have made the travelling support's day but Livingston held on for a narrow win and the virtual certainty of the Second Division championship.

The classic match struck a chord with the media. Anthony Haggerty of the *Daily Record* said that 'quite simply, this was an incredible game of football'. The manager was less than pleased: 'It was all down to bad defending and the game was lost in the first 22 minutes. To be honest I think it was just a freak situation – they just seemed to score at will. In their first five attacks they scored four goals. We had a mountain to climb after that. It looks as though we have lost the title on the second last day of the season.' Livingston manager Ray Stewart thought it was a great advert for football: 'It's the most exciting game I've ever been involved in as a manager.'

Livingston now only needed one point to be champions. Not surprisingly, they gained that the following week by defeating already-relegated Forfar 2-1. This news filtered through to Inverness as Caley Thistle ended the season with a 1-1 draw against Alloa. Iain Stewart scored the home goal and thus maintained an unbeaten home league record for the season. Steve Paterson summed up the season: 'From day one there was a good spirit among the players. We maintained a high level of consistency and never really hit a rocky patch. At the same time there was no purple patch – it was just steady progress and that was reflected in winning promotion with five games to go. That spoke volumes for the season.'

Caley Thistle finished in second spot with 72 points, five behind Livingston. In 39 league and cup matches they scored 85 goals and conceded 54. In a season dogged by injury, Iain Stewart only made six appearances and scored two goals – in successive weeks against Livingston and Alloa. The goal-scoring crown worn by Stewart for three seasons passed to Scott McLean. Now fully fit after his year out through injury, he was top marksman with 20 goals. Midfielder Barry Wilson capped an excellent season with 14 goals and was closely followed by Duncan Shearer on 13. The 85 goals were shared by 13 players with two own goals in the league and one in the Scottish Cup. Mike Teasdale repeated his 1996-7 feat of starting all matches. His 39-appearance total was matched by Paul Sheerin and Barry Wilson, but their figures included substitutions. Charlie Christie and Richard Hastings both achieved career totals of 150 appearances, with Mike Teasdale, Barry Wilson and Paul Cherry passing the 100 mark.

The reserve side had a good season with three cup wins and a third spot finish in the North Caledonian League. On 10 October in Inverness the Chic Allan Cup was secured by beating Balintore 3-0. On 27 February Golspie Sutherland were defeated 2-0 at Tain in the final of the PCT Cup, then the teams met again in the Football Times Cup final on 8 May. This time Golspie were beaten 7-1. Between 31 May and 4 June the SFA held a triangular Under-21 tournament featuring Scotland, the Republic of Ireland and Northern Ireland. Elgin hosted one game and two were held at Caledonian Stadium. In mid-season an ICT Girls team was constituted under the guidance of coach Ian Davidson.

There were a number of changes to the board during 1998-9. Craig Maclean left but Ian MacDonald, Ron Shiels, Harry Brown and Alan Nelson joined. Local solicitor Ian MacDonald would still be in post at the end of the club's first decade but the other newcomers would only serve for a short period. Norman Miller moved to the honorary position of life vice-president and Roy McLennan became vice-chairman. In March Gary Thompson joined the staff as commercial manager.

SUPER CALEY GO BALLISTIC
1999-2000

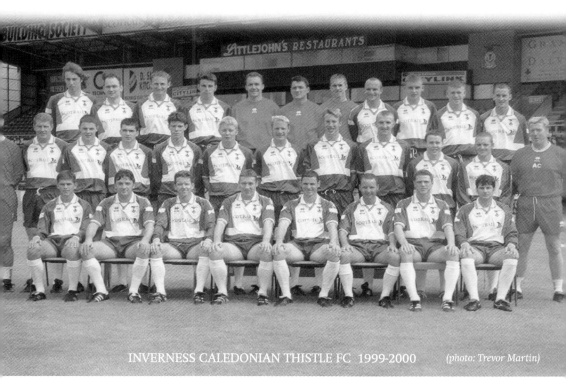

INVERNESS CALEDONIAN THISTLE FC 1999-2000 *(photo: Trevor Martin)*

(*Back*) Mike Newlands, Iain MacArthur, Mike Teasdale, Scott McLean, Les Fridge, Jim Calder, Ally Ridgers, Paul Cherry, Grant Munro, Andrew Allan, Paul Sheerin

(*Middle*) Steve Paterson (manager), Duncan Shearer, David Hind, Jordan MacDonald, Graeme Stewart, Barry Robson, Martin Bavidge, Ross Tokely, Bobby Mann, Scott Kellacher, Martin Glancy, Alex Caldwell (assistant manager)

(*Front*) David Craig, Stuart Golabek, Charlie Christie, Barry Wilson, Mark McCulloch (captain), Iain Stewart, Richard Hastings, Gary Farquhar

GOING BALLISTIC!

On 8 February 2000 the name of Inverness Caledonian Thistle reverberated around the world as the team that had just pulled off the greatest ever shock in Scottish football. Not only had Celtic been comfortably beaten 3-1 in the Scottish Cup but it happened at Celtic Park. The victory spawned the classic *Sun* headline 'Super Caley Go Ballistic Celtic Are Atrocious' and the aftershock brought down the Celtic management team. The cup had been very far from Steve Paterson's thoughts when he contemplated the club's first season in Division One: 'The aim is consolidation with a capital C. I hope people see my aim as a realistic one and that is to try and establish the club as a worthy First Division outfit. The season will be all about surviving – and that is not being unambitious.' Before the Scottish Cup euphoria there was to be a disappointing defeat in the final of the Bell's Challenge Cup but, more importantly long term, Paterson's target of league survival would be achieved.

From 2000-1 the SPL was to be increased to 12 teams. The top two in the First Division at the end of 1999-2000 were to be promoted automatically, with the third team going into a play-off against the tenth-placed Premier team. Only one team was to be relegated from Division One (in the event this was Clydebank), so there was less pressure than usual. It certainly did not seem that way at first.

Lack of cash meant few signings and a heavy reliance on the squad that had gained promotion. Stuart Golabek came from Ross County and Kevin Byers from Raith Rovers. In September Canadian internationalist Davide Xausa arrived via Dutch side Dordrecht 90 and Dennis Wyness joined from Aberdeen. Wyness was not an instant success in the goal-scoring stakes (it took 17 games until the first of his eventual 80 goals), but he worked hard and Steve Paterson was always confident that his natural ability would bring success. He signed after three months on loan and repaid the management team's faith in him many times over before leaving for Hearts in May 2003. On the downside, defenders Paul Cherry and Iain MacArthur retired through injury – both had played major parts in two promotions. Scott McLean left for Queen of the South in December and Barry Robson spent October to April on loan to Forfar. A deal was signed with Errea of Italy to be the club's new kit supplier.

Most of the pre-season friendlies were against Highland League opposition, but a stronger challenge was faced at Forfar on 17 July and, after a poor performance, it ended 2-2. On the same day a young team (strengthened by the experience of Jim Calder) represented the club at the Keyline Challenge Cup in Oban and were joint winners with Clyde. The next Saturday Dundee came to Inverness as the main pre-season attraction: Dundee won 2-1. The first competitive match took place on 31 July – away at Stenhousemuir in the first round of the CIS Insurance Cup. It proved to be a stroll in the sun as Caley Thistle won 3-1. The victory was set up by two first-half Scott McLean goals, with the opener in one minute 34 seconds being the first goal of the season in Scotland. Barry Wilson added a third in the second half, then 'The Warriors' managed a consolation goal in the dying minutes.

The start of the league campaign on 7 August was another matter, as the reality of First Division life hit – a 4-0 defeat away to newly-relegated Dunfermline. Caley Thistle were dealt a hard blow when an early injury to Barry Wilson saw him stretchered off: then substitute Andrew Allan was red-carded in the 66th minute. It was all downhill after that. At half-time Dunfermline held a narrow 1-0 lead but it was 2-0 in 61 minutes. Two more were added after Allan's dismissal.

The first match in the resurrected League Challenge Cup took place the following Tuesday. The competition name had been changed to the Bell's Challenge Cup and the new arrangement was for games every second Tuesday. Caley Thistle's successful run led to a hectic schedule. The home cup match was also the first of three games in 11 days against St Mirren. It was a very dull affair with the deadlock only broken by an 88th-minute Mike Teasdale headed goal. On the 14th Falkirk came north and the result was more disappointment in front of 3022 spectators – the highest crowd of the season for a home league match. Caley Thistle led twice through Paul Sheerin and Ross Tokely, but twice Falkirk came back. Then, with three minutes left, the Bairns grabbed the winner.

The following Tuesday St Mirren came back to Caledonian Stadium in round two of the CIS Insurance Cup. It was all very even for 90 minutes, but in extra time a Paul Sheerin penalty goal and a fine effort from new signing Kevin Byers made it 2-0. Just four days later Saints gained revenge in the league at Love Street with a 3-2 win. Ross Tokely's dismissal in 21 minutes was a major setback, but a Paul Sheerin penalty gave Caley Thistle a 29th-minute lead. It was short lived, as three quick goals from Saints ended the contest. Mike Teasdale pulled one back late on, but the first point was still proving elusive.

GOING BALLISTIC!

The busy month continued and for the third Tuesday in a row there was a cup-tie. This time it was at Firhill against ground-sharing Hamilton. Iain Stewart scored two of the goals in the 3-0 win and these were to be his only strikes of another injury-ravaged season. The seventh game of the month took place on the 28th at Ayr's Somerset Park. For nearly 90 minutes it looked as if the scoreline would remain blank, but a Glynn Hurst goal close to the whistle gave Ayr all three points – another major disappointment. Not surprisingly, Caley Thistle finished August propping up Division One.

First win in First Division

The league duck was broken on 4 September when a Martin Glancy goal earned a 1-1 draw at home to Morton. The visitors' Harry Curran was sent off in 72 minutes at 1-0 but despite the man advantage it was the Greenock side that equalised. A week later troubled Clydebank came to Inverness and the first win finally happened. Paul Sheerin scored the only goal with a penalty, but the game was marred by a bad shoulder injury to striker Davide Xausa on his debut. Paterson was relieved: 'It was vital that we got the victory and we had to work hard. You could feel the tension but we got there and everyone is delighted.' The next day Caley Thistle won the North Cup at Forres by defeating Lossiemouth 3-0.

Another Tuesday and another cup-tie. Clydebank made the trip north for the Quarter Final of the Challenge Cup and were beaten 2-0 thanks to goals from Martin Glancy and Barry Robson. September's league card was completed by a 2-2 draw at Livingston and a 2-0 home defeat at the hands of Raith Rovers. The Livingston game on the 18th had the atmosphere of a local derby thanks to the history of exciting encounters between the sides. Livi's Brian McPhee scored in the 26th minute then, before half-time, Martin Bavidge and Paul Sheerin made it 2-1. McPhee equalised in the second half. It was disappointing to surrender the lead but a draw was about right. The 2-0 defeat to Raith on the 25th was mainly down to a poor first-half performance. A spirited second-half fightback proved fruitless. The league win against Clydebank had earned a climb to eighth place, but by the end of September there was a slip to ninth.

This was not quite the end of the September action. The semi-final of the Bell's Challenge Cup took place on Tuesday 28th with a home tie against arch-rivals Livingston. Despite the prize of a cup final spot, it was a low-key affair in front of a sparse crowd. The battle of two off-form teams was settled by an 88th-minute Paul Sheerin goal. The semi-final victory ensured a November cup final place against Alloa. September's exploits earned Steve Paterson his eighth 'Manager of the Month' award and his first in Division One.

The opening game of October was an away visit to Airdrie on the second. Airdrie took a deserved 35th-minute lead and looked like taking all three points. Martin Glancy's 72nd-minute equaliser changed that and late pressure nearly gave Caley Thistle victory. While the first team were toiling in Airdrie, the reserve side were in nearby Coatbridge demolishing Albion Rovers in the Second XI Cup. They won by the remarkable margin of 12-2, with Graeme Stewart scoring four. On 12 October there was yet another Tuesday cup-tie in the third round of the CIS Insurance Cup, at home to SPL team Motherwell. Having run them so close two years earlier, hopes were high. It was another near thing, but the visitors narrowly won 1-0. Scorned first-half chances could have turned the game, but Lee McCulloch scored the only goal just after half-time. Paterson reflected on his team's display: 'I felt that at no time were we shown up and we probably made more chances than I expected.'

There was another First Division landmark at Falkirk on the 16th – the first away victory. Falkirk's cause was not helped by an 8th-minute own goal from Scott Crabbe, then a red card for Jamie McQuilken. Scott McLean sealed the win with an 85th-minute goal to make it 2-0. Steve Paterson was a happy man: 'I'm delighted to get our first away win of the season. In the first quarter of the season we weren't getting the rub of the green but today we did.' Some small revenge was gained over Dunfermline for the August defeat in the home game the following week. The Pars took the lead in 28 minutes through Steven Hampshire and held it until Martin Bavidge netted with a glancing header a minute from time. The final game of October took place at Cappielow on the 30th against nomadic Clydebank, resulting in a comprehensive 3-0 win. This ensured a climb to seventh place and opened up an 11-point gap over Clydebank at the foot of the table.

Caley Thistle made it five games undefeated on 6 November with a fine 2-0 home win against Livingston. The highlight was Stuart Golabek's first goal for the club in 75 minutes – a 20-yard piledriver which gave Ian McCaldon no chance. Scott McLean added a second in the final minute. The good run ended the following Friday with a traumatic 5-1 defeat at Cappielow. The match against Morton had been rescheduled because Scotland were playing England in a Euro 2000 qualifier at Hampden the next day. The break from the established routine clearly upset the team: it was a disaster. Morton's early lead was pegged back by Ross Tokely before Morton went 2-1 ahead just before half-time. The defence went to pieces in the second half, losing three more goals.

Bell's Challenge Cup final

The final of the Bell's Challenge Cup took place at Airdrie's Shyberry Excelsior Stadium on Sunday 21 November 21 against Alloa Athletic. After a strong build-up, over 2000 fans made the journey south.

The team that represented Caley Thistle in its first senior cup final was Les Fridge, Ross Tokely, Richard Hastings, Mike Teasdale, Mark McCulloch, Paul Sheerin, Barry Wilson, Davide Xausa, Dennis Wyness, Charlie Christie and Stuart Golabek. Substitute Kevin Byers replaced Golabek mid-way through the second half and, during extra time, Martin Glancy and Martin Bavidge came on for Wyness and Xausa.

To the neutral the game was exciting, but for Caley Thistle fans it was to end in disappointment. Little separated the sides, but underdogs Alloa were always in the driving seat. Alloa's Gary Clark scored in 20 minutes, Wilson equalised nine minutes later then Mark Wilson put Alloa back in the lead in 33 minutes. A Sheerin penalty straight after the restart made it 2-2 but Martin Cameron very quickly restored Alloa's lead. Sheerin's second penalty goal in 56 minutes led eventually to extra time. Cameron scored his second in 104 minutes, then Sheerin completed his hat-trick with just eight minutes left to take it to the dreaded lottery of penalties. It was 4-4 – after the regulation five attempts each – before the inevitable hero and villain emerged.

Goalkeeper Mark Cairns has to take the credit for Alloa's victory – he scored to make it 5-4 then saved Teasdale's kick to win the cup. The Caley Thistle manager blamed his defence for failing to contain two-goal Martin Cameron and he even asked a patrolling policeman for assistance: 'Could you not arrest those two centre backs for loitering?' He acknowledged that it was a great game: 'It was a great advert for Scottish football but to score four goals in a cup final and still finish on the losing side is surely not right.'

The loss of four goals was especially disappointing as Caley Thistle had not conceded a goal in the four games leading up to the final. Alloa boss Terry Christie echoed Paterson's views: 'I thought it was a terrific game but some of the defending was a bit suspect. Caley Thistle just kept coming back at us and coming back at us.'

There was a cup victory the following midweek at Mosset Park, Forres, when the hosts were crushed 6-0 and the Inverness Cup retained. Martin Bavidge was top scorer with two. November finished with two league home games. On Saturday 27th Airdrie were beaten 2-0 thanks to Barry Wilson and Davide Xausa – and it could easily have been more. On the following Tuesday Ayr United made the long trip to Inverness amidst gales and rain. The pitch was very wet and the continuing heavy rain put the game in doubt – even once it started many feared abandonment. The conditions prevented good football and the 1-1 score seemed fair all round. Charlie Christie scored the home side's goal with ten minutes left to earn a point. The two league wins and a draw in November led to a small but important climb to sixth.

December was less successful, starting with a 4-2 defeat away to Raith Rovers. The game only just survived the Scotland-wide snow. Paul Sheerin once more slotted home a penalty to make it 1-1 in 14 minutes, but Alex Burns scored twice close to half-time. There was still time for Martin Bavidge to pull one back before the interval, but Paul Browne's goal from close range in 73 minutes ended the contest. The following week was better – Barry Wilson scored to earn a 1-1 home draw against league leaders St Mirren – but there was more disappointment on the 18th, with defeat at Dunfermline. It was 0-0 until the last minute, with Caley Thistle holding their own until Andy Tod's 90th-minute header decided the match. The last game of the year took place at home on Monday 27 December against Clydebank. Live television coverage of Rangers against Celtic put the kick-off time back to 3.30 pm which allowed a piece of history to be made. Two goals each from Paul Sheerin and Barry Wilson earned the 4-1 win, with Wilson's 87th-minute strike proving to be the last Scottish league or cup goal of the millennium. Caley Thistle turned the year in sixth place.

At the club's AGM on 29 December 1999, Dougie McGilvray announced that he was stepping down as chairman to make way for new blood. He felt it was time to concentrate on his own business which had been neglected in favour of football commitments: 'The pressure of running my own business, which has an increasingly international dimension, has convinced me that I cannot devote the time to be chairman of the Board. I have had four highly enjoyable years in that role but in recent months I have been liaising with a working party of major shareholders to enable the club to enter the millennium with a new approach to address the financial problems which, in common with so many other clubs, we have endured.' On taking office, McGilvray made the bold prediction that the club would be in the Premier League within eight years. At the time this was seen as an impossible goal but on stepping down he pointed out that the First Division had been reached in half that time and further progress was still possible. At the same AGM two new directors were elected to the board – new chairman-elect David Sutherland, chairman of Inverness-based construction company Tulloch PLC, and Ken Mackie, former chief executive of Raigmore NHS Trust. The Queen's New Year Honours List for 2000 was published on Hogmanay and it included an OBE award to life president Jock McDonald for services to the whisky industry.

January started with Barry Wilson making his place in football history even more secure. On Monday 3 January at Livingston the kick-off was brought forward to 1 pm due to floodlight problems. Wilson's close-range headed goal in 72 minutes was the first of the new millennium in Scotland and completed an historic double. Brian McPhee equalised in 82 minutes and it ended 1-1. Davide Xausa was sent off with three minutes left for a second booking. On 8 January Morton came to Inverness and were soundly whipped 6-2 in revenge for November's disaster in Greenock. Surprisingly, it was 0-0 at half-time, but the floodgates opened in the second half, with Barry Wilson netting two of the goals.

David Sutherland becomes new chairman

David Sutherland took over as chairman on 10 January 2000. Sutherland had no formal football connection up to this point but was a well-respected, high-profile business figure in Inverness. His aim was financial stability: 'The AGM gave us clearance to introduce a new £2 million share issue which will be launched in the spring and a good response would be a major boost. I and others are ready to put some money into this share issue but there is no way that I would seek to have a shareholding which controls the club. I see my role as working hard behind the scenes rather than shouting from the rooftops and I'm going to concentrate on using my business experience to benefit the club.' He knew that the club had financial problems which had to be addressed as a matter of priority, but he was unaware of the true scale of the escalating debt until he took office.

A frozen pitch at Ayr on 15 January led to a late postponement of the league game. The team were having their pre-match meal and supporters were well on their way when the surface was ruled unplayable. The supporters' club bus diverted to watch Dunfermline against Falkirk, so the day was not entirely wasted. A 1-1 home draw with Raith Rovers on the 22nd turned out to be the last game of January. It took a late Martin Glancy goal to gain a welcome point and maintain sixth place.

Going Ballistic!

The greatest chapter in the club's short history started on Sunday 9 January 2000 when Craig Burley drew the club's name out of the drum just after that of Celtic in the draw for round three of the Tennent's Scottish Cup. First Division status meant direct entry to this round along with the SPL members. This started a chain of events which would rock Inverness, Scotland and the rest of the football world. The players, officials and fans were ecstatic – particularly the chairman and finance director who were toiling to reduce the debt and keep the club afloat. The revenue from the cup saga was to prove a lifeline. Steve Paterson described the draw as 'brilliant for the club and the town. A good way for me to mark my fifth season at the club.' Barry Wilson cheekily thought 'it's really nice to get a bye!' With both Celtic and Rangers supporters in the Caley Thistle ranks, an extra edge was added to the tie. One Inverness fan approached coach Duncan Shearer claiming that it would be four apiece – four for Moravcik and four for Viduka!

At the time Celtic were trailing Rangers in the SPL by a considerable margin – six points when the cup match should have been played and nine by the time it was – but they were still a major force in Scottish football. They seemed to be taking nothing for granted when head coach John Barnes and his assistant Eric Black came to Inverness on a spying mission at the home draw with Raith Rovers. Both were in jovial mood and Steve Paterson admitted that they were unlikely to be worried: 'I don't think John Barnes will be losing much sleep from what he saw. We will have a somewhat different approach for Parkhead.'

Initially Caley Thistle were only allocated 3000 tickets, but after representations this was doubled.

Ticket sales were brisk: 4000 fans set off south on Saturday 29 January by every means of transport available, including a special train. The team stayed at a Livingston hotel the night before and made their way to Celtic Park in the morning. Inverness fans began to stream into Glasgow, approaching the game with a mixture of excitement and trepidation. No one could possibly have anticipated what was to happen next.

After a night of gales, Celtic Park's new Lisbon Lions stand was deemed dangerous because of loose guttering and the match was called off just 45 minutes before kick-off. The players were on the pitch when the news came through on BBC Radio Scotland and most fans were swarming around the turnstiles. Regular travelling fans were used to snow and frozen pitches leading to cancellations, but this was an amazing turn of events at a top-level ground. There was no choice but to turn around and head home. The train travellers had to wait many hours for their return trip and most resorted to an unscheduled day's shopping in the city.

The match was rescheduled for Tuesday 8 February but first there was a league match to play at Airdrie on the fifth. The Celtic tie should have been Steve Paterson's 200th game in charge, but in the event it was the Airdrie match. It ended in a convincing 4-1 win, all came through unscathed and preparations were made for the return trip to Glasgow.

Celtic accepted responsibility for the earlier debacle and allowed Caley Thistle to keep the money from Inverness ticket sales to pay for fans' transport. This placated those who would otherwise have paid twice – but not the supporters unable to make it south midweek. The row about possible ticket refunds was taken up by local Trading Standards Officers and rumbled on for months. Normal practice at the time was to print 'non-refundable' on the back of each ticket, but the legality of this was challenged and eventually the SFA rules were changed. The missing fans were desperately unlucky not to be able to witness history in the making as their team pulled off an astonishing – and well deserved – win. The 3-1 result was dubbed the greatest Scottish football shock since Berwick Rangers defeated Rangers in 1967. Inverness fans dismissed Berwick's claim as their achievement, whilst dramatic, was at home by just one goal.

Because of the evening kick-off, the team travelled down on the day of the match and fans once more crowded the A9. A fleet of free buses left Caledonian Stadium and all the passengers were in good shape. Once more, a good day out was anticipated and the general hope was that the team would not be humiliated. The black humorists joked about a cricket score, but most fans were confident of a good performance from a side holding its own in the First Division. The Caley Thistle starting line-up was Jim Calder, Mike Teasdale, Stuart Golabek, Bobby Mann, Richard Hastings, Paul Sheerin, Ross Tokely, Mark McCulloch, Barry Wilson, Charlie Christie and Dennis Wyness. All three substitutes were brought on in the closing minutes – Kevin Byers, Martin Glancy and Martin Bavidge.

Celtic started the match with flair, but the visitors' defence held out. The home fans were stunned when Caley Thistle took the lead in 16 minutes. Sheerin sent in a precision cross from the left and a glancing header from Wilson gave Jonathan Gould no chance. A minute later Mark Burchill equalised and the Caley Thistle fans thought their moment of glory had passed. In the 24th minute Caley Thistle again took the lead when a Mann header was deflected by Lubo Moravcik past Jonathan Gould. The goal went into the history books as an own goal but Mann has always insisted it was his and he has a very strong claim: 'Paul Sheerin sent in a corner and I headed it towards goal. It bounced off Moravcik before going in but I had done enough to get the credit.' Outstanding defensive work, including heroics by Jim Calder, kept the lead intact until the interval. The away fans were behind Calder's goal in the first-half and had a poor view of their side's goals – they relied on the video screen replays for a proper look and confirmation that it was no dream!

Ian Wright replaced Mark Viduka at half-time – it emerged later that the substitution was the result of a row in the Celtic dressing room. There have been many versions of what happened but those involved have kept details very quiet. The expected Celtic revival in the second half never happened and confidence began to grow in the Caley Thistle ranks. In the 57th minute, Regi Blinker brought down Wilson, and Sheerin prepared to take the crucial penalty. Celtic fans were packed behind Jonathan Gould's goal – the whistling was deafening. The tension was unbearable, but Sheerin did his best to keep cool – his only thought was 'Please go in!' He stepped up, sent Gould the wrong way and it was 3-1. With over 30 minutes left, the Caley Thistle camp still expected an onslaught and all eyes were on the clock. As the minutes moved into single figures the realisation began to strike that Celtic were not going to recover. The unthinkable was about to happen. With two minutes left, substitutes Glancy and Bavidge combined to set up a good chance, but indecision as to who was to shoot allowed the Celtic defence to clear. By this time thousands of home fans had walked out and there were vast gaps in the stand when the final whistle blew. The remaining Celtic fans sportingly applauded the Caley Thistle players. The fans then turned on their own management team.

It was fitting that former Celt Charlie Christie should be named 'Man of the Match' – he ran the midfield and the game was undoubtedly the highlight of his career. The travelling support went wild as their team took a bow. Outgoing chairman Doug McGilvray shared the magic moment trackside with his successor David Sutherland.

The glorious aftermath

The media had a field day. Ian Paul in the *Herald* compared the result with Berwick's defeat of Rangers in 1967: 'It has taken 33 years to outdo it but Berwick Rangers' infamous defeat of Rangers in the Scottish Cup of 1967 was finally overtaken in notoriety by this glorious Highland fling at Parkhead when the youngest club in the country...left Celtic, mighty Celtic, beaten, bothered and humiliated.' BBC Radio Scotland had been featuring live commentary of the Aberdeen/Livingston cup-tie that night but transmission was switched to Celtic Park as the drama unfolded.

Future *Highland News* sports editor Paul Chalk was only 12 months into a news traineeship when he found himself covering the biggest story ever in Highland football. Although news was the way to learn the on-the-job basic methods of journalism, sports reporting was always his goal. When the then sports editor Bernard Salmon decided to take a week off, before discovering Caley Thistle had been paired with Celtic at Parkhead, he offered the task to Paul. It was a real baptism of fire – delayed somewhat by the postponement of the match. For the revised date, Paul travelled on a supporters' bus and for a local reporter covering the team who caused such an upset it was a proud few hours. Such was the mayhem of the interviews afterwards that Paul missed the bus back but luckily met the next-morning deadline by virtue of a spluttering fax machine.

Elements of the press focused more on the fact that Celtic had lost rather than the fact that Caley Thistle had won. Captain Mark McCulloch summed it up: 'Most of the press seem to be more interested in the demise of Celtic whereas it should certainly concentrate on the fact that we won fair and square. Eleven against eleven. We played better than them, we scored more goals than them and we defended better than them – we wanted it more and we won.' Defender Mike Teasdale echoed the thoughts of many players that the postponement of the first game set up the victory: 'The players were nervous the first time we went down but by the time the match was played these nerves had subsided and we were better prepared mentally for the game.'

Teasdale's brother John (former Elgin City manager) is a Celtic supporter now resident in Los Angeles. He watched the match on TV in the local Celtic Supporters' Club and for the first time in his life cheered on the opposition. Unsurprisingly, he was the only Caley Thistle fan in the club but there was a reluctant agreement that the Inverness side deserved their historic win. Ross Tokely 'never wanted the night to end or to forget it in my life'. Goalscorer Paul Sheerin said 'it was the best moment in my career to date'. Charlie Christie recalled the moment at the end of the match when he ran to the Inverness fans in celebration: 'A Celtic fan called out my name and I expected abuse but he threw me a scarf which is now tied around my 'Man of the Match' award.' Christie's only criticism was with some aspects of the coverage: 'Somebody said we were 16-1 to win which in 90 minutes of football is a nonsense. We are sixth in the First Division – not a part-time Third Division team any more.'

For Coventry-based fan Dave 'Gringo' Wilson, the postponement of the first match was a nightmare. His train journey north with son Robert started at 6 am and the usual travel tension was compounded by a line closure between Preston and Carlisle. The bus replacement worked a treat and they reached Glasgow in plenty of time. A short trip to the East End – then everything started to go wrong. When the match was called off Dave and Robert had to turn around and head back south. They reached home just after midnight – 18 hours travel and no football. Despite difficulties getting off work and school, Dave and Robert headed off on another marathon trip for the rearranged game. It was all rather different this time. Like all who were going back into the city after the game, Dave was concerned about the reaction of the Celtic fans but while they were disgusted at their team's performance, most were good sports, wishing Dave and Robert a safe journey home. There was some tension when one Celtic supporter approached looking rather unhappy, but he just wanted to swap scarves. Then it was the sleeper to London and a train back up to Coventry. Robert's penance for the time off school was to write a match report – in the circumstances it was a pleasure.

There were two Caley Thistle club buses parked next to the main entrance of Celtic Park – the team bus and one which brought staff, volunteers and players' families. As Celtic fans gathered to protest, the family bus was completely hemmed in by the crowd and escape seemed impossible. Suddenly, as if at a pre-arranged signal, the fans formed two neat lines and allowed the bus to move. To a man and woman they clapped and cheered as the bus drove away, much to the relief of the occupants. Directors, supporters and players all paid tribute to Celtic for their attitude on what was clearly a night of bitter disappointment – they showed nothing but courtesy and generously praised their Inverness conquerors. On that evening, sportsmanship was alive and well in the east end of Glasgow.

The journey up the A9 was a pleasure as the match was relived. Fans stopped at hostelries on the road home for a refreshment or two and to watch the late-night highlights on television. This also served to convince those still in a daze that it was all real. Many were late for work the next day. Many did not make it at all. The club flag was raised by Highland Council at the Town House in celebration and a media frenzy began which, for the next few weeks, overwhelmed the club. The team stopped in Bridge of Allan on the way home to celebrate and to see TV highlights for themselves. They reached Caledonian Stadium in the early hours to find a media pack looking for photographs and quotes. The press were persuaded to leave the players until the next day on the promise of interviews with all. In the event, some players could not be rounded up for two days!

Goalkeeping hero Jim Calder described reporters and TV crews turning up at his house: 'I think that was my 15 minutes of fame.' The scoreline sent shockwaves around the football world: reports even appeared in the *Buenos Aires Herald* and Saudi Arabia's *Arab News*. E-mails arrived at the club from all over the world, including one from Sweden which noted the club's first ever mention in the Swedish papers. In Ian Rankin's bestseller *The Falls* fictional detective Inspector Rebus smiles at the famous *Sun* headline and refers to it as a 'modern classic'. Life president Jock McDonald's Tomatin Distillery produced a special edition whisky and each squad member was presented with a personally-inscribed bottle. Local MP David Stewart had promised a bottle of champagne for every goal scored – he did not reckon on three, but was delighted to keep his word.

Celtic chief executive Allan MacDonald issued a press statement the next day: 'Last night's performance was totally unacceptable to myself and my fellow Directors and simply not good enough for the Celtic support. I am addressing this situation as a matter of urgency with our Director of Football, Kenny Dalglish, who is returning this evening from club business overseas. The situation will be fully reviewed immediately on his return.' Dalglish returned from Spain to a waiting storm. The review promised by MacDonald led to the sacking of manager John Barnes, his assistant Eric Black and coach Terry McDermott. Dalglish took temporary charge of the team, but eventually was shown the door.

The Parkhead win led to the Inverness side being named Tennent's Team of the Round. Not surprisingly the crowd of 34,389 was a season record. The match was filmed by Celtic, who produced a video, 'A Night to Remember', for sale in Inverness. It is appropriate that the 1958 Kenneth More film of the same name told the story of the sinking of the Titanic – for Titanic read Celtic, but Caley Thistle were certainly much more than a floating iceberg! Berwick's 1967 goal-scoring hero Sammy Reid came to Inverness for a photo call with the Inverness heroes and thought comparison between the two feats was unfair: 'It is debatable because Berwick were playing in a lower division as well – back then we were a Second Division side and Rangers were in the First Division. Rangers had also been in the Cup Winners' Cup Final that year.'

Celtic youngster Liam Keogh, who was to join Caley Thistle in the summer of 2002, watched the match from the stand: 'It was almost unbelievable to witness what was unfolding on the field that night. In the aftermath of the game nobody knew what was happening regarding the manager, but the defeat proved to be the final nail in the coffin for John Barnes.' After the dust settled Celtic fans looked back on the debacle as a blessing in disguise. The club realised that it was time for a drastic change and this led to the start of the very successful Martin O'Neill reign. At the time, it was all gloom and doom.

There was a management change at Caley Thistle in February 2000, but the circumstances were less dramatic than those at Celtic. The Scottish League voted to admit Elgin City and Peterhead to Division Three from the start of 2000-1; Caley Thistle assistant manager Alex Caldwell was appointed to take charge of Elgin. Caldwell had been at Paterson's side since the start of 1995-6 and he was the one that could be heard driving the players from the side of the pitch while the manager sat deep in thought. Caldwell's departure was delayed by the cup run, at which point Duncan Shearer took over his duties. The former Scotland international had been appointed first-team coach in May 1998 while continuing to play. He joined Steve Paterson in the dug-out for the first time on 12 February – two weeks before Caldwell finally left. Shearer took over Caldwell's role as the vocal half of the partnership: 'Some people call us the good and the bad men, just because I jump up and down out there. Steve has his own character and any instructions are passed on by me to the team. If they are not carried out then there's trouble.'

Defender Richard Hastings had little time to take part in the Parkhead celebrations, as he had to fly out to join the Canadian squad preparing for the Gold Cup in California. He spent a sleepless night in a Glasgow Airport hotel before leaving early the next morning. Both he and Davide Xausa were in the squad when the Celtic game should have been played – there was a risk that both would have to head for the USA before the revised date, as two days later Canada were to play Costa Rica. Eventually it was agreed that Xausa would miss the tie and Hastings would fly out immediately after it. Paterson felt that he had enough cover up front to allow Xausa to go, but he could not spare Hastings.

Aberdeen next

Hastings and Xausa were both missing from the team that faced Aberdeen at home in the fourth round. Sky Television had chosen this tie for live coverage when the draw was made and, even before the Celtic match had been played, commentators were referring to a future Celtic/Aberdeen pairing. The publicity surrounding Caley Thistle ensured Sky a bumper audience and a good pay day for the club. A record crowd of 6290 packed Caledonian Stadium on Sunday 20 February after a ticket scramble, and the atmosphere was tremendous. It was 0-0 at half-time, but Mark McCulloch and Ross Tokely had both come very close. Five minutes into the second half, a powerful Bobby Mann header made it 1-0 and this time there was no doubt about the scorer. Aberdeen moved up a gear, but the home side held out for 30 minutes. Arild Stavrum forced a great save from Jim Calder before Cato Guntveit headed an equaliser to force a return match. Paterson felt that a replay would put the pressure back on Aberdeen: 'It seems strange to say it but a lot of pressure was on us in the first game, despite the fact that clearly we should have been the underdogs. I felt that there was a definite expectation on us to do well and prove that the Celtic game was no fluke.' Aberdeen manager Ebbe Skovdahl praised his opponents: 'You cannot write Inverness off. No doubt they will go into the game thinking they have nothing to lose and everything to gain. What we showed against them is not the way I want to play football.'

The match went to an evening replay in Aberdeen nine days later and Richard Hastings and Davide Xausa returned from the USA in time to take part. There was little action in the first half, apart from Jim Calder tipping a shot from Rashid Belabed onto the bar. The second half was action-packed and could have gone either way. A deflected chip from Ross Tokely came agonisingly close then Aberdeen's international keeper Jim Leighton saved from Barry Wilson. The only goal came in 75 minutes when Arild Stavrum headed past Calder. A minute later Zerouali closed in on goal and, as Calder came out, his foot stuck in the ground and he went down injured. Zerouali shot towards the empty net but Stuart Golabek hit it off the line with his knee. In 83 minutes Martin Bavidge was through but he was brought down on the edge of the box by Mark Perry. Caley Thistle came very close twice in the dying minutes. Tokely and Bavidge set up Dennis Wyness but he skidded on the sandy surface and it slid past. With a minute left, the ball fell neatly for Paul Sheerin 20 yards out and he hit a superb volley which seemed net-bound. Leighton pulled off a world-class save and Aberdeen held on to win. The result was a disappointment, but Caley Thistle's place in history was already secure.

Duncan Shearer admitted that nerves had played a part on the night: 'When we beat Celtic nobody expected us to go there and win but after that result people really thought we could beat Aberdeen. It would not have been that much of a shock and I think the players were aware of that.' Aberdeen goal-scorer Arild Stavrum thought that Caley Thistle were the better side up to his goal: 'I was really impressed by Inverness and we knew from the first game that they were very capable. It was not an easy game and we are just glad to be through.'

Supporter David Jardine went to Glasgow on the day of what he describes as the 'fluttering guttering' and was able to make it back down for the historic victory. The fourth-round Aberdeen tie proved more of a challenge. A pre-booked holiday in Spain took priority, so the search was on in Barcelona for a TV showing the match. A successful scouting mission led to a sports bar with 30 screens and a barman who agreed to show the Inverness cup match on one of them. There was stiff competition: Barcelona were also on TV that night and David shared the bar with hordes of enthusiastic Spaniards. Football camaraderie ensured that when the TV replay of Bobby Mann's goal was shown the Spaniards joined in with David's cheers. They also sympathised when Aberdeen equalised! He made it home in time for the Pittodrie replay – but there was to be no happy ending.

In most other seasons, a good cup run could have led to league problems but Clydebank were deeply buried at the foot of Division One so, with only one team going down, there was no chance of relegation. There were two more February league games before and after the first Aberdeen cup-tie. St Mirren were the benefactors of the Celtic cup hangover when they won 2-0 at Love Street on 12 February. A jaded Caley Thistle side, with four regulars missing, created little against the top side and were well beaten. Another poor performance, sandwiched between the Aberdeen cup games, led to a 3-0 defeat at the hands of Falkirk. There were few chances, but Falkirk took three of them. Sixth place was maintained by the end of February, despite only gaining three points.

Division One status was mathematically assured when Dennis Wyness earned a 1-0 victory at Cappielow against Clydebank on 4 March, playing in front of a crowd totalling only 168 – a record low for Caley Thistle. The rearranged game at Ayr took place on Tuesday 7 March and resulted in a well-deserved 3-1 win, despite Ayr taking an early lead. On the 18th Livingston were thrashed 4-1 at home, with Davide Xausa scoring a hat-trick against the club he was to join a year later. Livingston's unusually poor display was partly explained by the sacking of manager Ray Stewart a few days earlier. They lost Graham Coughlan to a red card in 79 minutes, but the game was over before that. A lacklustre 1-1 home draw with Ayr United on the 25th ended March – it was a day for the Wilsons, with Marvin scoring for Ayr and Barry for Caley Thistle. Sixth place in the league was retained. On 26 March the stadium was used for a rugby match for the first time, when Caledonian Reds played Edinburgh Reivers.

On April Fool's Day it was back to Cappielow for the fourth time and a 2-0 win against Morton. Former captain Mike Noble became the fourth Caley Thistle player to be granted a testimonial and St Johnstone provided the opposition on 4 April. Noble scored the second goal of the 2-0 win from the penalty spot. Injuries and suspension ravaged the squad ahead of the Raith Rovers game the next Saturday and, as a result, three Skillseekers were in the Kirkcaldy starting line-up. Not surprisingly, Raith won 2-0. There was a disaster on the 15th, when Airdrie inflicted a 5-1 defeat in Inverness. After beating them 4-1 in February on their own territory, this came very definitely under the heading of unpredictable. Niall Thompson scored a hat-trick as Caley Thistle put on a dreadful display and Airdrie took full advantage. Les Fridge salvaged some pride with a 72nd-minute penalty save and Dennis Wyness hit a consolation goal. It was little better the following week, when Dunfermline came north and ensured promotion with a 2-1 win.

There was a strange atmosphere at Falkirk on the 29th as this was supposed to be the last ever game at Brockville. The ground facilities were not up to SPL standards so, despite lying third, Falkirk were denied a play-off place. They did, however, have plans to sell up and build an SPL-friendly stadium. The day was a cross between a carnival and a wake. Bairns' fans even carried a suitably-inscribed coffin into the stadium. A 2-2 draw satisfied all, and in the event Brockville was to survive another three years. Caley Thistle's hero of the day was Les Fridge, who saved two penalties from Scott Crabbe.

Champions-elect St Mirren arrived in Inverness on 6 May in celebratory mood and were clapped on to the pitch by the home players and fans. The respect ended there, as they were unexpectedly thumped 5-0. It was 3-0 at half-time and some Saints' fans walked out. Those that remained endured more misery, but decided not to let this stop the celebrations. They cheered each Caley Thistle goal – then invaded the pitch at the final whistle. The playing area was only cleared after their team reappeared to take a bow. Captain Mark McCulloch scored a brace and Barry Wilson scored one – both on their final appearances before transfer. Davide Xausa and Martin Bavidge added the other goals. Despite scoring, it was an unhappy afternoon for Xausa, as he damaged teeth after colliding with a post. This led to an unusual tannoy plea for the services of a dentist.

GOING BALLISTIC!

Sixth place in first season

Caley Thistle finished the season in sixth place with 49 points – a satisfying end to a remarkable season. In 47 league and cup games they scored 80 goals and conceded 64. The 80 goals were shared by 16 players with two own goals. Captain Mark McCulloch made the most appearances with 46 out of a possible 47. Paul Sheerin was three behind on 43. Mike Teasdale, Jim Calder and Barry Wilson passed the 150 career-appearance milestone, whilst Ross Tokely, Mark McCulloch and Paul Sheerin notched up 100 appearances. Sheerin was top goal-scorer with 17 – a remarkable tally from midfield. The manager was pleased with the debut season in the First Division after a difficult start: 'It took a bit for them to find their feet but a lot of the younger lads now look comfortable First Division players. After the cup it might have been easy for the season to fall flat because we were safe from relegation but the lads kept it going really well.'

Canada were victorious in February's Gold Cup in California with more than a little help from Richard Hastings and Davide Xausa. This highly prestigious competition on the American continent is organised by the tongue-twisting Confederation of North, Central America and Caribbean Association Football. Twelve countries took part following pre-qualifying tournaments throughout CONCACAF's vast area of operation. Hastings played for Canada in all the matches, including the final, and was named 'Rookie of the Tournament'. The quarter-final match against pre-season favourites Mexico went to extra time and Hastings scored the Golden Goal that took them through to the semi-final. This feat alone led to tremendous media attention for the young defender, which went into overdrive when Canada beat Colombia 1-0 in the final to take the cup. Hastings played in the final but Xausa was bitterly disappointed to miss out due to a shoulder injury. As with the Celtic Park triumph, Hastings had no time to celebrate – both he and Xausa had to return post haste to Scotland for the Scottish Cup fourth-round replay against Aberdeen.

An Under-12 team coached by Charlie Christie won the Forres Soccer Sevens Cup for the second year in succession. For the first time the club entered the East of Scotland Reserve League, but the reluctance of teams in the south to travel led to all games being played away from home. A team also entered the Reserve Cup. Two girls' teams represented ICT over the season, spearheaded by the Under-16s, who were very successful and ended up winning the League Championship as well as seven cups. Finella Annand, Shelley Grant and Suzanne Grant were called up to the Scotland squad in April and Finella captained the international team in three matches. Their achievements were rewarded with a civic reception hosted by Inverness Provost Bill Smith. At the end of 2000-1 the team amalgamated with Ross County to form Inver-Ross Ladies team. This arrangement lasted until summer 2003 when a separate ICT Ladies team was created and entered in division three of the Scottish Women's League from 2003-4.

When David Sutherland took over as chairman in January 2000, Ken Thomson became vice chairman and Ken Mackie took on the role of financial director. In March former player Graeme Bennett returned from Clach as director of football. Alan Nelson and Harry Brown left after short periods of service and the board was gradually cut to six members. The rapidly deteriorating economic situation dominated meetings of the new board. The cup run proved a life-saver, but there was still the small matter of a £2 million overdraft. In March the chairman wrote to all shareholders spelling out the position and asking for their support for his rescue plan. A further share issue was announced, allied to more drastic measures in 2000-1 to prevent bankruptcy. In a strange turn of events, Sutherland temporarily resigned as chairman on April 3 due to a conflict of interest over a legal dispute between the club and his company Tulloch Construction concerning land adjacent to the stadium. The issue was quickly resolved and Sutherland resumed office three days later.

In January the medical team was strengthened by the arrival of physio Emily Goodlad. Emily was contracted to treat players at the stadium during the week and the club agreed to allow some use of the treatment room for private patients. Emily would eventually replace Ian Manning in the trackside role when he retired at the end of 2001-2.

CHAPTER 10

TO KILMARNOCK – TWICE
2000-1

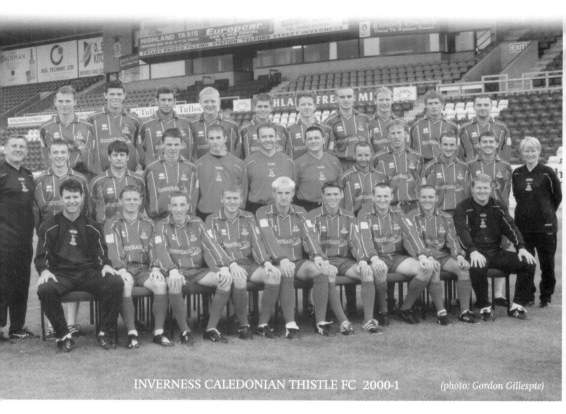

INVERNESS CALEDONIAN THISTLE FC 2000-1   *(photo: Gordon Gillespie)*

(*Back*) Neil MacDonald, Graeme Stewart, Davide Xausa, Barry Robson, David Craig, Charlie Christie, Grant Munro, Martin Bavidge, Dennis Wyness, Stuart Golabek

(*Middle*) John Docherty (coach), Tony Low, Gary Farquhar, David Hind, Ally Ridgers, Les Fridge, Jim Calder, Iain Stewart, Ross Tokely, Paul Sheerin, Roy McBain, Emily Goodlad (physio)

(*Front*) Steve Paterson (manager), David Bagan, Kevin Byers, Andrew Allan, Bobby Mann (captain), Richard Hastings, Mike Teasdale, Martin Glancy, Duncan Shearer (assistant manager)

Despite a tight budget, Steve Paterson steered the team to a top four place in Division One. There was also cup excitement – but not on the scale of the previous season. Economic difficulties hit home when two prominent players left in the close season for Livingston – Mark McCulloch and Barry Wilson were both out-of-contract and there was no possibility of matching the sums on offer at the West Lothian club. Bobby Mann took over the captaincy and Steve Paterson signed an extended contract. In July, Charlie Christie was appointed player/coach with responsibility for Skillseekers and younger players. Christie was delighted to take on this new role: 'I always hoped that I would get involved in the coaching side with Caley Thistle and I'm pleased that it has finally come along.' Paterson said that Christie had been elevated to reward him for services to the club: 'Charlie has been here since the merged club came into being and had long service with Caley before that. He deserves to have some future in the game to look forward to when his playing days are over.'

Roy McBain arrived in the close season from Ross County, and Scottish Cup medal-winner David Bagan signed from Kilmarnock. In September Stuart McCaffrey came on loan from Aberdeen and joined the club formally in December. In March 2001 Davide Xausa also took the road to Livingston for financial reasons. A small transfer sum was involved to reflect the short time left on his contract.

There was the usual round of pre-season friendly visits to Highland League grounds as well as participation in the annual Keyline Challenge Cup in Oban on 15 July. The pre-season build-up also included a visit to Inverness by Mansfield Town on 20 July, together with a few hardy supporters who had turned their team's Scottish tour into a holiday. It was spoiled somewhat by Caley Thistle's 5-2 victory. Aberdeen, the top attraction, were beaten 1-0 on 22 July thanks to an Iain Stewart strike. On 15 July Caledonian Stadium was the venue for a charity 'Music Against Cancer' concert headlined by Bob Geldof. The attendance was disappointing, but the Cancer Research Campaign made money and it was shown that the stadium could handle such an event.

The competitive season started on 5 August with a league visit by Airdrie and a change of rules – five substitutes were now allowed and any three could play. The Spanish-dominated Airdrie team was battling extinction and the line-up had been hastily assembled by new manager Steve Archibald. The

Wilson Robertson, scorer of the club's first
competitive goal on 9 August 1994
(photo: Gordon Gillespie)

Alan Hercher heads home the club's first league
goal on 13 August 1994
(photo: Gordon Gillespie)

First chairman John 'Jock' McDonald
(photo: Ken MacPherson)

1994-5 player/manager Sergei Baltacha
(photo: courtesy Coca-Cola)

Steve Paterson takes over as manager in May 1995
(photo: Trevor Martin)

Alex Caldwell became assistant manager in June 1995: his partnership with Steve Paterson lasted until February 2000
(photo: Gordon Gillespie)

On 20 January 1996 Mark McAllister became the first player to reach the 50-appearance milestone
(photo: Gordon Gillespie)

Chairman Dougie McGilvray welcomes new signings Mike Teasdale and Brian Thomson in December 1995
(photo: Trevor Martin)

Inverness Provost Bill Fraser cuts the first ceremonial turf at East Longman for the new Caledonian Stadium on 3 October 1995, watched by Mike Noble, Graeme Bennett, Danny MacDonald and Charlie Christie
(photo: Trevor Martin)

Scottish Cup quarter final against Rangers at Tannadice on 9 March 1996: John Scott after swapping shirts with Paul Gascoigne
(photo: Ken MacPherson)

Jim Calder receives his 'Man of the Match' award from John Howie of sponsors Tennent after the Rangers cup tie
(photo: Ken MacPherson)

Iain Stewart is the club's all time top goalscorer with 82 goals in 144 appearances. 1996-7 Third Division Player of the Year
(photo: Gordon Gillespie)

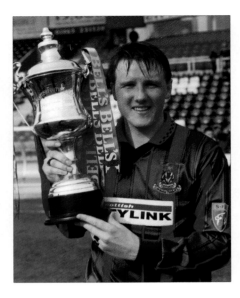

Celebrations after Scottish Cup penalty shoot-out victory over Stranraer on 15 January 1997: Graeme Bennett, Iain Stewart, Paul Cherry and Richard Hastings
(photo: Gordon Gillespie)

Captain Mike Noble with the Third Division Championship trophy on 3 May 1997
(photo: Ken MacPherson)

Canadian internationalist Richard Hastings
(photo: Trevor Martin)

Les Fridge pulls off a great save against Motherwell in a Coca-Cola-Cup tie on 9 August 1997
(photo: Gordon Gillespie)

Duncan Shearer arrives from Aberdeen, September 1997
(photo: Trevor Martin)

Barry Wilson made 156 appearances and scored 45 goals between 1996-7 and 1999-2000: he returned to the Club in August 2003
(photo: Trevor Martin)

Brian Thomson: joint top Second Division scorer 1997-8 with 20 goals
(photo: Trevor Martin)

Davie Ross: 105 appearances and 10 goals between August 1995 and March 1998
(photo: Trevor Martin)

1997-8 joint captains Iain MacArthur and Paul Cherry
(photos: Gordon Gillespie (left), Trevor Martin (right))

Pescanova North Caledonian League champions 1997-8. Second team, after beating Golspie 3-0, 9 May 1998.
(Back) Peter Calderwood, David Hind, Michael Rae, Fraser Gow, Alan McLeod, Sandy Silvestri,
Kenneth Macdonald, Jordan MacDonald
(Front) Kevin Sweeney (assistant manager), Neil McCuish, Mike Noble, Pescanova representative, David Craig,
Grant Munro, Steven Sanderson, Andrew Allan
(Standing, right) John Docherty (manager)
(photo: Clive Grewcock)

Scott McLean, club's top scorer in 1998-9 with 20 goals and also runner-up Second Division top scorer *(photo: Trevor Martin)*

Mark McCulloch, captain 1998-9 and 1999-2000
(photo: Trevor Martin)

Bell's Challenge Cup final against Alloa Athletic 21 November 1999. Paul Sheerin's hat-trick was not enough. Alloa won the cup in a penalty shoot-out
(photo: Ken MacPherson)

Bobby Mann being congratulated by
Paul Sheerin, Dennis Wyness and Mark
McCulloch after goal number two
(photo: Ken MacPherson)

Barry Wilson scored the first goal and
celebrates at the final whistle with
Mike Teasdale
(photo: Gordon Gillespie)

Tennent's 'Team of the Round'
(photo: Trevor Martin)

Paul Sheerin slots home goal number three
from the penalty spot and seals the victory
(photo: Ken MacPherson)

Charlie Christie celebrates the dramatic
4-3 Scottish Cup win against Ayr United
on 27 January 2001
(photo: Ken MacPherson)

Roy McBain celebrates scoring against his former
club Ross County on 31 March 2001
(photo: Ken MacPherson)

Martin Bavidge: 19 goals in 122 appearances
between 1998-9 and 2001-2
(photo: Ken MacPherson)

Midfielder Russell Duncan signed from
Aberdeen in August 2001
(photo: Ken MacPherson)

Mike Teasdale with the Inverness Cup
after captaining the team that defeated
Ross County 3-2 on 11 December 2001
(photo: Phil Downie)

Bobby Mann, captain from
2000-1 to 2003-4
(photo: Ken MacPherson)

3-1 Scottish Cup victory against Hearts at Tynecastle 26 January 2002:
two of the goalscorers Ross Tokely and David Bagan
(photos: Ken MacPherson)

Outgoing chairman David Sutherland (left)
passes the ball to his successor Ken Mackie
in May 2002
(photo: Ken MacPherson)

Summer 2002 signings Mark Brown
and Liam Keogh
(photo: Trevor Martin)

Bell's awards for November 2002: First
Division 'Player of the Month' Barry Robson
and 'Manager of the Month', for the third
month in a row, Steve Paterson
(photo: Ken MacPherson)

Paul Ritchie after scoring against
Celtic in the CIS Insurance Cup
on 23 October 2002
(photo: Trevor Martin)

Richie Hart celebrates his goal against St Mirren on 2 November 2002
(photo: Ken MacPherson)

Dennis Wyness: First Division Player of the Year 2002-3 and top First Division scorer with 27 goals
(photo: Ken MacPherson)

Barry Robson in action during the Scottish Cup semi-final against Dundee on 20 April 2003
(photo: Ken MacPherson)

John Robertson became manager on Boxing Day 2002; Donald Park joined him as head coach on 3 January 2003
(photo: Ken MacPherson)

Defender Stuart Golabek heads away under pressure from Aberdeen's Scott Booth on 19 July 2003
(photo: Ken MacPherson)

Charlie Christie played in all ten seasons and made 314 appearances: a club record
(photo: Ken MacPherson)

Defender Grant Munro broke through into the first-team squad in 1998-9 from the youth system, and is now one of the longest-serving players at the club
(photo: Ken MacPherson)

Stuart McCaffrey celebrates with David Bingham after scoring against Queen of the South on 6 December 2003
(photo: Trevor Martin)

Bell's Cup victory over Airdrie United on 26 October 2003:
goalscorers Steve Hislop and David Bingham celebrate with manager John Robertson
(photos: Ken MacPherson)

Mark Brown makes a seemingly impossible save against St Mirren
in the 4th round of the Scottish Cup 7 February 2004
(photo: Ken MacPherson)

A Barry Wilson wonder goal against
Motherwell earns a place in the 2003-4
Scottish Cup semi-final
(photo: Ken MacPherson)

First Division top-of-table clash and effective
title decider against Clyde 8 May 2004: Steve
Hislop heads the winning goal
(photo: Ken MacPherson)

Goalscorers Barry Wilson, Paul
Ritchie and David Bingham
(photo: Trevor Martin)

Bobby Mann after receiving the First Division
Championship trophy from Lord Macfarlane
(photo: Trevor Martin)

Celebrations after presentation of the trophy and medals.
(photo: Trevor Martin)

travelling fans had no idea who was in their team but came north sporting sombreros and clutching toy donkeys. The festive atmosphere disappeared when Caley Thistle beat them 2-0. Three days later it was off down the well-trodden path to Peterhead for the first round of the CIS Insurance Cup. This was a familiar destination for friendlies and the Buchan Cup but this was different. Balmoor Stadium was now a senior venue and the SFL newcomers proved hard to beat. The Inverness side were clear favourites and were cruising 2-0 at half-time through Iain Stewart (who would join Peterhead two months later) and Davide Xausa. Penalties brought Peterhead back into the game midway through the second half. Ross Tokely handled, but Les Fridge saved Scott Paterson's spot kick. The referee ordered a retake and Craig Cooper stepped up to score. Stuart Golabek brought Paterson down and Cooper again scored to make it 2-2. Bobby Mann saved the day with 13 minutes left when he headed home a Richard Hastings cross.

The rest of August was dismal – three league defeats, one cup victory and one cup defeat. On the 12th at Livingston it was 3-1 for the home side with goalkeeper Les Fridge both a hero and villain. At 1-0 down he saved a penalty from Scott Crabbe, then, in the dying minutes, he dropped the ball at the feet of former (and future) Caley Thistle favourite Barry Wilson, allowing him to score the winner. Iain Stewart scored the consolation goal. One bright spot was the 3-2 away victory against Alloa on Tuesday 15th in round one of the Bell's Challenge Cup. At 2-0 down Iain Stewart scored a brace to bring it back to 2-2 – then Martin Bavidge hit a late winner. This game marked Charlie Christie's 200th appearance. On 19 August Falkirk came to Inverness, dominated and won 3-2. Martin Bavidge scored both Caley Thistle's goals, but was robbed of the chance of a hat-trick by the referee's whistle. He was through on goal seconds over the 90 minutes when the referee blew for full time.

The following Tuesday, Airdrie came back north in round two of the CIS Insurance Cup. Their 2-0 win reversed the earlier league score. A 4-1 away defeat to Raith Rovers the following Saturday completed a month to forget and led to a poor eighth place. The goal at Kirkcaldy , scored by Iain Stewart, was his 82nd for the club. It would also be his last.

September started with the announcement that four players had been transfer-listed – Dennis Wyness, Gary Farquhar, Kevin Byers and Martin Glancy. Wyness would eventually realise his full potential and become a major player at the club, but the others were to leave. The first September game was a disappointing 2-1 home defeat in the second round of the Bell's Challenge Cup at the hands of Stranraer. Hastings and Xausa were on international duty with Canada, but this was no excuse – Caley Thistle created enough chances to win. All they eventually managed was a Martin Bavidge consolation. Paterson was furious: 'It must rank as the worst result since I've been here – and it comes seven months after our best result. It just highlights the high points and low points of football.'

The 2-1 home defeat by Clyde on the 9th led to a slip to the foot of the division, but the performance was better and gave some hope for the future. Caley Thistle held the lead for nearly an hour thanks to David Bagan's debut goal, until a disputed penalty award, and an equaliser, in 62 minutes. Continued protests led to a red card for Stuart Golabek. The game then turned Clyde's way and they scored what proved to be the winner.

On 16 September the derby matches with Ross County returned after a three-season gap. The first was at Caledonian Stadium where County took the points with a 54th-minute penalty goal after a hotly-disputed award. Caley Thistle had been well ahead in the first half but could not score. County played the last 15 minutes with 10 men after Eddie Cunnington's dismissal, but still held on to win. A 4-1 away win at Alloa on the 23rd improved matters, despite the low crowd of 584 – the worst of the season. It was an excellent performance, marred only by a red card shown to Richard Hastings, who had just returned after being hospitalised with concussion while playing for Canada in Trinidad and was making his 199th appearance. The opening goal at Alloa came from Barry Robson on his return from a loan spell at Forfar. A busy September was completed on the 30th at Ayr and an exciting 3-3 draw. With 20 minutes to go, Ayr seemed comfortable at 3-1, with the only ICT goal coming from Davide Xausa. Very late goals from Paul Sheerin and Bobby Mann rescued a point. After the ups and downs of the month Caley Thistle recovered slightly to maintain eighth place.

Results improve

Things looked up a little in October with two wins, a draw and a defeat. On the 7th Morton were hammered 4-0 at home with a double from Martin Bavidge and one each from David Bagan and Roy McBain (his debut goal). This should have been Iain Stewart's last match before his transfer to

Peterhead, but injury prevented a farewell appearance. He left behind a record of 82 goals in 144 matches, which would prove hard to beat. Dennis Wyness did eventually come close with 80 goals in 159 appearances. The 14th saw the third game of the season against Airdrie – this time a bad-tempered affair at New Broomfield. Airdrie took the lead in 58 minutes, but Paul Sheerin pulled one back just three minutes later. Austin McCann's punch at Ross Tokely in 70 minutes reduced Airdrie to ten men, but they held out until Davide Xausa's winning goal four minutes from time. Spanish tempers flared and Jesus Sanjuan was sent off close to the whistle for a second yellow card.

On the 21st hostilities were resumed against Livingston in Inverness and they left with a point after an action-packed draw. The ex-Caley Thistle double act of Mark McCulloch and Barry Wilson made it 2-0 before the hour mark. Wilson sent over two trademark corners and McCulloch headed them both home. A strong fightback led to goals from Roy McBain and Paul Sheerin. Bobby Mann collected a second yellow card near the end, but Livingston could not capitalise and it finished 2-2. The following week Raith came north and took a similar two-goal lead. An injury-hit Caley Thistle could only pull one Paul Sheerin goal back but, despite this setback, there was a climb to sixth place.

In November there were continuing injury problems and a struggle to find a squad of 16. A 1-1 draw at Clyde on the 4th was good in the circumstances – especially as Martin Bavidge's dismissal resulted in playing with ten men for the whole of the second half. Dennis Wyness had given the visitors an early lead, but Clyde equalised with 15 minutes left. The following week, a determined Alloa side fought hard in Inverness and were only defeated 2-1 thanks to spectacular goals from Mike Teasdale and Paul Sheerin.

On 18 November it was derby time in Dingwall and another classic encounter. It resulted in a 3-0 win and County ending with nine men. Dennis Wyness did most of the damage with two goals. Mike Teasdale scored another memorable goal to make it 3-0. County's frustration flared up in the second half and both Darren Henderson and Alex Bone earned second yellow cards. Protests by Bone led to two more red cards. Teasdale earned the 'Man of the Match' award – a rare feat on 'enemy' territory! It was back down to earth the following week and a 2-0 defeat by Morton at a boggy Cappielow. Morton took an early lead and hung on tenaciously with defensive football. They scored a second on the break and, despite some good play, the visitors could achieve nothing. The month ended with a one place climb to fifth and the loss of Martin Glancy to Clydebank.

7-3 against Ayr

The opening match of December was a dramatic home league encounter with Ayr. In years to come, supporters will still be talking about it. Despite the windy conditions, two attacking teams provided a great spectacle and it rained goals. Mike Teasdale's purple patch continued: he opened the scoring in eight minutes. Ayr replied quickly, through Eddie Annand and Hugh Robertson, then Paul Sheerin equalised from the penalty spot after Dennis Wyness had been brought down. Just before half-time Wyness made it 3-2, then Glynn Hurst equalised after the restart. At that point it could easily have gone either way, but Caley Thistle amazingly scored four more in the last 30 minutes. David Bagan lobbed Craig Nelson, then scored his second in spectacular style – a rocket shot from 18 yards after a Sheerin/Teasdale 1-2. Wyness completed his hat-trick near the end with an overhead kick, then a tap into the empty net, after neatly rounding Nelson. Ayr finished the match with ten men after Craig McEwan's dismissal in 81 minutes for a late tackle on Roy McBain. It finished 7-3 – a record club aggregate score which still stands. Paterson thought it was 'arguably the best 90 minutes of attacking football by Caley Thistle in my time as manager... anybody here today would have to admit that was one of the best games they've seen in a long time.'

The 2-2 draw at Falkirk the following week was rather an anti-climax, but a point was welcome in the wind and heavy rain. The Bairns were 2-0 up after 20 minutes, but Dennis Wyness and Paul Sheerin scored in the second half. Referee John Fleming was injured after 71 minutes and replaced by assistant Joe Heggie. In another high-scoring game on the 16th, Airdrie were hammered 4-0 at home. Although Airdrie were in financial turmoil, their Spanish contingent played good football and it was a satisfying win. The score could have been higher but Paul Sheerin uncharacteristically missed a penalty and Javier Broto in the Airdrie goal was in excellent form. The win was set up by David Bagan's 7th-minute goal and the second came close to the end of the first half in spectacular style. Charlie Christie strode through the Airdrie defence, played a one-two with Davide Xausa then flicked it over the advancing Broto. Xausa and Wyness completed the scoring. This was Wyness's seventh goal in six games – more than enough for him to be taken off the transfer list. The striker was delighted that his future was secure: 'It was frustrating sitting on the bench every week and when I got my chance I grabbed it with both hands.' It was all to work out rather well for both parties. Wyness played in a consecutive 119 games from 21 October 2000 up to his final match for the club at the end of 2002-3. He would be top goalscorer for three seasons in a row and net 80 goals in total,

December's final game was a home draw with Clyde. It was not a game to write home about but there was a fine goal from Davide Xausa to savour. David Bagan's goal on the half-time whistle gave Caley Thistle the edge but Clyde took a 2-1 lead midway through the second half. A Xausa solo effort made it 2-2. The point ensured another step up to fourth place. From tenth in early September to fourth by the end of the year was a major achievement. The unbeaten December run led to Steve Paterson being named Bell's 'Manager of the Month' and Dennis Wyness 'Player of the Month'.

For the first time since 1996-7 there was a New Year derby match, which went ahead at Caledonian Stadium on January 2 after a major snow-clearing operation. The crowd of 5291 was the top home league total for the season. It was quite a match, played in a better spirit than earlier encounters. Paul Sheerin gave Caley Thistle the lead in 12 minutes, but by half-time County were 3-1 ahead. Defeat seemed a certainty until a late onslaught on the County goal. Dennis Wyness hit two goals in quick succession to gain a point. The first came in the 89th minute with a flick-in from a Roy McBain cross. With two minutes of injury time on the clock, a Barry Robson header beat Garry Hamilton and came back off the post. Wyness was well positioned for a tap-in to make it 3-3 with the last kick of the game.

On 6 January it was down to Alloa in confident mood, but a stubborn Wasps' side held out for a point. Despite first-half dominance, only a Davide Xausa strike separated the teams. Alloa were stronger after the break and gained a point. With five minutes left, Gareth Evans scored. A bone-hard pitch at Ayr on the 13th made good football difficult and had put the game in doubt. Ayr dominated and scored in only three minutes through Pat McGinlay. An error by Ayr goalkeeper Marius Rovde gifted Dennis Wyness the equaliser in 22 minutes when he dropped a Davide Xausa cross at the striker's feet. Ayr took command in the second half, but the Caley Thistle defence held out for a point. This was the last league game of the month and fourth place was retained.

GOING BALLISTIC!

The Morton home game due to be played on 20 January was postponed due to a frozen pitch, breaking a fine record. It was the first senior match to be cancelled at Caledonian Stadium – a remarkable tribute to the Moray Firth location and the skills of groundsman Tommy Cumming. This blank Saturday meant that Ayr were the next opponents in a home Scottish Cup third-round tie on the 27th. The reputation of the two teams for producing goals and thrills was enhanced by this tremendous match. Ayr were well ahead 3-0 at half-time and it looked all over. In a stunning second-half comeback Caley Thistle scored four times in 18 minutes to win. Paul Sheerin started the blitz in 54 minutes from 20 yards, Bobby Mann netted a free kick from the same spot and Davide Xausa then made it 3-3 from 22 yards. Excitement was at fever pitch – a rare event for the normally reticent Inverness crowd. Four minutes later Dennis Wyness scored the winner with a carbon copy of his goal a fortnight earlier – Rovde dropped it and Wyness was again in the right place at the right time. Paul Sheerin's five-star performance earned him the title of Tennent's 'Player of the Round'. When fans reminisce about memorable matches this is one that is always mentioned – usually in the same breath as December's 7-3 league thriller. Steve Paterson was named Bell's 'Manager of the Month' for January, his second award in a row.

Inverness was granted city status in December 2000 to mark the new millennium and this reopened the debate regarding the team's name. 'Inverness City' had been mooted, but a poll at the Ayr cup game resulted in a 72% supporters' vote in favour of the status quo. In January 2001 an 'SPL2' was proposed and eight First Division clubs expressed interest – including Caley Thistle. Not surprisingly, the hope was that a formal link with the SPL would improve finances. In the event, nothing materialised.

February was dominated by cup activity, but first there was one league match at home to Falkirk. Frozen pitches meant that this was the only league match of the month. It ended 1-1 despite constant Caley Thistle pressure. Falkirk had taken an unexpected lead through Andy Lawrie, but Dennis Wyness headed a welcome equaliser. The visitors had come to defend and they were very successful. There was a potential problem in February with the imminent bankruptcy of Airdrie. The nine points already gained from Airdrie could be lost, which would bring relegation worries. In the event Airdrie struggled on until the end of 2001-2.

TO KILMARNOCK – TWICE

Killie in the Cup

The fourth round of the Tennent's Scottish Cup threw up a home tie against SPL side Kilmarnock and started a saga which ran into March. There was plenty of pre-match hype and the all-ticket game on 17 February attracted a crowd of 5294. Caley Thistle took the game to Killie in the first-half, but it was the visitors who should have taken the lead. They were incensed when a goal was chalked off right on the half-time whistle. Andy McLaren hit the bar, the ball bounced down – and clearly crossed the line. Unlike Geoff Hurst's similar effort in 1966, the linesman was convinced that it was not a goal. McLaren's day went further downhill when he was red-carded with 20 minutes left for an off-the-ball kick at Paul Sheerin. Killie's Gary Hay netted in 80 minutes but he was offside. As time ran out, a replay looked a certainty – then, with seconds remaining, Barry Robson scored with an 18-yard half-volley. Celebrations of another SPL scalp were cut short when, two minutes into added time, Gary Hay headed an equaliser. A trip to Kilmarnock was required. Kilmarnock manager Bobby Williamson was happy to take a draw: 'We came within a few seconds of going out of the Scottish Cup in Inverness but credit to the players for keeping going right to the final whistle.' As the equaliser followed Robson's goal, Paterson went 'from the heavens to the depths'.

Eight hundred fans made the midweek journey to Rugby Park on the 28th but it proved abortive. Undersoil heating was to become an emotive issue three years later and fans were to recall their experience of Kilmarnock's system. Despite freezing weather, Kilmarnock were confident that their heating would keep the pitch soft. However, sections were hard and the referee had no choice but to abandon the match after 27 minutes at 0-0. Stories abounded as to the reasons for the frozen pitch but it emerged later that the undersoil heating had been switched off overnight because of neighbour complaints. Kilmarnock claimed that the pitch had been playable earlier in the day but weather conditions deteriorated during the game. This was backed up by referee Dougie McDonald, who denied claims that conditions were unplayable before kick-off: 'Temperatures got slowly colder and colder. There were patches of very soft ground where the undersoil heating was working well but other patches which were very hard. The difference between hard and soft made the conditions absolutely treacherous.'

The ill-fated match started controversially when Kilmarnock were awarded a penalty after only two minutes, but Jim Calder continued his amazing record by saving Andy McLaren's kick. Caley Thistle were enjoying a good spell when time was called. A few minutes before the 'final' whistle, referee Dougie McDonald alerted police and stewards to enable contingency plans to be put into action.

Despite being given vouchers for the revised date, the visiting fans were quite rightly livid. Chairman David Sutherland came over to speak to a large number as they left the stand and promised something would be done: 'I'm very upset and angry for our fans and I shall be writing a strongly-worded letter to the SFA to voice my full feelings. I feel pretty aggrieved and I just cannot believe something like this could happen at a big club like Kilmarnock.' Sutherland also vowed to seek financial help for supporters who would now need to repeat the trip less than a week later. After venting their anger on the referee and Kilmarnock, the fans had no choice but to set off on the long trip home. The *Daily Record* headline 'Shambles' summed it up well. There was something rather familiar about the episode in view of the Parkhead 'fluttering guttering' debacle, but this time there was to be no happy ending.

Cup sponsors Tennent paid for 12 buses to take fans to the re-scheduled replay on 6 March and, perhaps not surprisingly, the travelling number increased to 1000 despite it again being in midweek. Few of the additional 200 away fans had to pay as, amidst the chaos of the abandoned match, the stewards generously issued vouchers in handfuls to try to stem the tide of anger! Killie had the better of the first half and had two good penalty claims turned down. Jim Calder had two outstanding early saves and at half-time it was 0-0. Just after the break a Davide Xausa free kick was pushed away by home keeper Gordon Marshall then, in 51 minutes, Xausa gave Caley Thistle the lead from close range. Kevin McGowne equalised on the hour mark after a goalmouth scramble, then Paul Wright converted a penalty four minutes later for the winner. Dennis Wyness nearly forced extra time in the dying seconds, but his shot was cleared off the Killie line. The crowd of 6528 was the highest for any ITC match all season.

Paterson had no complaints: 'I feel we could have played better. It needed everyone playing at the top of their game but not everyone did. Killie deserved to win.' Williamson was very relieved: 'We had most of the game in the first half but there wasn't much in it. We played with a lot of spirit when we went behind and battled on. Thankfully we did enough to pull it out of the bag.'

TO KILMARNOCK – TWICE

Back to the League

It was back to league business and a busy March catching up with postponed matches. Six were played – three at home and three away including the final derby of the season. There was no major cup backlash as this heavy programme was completed with two draws and four wins. A visit to Kirkcaldy on the Saturday following the second Kilmarnock trip ended in a 1-1 draw with Raith Rovers despite Dennis Wyness giving a 51st-minute lead. There was clearly some fatigue and the Raith hoodoo continued. On 13 March Morton were beaten 4-2 at home: it could have been more. Dennis Wyness scored his second hat-trick of the season and David Bagan hit the fourth. A rather dour home match on the 17th against Alloa ended in a 2-0 win, including a bizarre goal early in the second half. Alloa defender Steven Thomson attempted to head back to Guido Van de Kamp but the goalkeeper was on his way out to collect and the two collided. Dennis Wyness helped the ball on its way into the empty goal. Barry Robson added the second with a solo effort four minutes from time.

The elusive first victory over Raith came on 23 March at home. The match was played on a Friday night, as Scotland faced Belgium in a World Cup qualifying match the next day. Memories of the Friday night drubbing by Morton in November 1999 came flooding back, but this time things were much better. Dennis Wyness scored both goals in the 2-0 win and Caley Thistle climbed to third in the league – a position which was held until early April. March's busy programme continued with a midweek visit to Clyde at Broadwood on the 27th and a 2-2 draw. The following Saturday Victoria Park staged the fourth local derby of the season but wind and rain spoiled it as a spectacle for the 5876 fans, the highest league crowd of the season. The points went to the Inverness side thanks to a 39th-minute goal from former Ross County player Roy McBain.

April's first match was a midweek rearranged fixture at Livingston on the 3rd. The long, unbeaten league run came to an end at the hands of two former players. Davide Xausa, making his first appearance for Livingston, scored two goals in their 4-1 win and Barry Wilson added the other two. Dennis Wyness scored Caley Thistle's consolation. A major road accident at Ballinluig had held up the Caley Thistle team bus and the match started 15 minutes late. The difficult journey arguably unsettled the players and Livingston were well ahead throughout. This led to a slip to fourth, but third place was regained on the 7th with a 3-0 away victory against Morton. Steve Paterson introduced fringe players and young Neil MacDonald grabbed the third goal with a spectacular first-time volley. The Caley Thistle cause was helped by some erratic goalkeeping from Andy Carlin, which saw him replaced at half-time.

Ayr came back north the following week and, unlike previous encounters, there was only one goal in it. The home side won 1-0 and the goal came after a Barry Robson corner was seemingly netted off the knee of Bobby Mann. Television pictures later confirmed that the last touch was by Dennis Wyness. On the 21st it was off to Airdrie and a meeting with new manager Ian McCall's revamped team. Steve Archibald had departed and most of his Spanish imports had gone with him. It ended 1-1 with Dennis Wyness increasing his season's tally to 25. Barry Robson was dismissed following hand-ball on the goal line.

Livingston came to Inverness on the 28th, their narrow 3-2 win securing their promotion to the SPL. A Paul Sheerin penalty gave the home side a 1-0 lead in 17 minutes, but former Airdrie striker David Fernandez equalised after 31 minutes. Barry Wilson made it 2-1 to Livi just before half time, with a Stuart McCaffrey own goal increasing the lead to 3-1 in 53 minutes. Sheerin scored with another penalty in the last minute, but it was too late. The Livingston fans invaded the pitch to celebrate their remarkable achievement. The financial reality of the six-year transformation from Meadowbank Thistle would eventually hit in February 2004, but for the moment they could look forward to top-flight football. In 2001-2 they would take the SPL by storm.

The last match of the season was away to Falkirk on 5 May. Third place was at stake. A draw would have been enough for Caley Thistle but a young Falkirk team edged it 2-1. This resulted in a fourth-place finish on 54 points, an excellent result considering the poor start. Charlie Christie appeared in all 42 games: nobody could match that. It took until November before Dennis Wyness scored but he ended as Club and Division top scorer with 26 goals. Both Wyness and Paul Sheerin were nominees for First Division 'Player of the Year'. A total of 84 goals were scored and 68 conceded in 43 league and cup matches. The goals were shared by 13 players.

Richard Hastings became the second player to reach 200 appearances in November 2000, while Ross Tokely passed the 150 milestone in April 2001.

Richard Hastings and Davide Xausa once more made many transatlantic trips on Canadian international duty. Niall Calder was capped for Scotland at Under-16 level in the Nordic Cup. ICT Girls' Under-16 goalscoring machine Suzanne Grant won the female Under-18 prize at the Inverness Area Sports' Council Awards for 2000. She also played and scored for Scotland Under-18s against Northern Ireland. Lorraine Cadden was also capped for Scotland and the team won more silverware.

Behind the scenes

In June 2000 Catriona Bisset was appointed to the newly created post of chief executive. She was the first female to hold such a top football job in Scotland and was previously managing director of the Littlejohn restaurant chain. This experience was to be put to good use in revamping the hospitality and catering sides of the club's business. The AGM of the PLC on 25 August saw the unveiling of the board's revival plan 'The Road To Premier League Football'. This envisaged the setting up of a charitable trust to take ownership of the stadium and shoulder the debt of £2m plus. The football club would lease the stadium back, raise cash for football purposes and move on free of debt. The charitable trust, via a property company, would service the debt by initiating developments around the stadium. Development had always been seen as the key to raising money to upgrade the stadium, and various plans had been mooted. At one time the hope was to build offices under new stands and therefore meet SPL criteria at low cost, but this plan fell through. The football club was originally to drive any developments but, when David Sutherland became chairman, he proposed the splitting of the business into football, operations and development arms. As the financial crisis deepened, something more radical was required and this led to the charitable trust.

A further share issue was also to take place early in 2001. The price caused much public argument with first 50p per share mooted then 66p. Existing shareholders would have seen their holding devalued overnight. The board were of the view that the true current value of each share was less than 66p but, in the light of the opposition, the price was set at £1. The prospectus for the share offer was issued on 1 January 2001 with a closing date of 30 March. Public debate surrounded the fact that shares would now be in a PLC without the major asset of a stadium. Former chairman Dougie McGilvray wrote to all shareholders expressing his misgivings: '...does it make sense to sell the crown jewels and leave the safe empty?' David Sutherland responded by pointing to the club's financial plight and inviting any shareholder with a better plan to come forward. The restructuring plan was voted through by shareholders on 1 March almost unanimously and the stadium was transferred to the new trust headed by former Inverness Provost Allan Sellar. Due to a poor response, the share issue was extended, but in the end only a disappointing £100,000 was raised.

In December 2000 an internal re-organisation of the administration staff was necessary when it was announced that Catriona Bisset would revert to a part-time consultancy role from 1 April. General manager John Sutherland left to be replaced by commercial manager Gary Thompson. There was great sadness in February with the death of receptionist Liz Robertson. She had worked at the club for nine years, first at the Greig Street offices then at Caledonian Stadium, and had always been a popular figure with players, officials and staff – despite her proud record of never having watched a match!

At the start of 2000-1 doctors Ian Smith, Derek MacLeod and Donald McVicar officially joined the ranks as assistants to Dr John MacAskill, although all had already deputised on occasions. Dr Ian Smith in particular had been a regular spectator since 1994-5 and had assisted medically for over four years. Drs Smith and MacLeod had also been involved with Scotland's youth squad. Physio Emily Goodlad was called up to the medical team attached to the Scotland women's team in preparation for the European Championships. Later she travelled with the team to Holland and Ireland.

The velvet revolution in the boardroom continued during summer 2000 with many departures. By the start of 2000-1 the board comprised just six members – David Sutherland, Ken Thomson, Ken Mackie, Roy McLennan, Ian MacDonald and Graeme Bennett. Roy McLennan left during the season to be replaced by Sandy Catto.

At amalgamation there were two social clubs, the Caledonian one in Greig Street and the Thistle premises in Baron Taylor's Street. Consideration was given to closing both and creating a sports bar/club in Church Street. This plan was abandoned for economic reasons and the upper floor Thistle club was sold on 1 May 2001. The Greig Street property was renamed the Inverness Caledonian Thistle Social Club and improvements made. The social club has gone from strength to strength under the stewardship of Ian West, who was named runner-up in a 2003 'Bar Personality of the Year' competition. It continues to make a major financial contribution to the football club.

CHAPTER 11

BROKEN HEARTS
2001-2

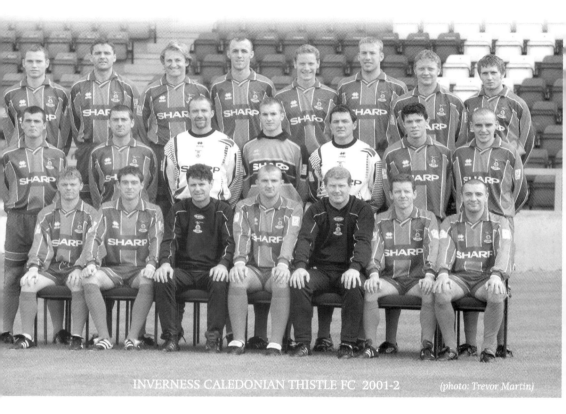

INVERNESS CALEDONIAN THISTLE FC 2001-2 *(photo: Trevor Martin)*

(*Back*) Neil MacDonald, Paul Ritchie, Mike Teasdale, Paul Bradshaw, Martin Bavidge, Ross Tokely, Barry Robson, Dennis Wyness

(*Middle*) Russell Duncan, Roy McBain, Les Fridge, Ally Ridgers, Jim Calder, Graeme Stewart, Grant Munro

(*Front*) David Bagan, Stuart McCaffrey, Steve Paterson (manager), Bobby Mann (captain), Duncan Shearer (assistant manager), Charlie Christie, Stuart Golabek

GOING BALLISTIC!

This season saw preservation of First Division status, more Scottish Cup exploits and another season of economic difficulties. The First Division was the tightest ever seen: with four weeks of the season remaining, any two from four teams could have been relegated. It was tense in Inverness until safety was assured with only three games left. The playing pool was depleted in the close season when influential midfielder Paul Sheerin signed for Ayr United and Richard Hastings went to Ross County. Both Ayr and Livingston had been interested in Sheerin and the club could not match the money available at either club. Out-of-contract Hastings had been a Bournemouth target and was linked with a club in the USA. This all came to nothing and Hastings accepted an offer from the club's arch-rivals in Dingwall. Kevin Byers left for Forfar after spending four months of 2000-1 on loan to Montrose. The gaps were filled with the summer signings of Paul Bradshaw, Russell Duncan and Paul Ritchie. In late August former Scottish international goalkeeper Nicky Walker also arrived on a one-year, part-time deal. Bradshaw's Inverness career was to be a short one – he never settled to full-time football, and left in September. Duncan, Ritchie and Walker became established first-team players. Barry Robson returned from an extensive loan period with Forfar and rapidly established himself as a key player.

In June an ambitious attempt was made for Inverness to be a Euro 2008 host city. This was seen as a golden chance to upgrade Caledonian Stadium to SPL standards but it proved academic. The Inverness bid was not ready to be submitted by the 31 July deadline and an eight-week extension was sought from the SFA. This was refused: Scotland's hopes were pinned on Glasgow, Edinburgh, Dundee and Aberdeen. Eventually a joint Scottish/Irish bid was beaten by Austria/Switzerland. On 5 July Sharp was unveiled as the new shirt sponsor with a lucrative two-year deal then, on the 9th, the transfer of Caledonian Stadium to a charitable trust was completed. The trust, chaired by former Inverness Provost Allan Sellar, took over the debt, which by now had reached £2.6 million, and assumed responsibility for all future improvements to the stadium. Chairman David Sutherland warned supporters that this would not translate to new signings in the short term: 'It does not mean that Steve has money to burn on players. The club still has to pay its way. However it does mean that the football operation will not face the massive constraint which has held it back.' General manager Gary Thompson left early in the season for personal reasons and Debbie Ross joined in August with the title of sales and promotion executive. The board increased to seven in February with the return of Roy McLennan.

At the Keyline Tournament in Oban on 14 July the team came second to Clyde, then played six pre-season friendlies – four against Highland League opposition, a 2-0 defeat at Forfar and a 2-0 home win against a Celtic XI.

The league campaign opened at Clyde on 4 August, with a Bobby Mann penalty goal securing a 1-1 draw. The short Bell's Challenge Cup run began at home to Forfar on Tuesday 7 August. After early Caley Thistle domination, with goals from Charlie Christie and Martin Bavidge, Forfar pulled back to 2-2 and extra time. Paul Ritchie scored the winner with five minutes left. Falkirk were the next league opponents, and the poor home record against the Bairns continued with a 2-1 defeat. Although Bobby Mann's penalty right on half time made it 1-1, Paul Wright scored a second late on and Falkirk held out to win.

Bell's Challenge Cup hopes came to an end at a very wet Alloa on the 14th. Gareth Evans put Alloa ahead in the first half and Paul Ritchie scored a late equaliser, but only after 'Man of the Match' Bobby Mann had hit the post with a penalty. Caley Thistle pulled ahead through Dennis Wyness just 45 seconds into extra time and looked comfortable. Alloa scored twice, Roy McBain was sent off and it ended 3-2 for the home side. There were no thrills at Firhill the following Saturday, where a dismal performance led to a 1-0 defeat by Partick Thistle. On the 25th it was slightly better, with a 1-1 draw away to St Mirren, but it took an 88th-minute Bobby Mann header to gain the point. Mann by now had scored all three of the club's league goals. August's two points left Caley Thistle in tenth place – but things were to improve.

On 1 September a benefit match for local Grade One referee Kevin Bisset was played at Caledonian Stadium between select teams representing the SPL and the Highland Area. Kevin was forced to quit refereeing after suffering two brain haemorrhages, but made a remarkable recovery and continues to be a regular Caley Thistle supporter. St Johnstone manager Sandy Clark took charge of the SPL team, and the Highland Select was jointly managed by Steve Paterson and Ross County's Neale Cooper. 1200 turned up to honour Kevin and the SPL side won 3-2.

GOING BALLISTIC!

A very strong squad crossed the Pentland Firth to Orkney for a match at Kirkwall's Pickaquoy Centre on 4 September. The game, against a team representing Orkney Amateur Football Association, attracted 500 spectators and ended with a 9-0 win for the visitors. The northern trip obviously worked wonders, as the first league win came in style the following Saturday with a 5-1 home drubbing of Arbroath. Dennis Wyness broke his league duck with a hat-trick.

Tuesday 11 September 2001 has gone down in history for reasons a world away from football: everyone remembers where they were when news of the New York World Trade Centre attack broke. The Caley Thistle team were on a bus en route to a CIS Cup match in Coatbridge – suddenly football seemed very unimportant. The tie did go ahead and a young Albion Rovers team were eventually beaten by two Paul Ritchie goals late in the second half. One minor consequence of the New York tragedy was the stranding of goalkeeper Nicky Walker, who had been in Texas on business. With all US airspace temporarily closed, Jim Calder deputised for a total of three games.

The opening local derby of the season at Dingwall on 15 September was very disappointing with a 2-1 defeat and the loss of Bobby Mann after two yellow cards. Barry Robson scored the only Caley Thistle goal. The changing fortunes of football were amply illustrated over the next two games. On Wednesday 19 September Raith Rovers were hammered 5-2 in Inverness, with Dennis Wyness scoring a record four goals. This result propelled Caley Thistle up the league from tenth to fifth. Then it was down to Airdrie on the Saturday with a squad of only 14, as the second team were playing Clach in the final of the North Cup at Grant Street Park. Hopes were high after the Raith result, but a rejuvenated Airdrie amazingly won 6-0. It was 5-0 at half-time, including an Owen Coyle hat-trick. Paterson had no excuses: 'It's hard to fathom after our midweek performance. We started sluggishly and paid for it. I don't know if we were so bad or if Airdrie were so good. I suppose it was a combination of both.'

Caley Thistle had reached the final of the North Cup after an incredible penalty shoot-out victory over Fort William in the semi-final. It was 1-1 after both 90 and 120 minutes: victory was only secured 9-8 on penalties. There were two heroes – Neil MacDonald and Ally Ridgers. MacDonald scored the equaliser in normal time then slotted home two penalties in the shoot-out. Young goalkeeper Ridgers scored with one penalty and saved three. There was to be no repeat of this success in the final: Clach won 2-0. For a long time it was 1-0 and Caley Thistle fought hard. Iain Polworth settled it with a goal in the last minute.

The CIS Cup

On 26 September the CIS second-round tie against Partick Thistle in Inverness was an exciting affair. Mike Teasdale scored in the 12th minute but by half-time it was 1-1. Barry Robson made it 2-1, Partick quickly equalised and it was on to extra time. With 116 minutes on the clock, former Caley Thistle striker Scott McLean gave Partick the lead from the penalty spot but Robson scored his second on the two-hour mark. The penalty lottery went Caley Thistle's way 4-2, with Robson converting the decider. The final game of a busy September was in the league against Ayr at home. It was Bobby Mann's 100th appearance and the away terracing was brightened by the bizarre sight of a dozen Ayr-supporting Elvis impersonators. They were disappointed to see their side go down 3-1, thanks to a brace from Paul Ritchie and one from Charlie Christie. Caley Thistle ended the month in sixth place. In late September Steve Paterson was touted in the press for the newly vacant St Johnstone manager's post and the Caley Thistle board stated that it would not stand in his way. Speculation ended on 5 October with the appointment of Billy Stark.

The first game of October was a classic CIS Cup-tie – a fine victory on penalties in round three away to new SPL side Dunfermline. Nicky Walker performed heroics in the early stages to keep the scoreline blank then, after 15 minutes, Martin Bavidge tapped in for 1-0 after goalkeeper Scott Thomson dropped a Bobby Mann free kick. Steven Hampshire equalised in 62 minutes and Dunfermline pressed for the winner. Walker continued his fine form and, in injury time, a Dennis Wyness volley was turned onto the bar. Into extra time, and Walker made a point-blank save from Jason Dair, then Bobby Mann headed a disallowed goal and was penalised for pushing. Despite efforts at both ends, it was on to penalties. There was no contest: Caley Thistle blasted home four in a row and Walker saved two out of three. Ross Tokely netted the deciding kick and the match was won. The result secured a CIS Insurance Cup quarter-final place for the first time and the match also marked Charlie Christie's 250th appearance. With Jim Falconer on holiday, the author was acting secretary for the Dunfermline match and is proud of his 100% record in the post!

There was no cup hangover as Caley Thistle thumped Clyde 5-1 at home the following Saturday. Dennis Wyness scored the first of a brace in 31 minutes, Paul Ritchie scored one and Martin Bavidge the fourth before Clyde salvaged some pride with a Ritchie McCusker penalty goal. Immediately after the kick-off Russell Duncan made it 5-1. A 2-1 win at Falkirk a week later was Caley Thistle's first away league success of the season, edging them up to third place. The Bairns had been on top and scored first. Second-half goals from Bobby Mann and Paul Ritchie earned the win after a second-half fight-back. On the 27th it was down to Arbroath's 'Fortress Gayfield' and a disappointing 3-2 defeat. The strong wind favoured Arbroath in the first half and at the break it was 1-1, with Paul Ritchie scoring the Caley Thistle goal. Arbroath goalkeeper Craig Hinchcliffe made some great saves in the second half, as the visitors tried to take advantage of the wind. The pace was frantic – and it was Arbroath who mastered the conditions. They made it 2-1, Ritchie equalised and Colin Mackinnon scored the winner. Dennis Wyness's goalscoring reputation was beginning to spread, and a Manchester City scout watched him at Gayfield. Paterson did not dwell on this defeat: 'I didn't get too carried away when we beat Falkirk and I am not going to get carried away because we were beaten by Arbroath.' Despite this setback, third place was maintained.

November was a topsy turvy month and included back-to-back visits to Ayr in the league and CIS Cup. It started with a disappointing home 2-1 defeat to St Mirren on the 3rd. A spirited fightback and a Dennis Wyness goal nearly earned a draw but not quite. A week later, things improved greatly, with the first ever win at Stark's Park against Raith Rovers. Nacha Novo gave Raith the lead in two minutes from the penalty spot, but Bobby Mann matched that in 11 minutes to make it 1-1. By half-time it was 2-1 thanks to Charlie Christie, while in the second half it was one-way traffic: Paul Ritchie, Ross Tokely and Barry Robson all scored to make the final score 5-1. An unfortunate piece of history was created in 77 minutes, when Jim Calder came on in place of the injured Nicky Walker – the club's first ever substitution of a goalkeeper in a competitive match.

On 17 November it was the first home derby of the season and a 3-0 win against a poor Ross County team. Mark McCormick's own-goal in 37 minutes set up the victory, with Dennis Wyness scoring twice in the second half. For the first time the 'Man of the Match' award was a joint one between Dennis Wyness and David Bagan. A week later, there was the first of two unsuccessful visits to Ayr in five days. A 3-0 defeat in the league was a poor dress rehearsal for the quarter final of the CIS Insurance Cup, but it was a closer game than the score suggests. Paul Sheerin came back to haunt his old club with Ayr's early opening goal, then David Bagan came close to equalising soon after. Ayr pulled away in the second half with two more goals.

With a Hampden semi-final place at stake the CIS Cup-tie created great excitement. Demand for places on the supporters' buses was high despite the midweek timing and the distance involved. The travelling fans were joined by the large central-belt support that can always be relied on to swell numbers for big matches in the south. It all started well when, in nine minutes, Ross Tokely headed home Barry Robson's corner – but Tokely turned from hero to villain a minute later. A rush of blood led to an altercation with Pat McGinlay and a red card. 80 minutes with ten men away from home is a tall order and Ayr soon took advantage. They scored two quick goals but Caley Thistle did not give up. Only a brilliant Craig Nelson save prevented Bobby Mann from equalising in the first half. A third goal in 56 minutes killed the game: Ayr added two more to make the final score 5-1. Assistant manager Duncan Shearer was disappointed that his team had missed out on a game at Hampden: 'The boys are feeling bad but Ross is feeling twice as bad as anyone else. It was just a heat of the moment thing and he has got to learn from that. He had just scored so he should have been high as a kite.' Paterson thought they had been well beaten at the end: 'I feel really sorry for guys like Charlie Christie who might not get another chance to play in a semi-final.' There was a one-place league drop to fourth by the end of November.

December was a poor month and resulted in a dip to fifth place. It started with two home 2-1 defeats by Airdrie and Partick Thistle. The Airdrie game was only three days after the Ayr cup-tie so there was definitely an element of a hangover. At 2-0 there was a resurgence, but Paul Ritchie's 61st-minute goal was all they had to show for it. Against Partick, Caley Thistle were in the driving seat for most of the time and deserved their 1-0 lead from a Dennis Wyness goal in 58 minutes. Martin Hardie scored two late goals to send the points to Maryhill. In the following midweek the Inverness Cup was recaptured from Ross County. The match was switched from Grant Street to Caledonian Stadium, which certainly helped the cause. It was 2-2 until 15 minutes from time, when youngster Neil MacDonald capped a fine display with the winner.

Freezing weather all week put the away game at Clyde on 15 December in doubt. An unexpected thaw allowed the game to go ahead although the programme had already been cancelled. Good goalkeeping at both ends (including a penalty save by Clyde's Kevin Budinauckas) kept it tight and it took a Bobby Mann own-goal to end the deadlock. The next game in Inverness against Arbroath was also in doubt because of a cold snap, but it survived a late inspection. As conditions deteriorated it was nearly called off at half-time. Caley Thistle were glad it continued as they ended a bad run with a 3-2 victory. A goalless draw against St Mirren in Paisley on the 29th ended a remarkable record. Caley Thistle always had a reputation under Steve Paterson of being an attacking team, and 160 games had passed since the last 0-0 draw on 4 April 1998 at home against Forfar. It was perhaps more remarkable that the visitors made it to Paisley, as heavy snow had made road conditions treacherous and only two First Division games survived.

At the AGM of the PLC on 13 December the chairman initiated lively discussion when he mooted a move from East Longman to somewhere more central to give easier access and attract more fans. Despite the success of the team over the years, the crowds at East Longman were disappointing. The numbers matched closely those achieved in the Third Division days, despite the climb up the league. It was not long before rumours started of a sale of the existing site to supermarket giants Walmart-Asda and relocation to the Bught Park. Although the club denied it in mid-February, speculation reached fever pitch towards the end of the season and there was much confusion. Despite the obvious hurdles (including the fact that the stadium site is held on a long lease from Inverness Common Good Fund), many were convinced that a move was imminent. Not least among interested parties were city athletes who feared this threat to the Queen's Park athletics track. Asda confirmed interest in moving to Inverness but emphasised that they were looking at various options. This was a saga that would run and run. At the AGM the chairman also announced that the players and management had agreed to take a 10% pay cut in the light of the club's continuing financial problems. Team captain Bobby Mann said: 'We feel there is something very positive at Caley Thistle and we want to help. This is our way of showing solidarity with the fans and directors.' In September there had been a real risk that reverting to part-time football was the only way out of the financial crisis, but a major economy drive had averted the threat.

The New Year opened with weather problems and the postponement of the local derby at Dingwall. Rain on top of ice caused a three-day delay to the Scottish Cup third-round match away to Arbroath, originally due to be played on the 5th. It turned out to be an important 2-0 victory. Barry Robson scored the first goal direct from a free kick just before half-time, Paul Ritchie adding the second six minutes after the break. The fourth-round draw produced the mouth-watering prospect of Hearts at Tynecastle. There were two league games to be negotiated before the visit to Edinburgh. Frozen pitches led to these being the only ones to survive January.

Before the home match against Raith Rovers on 12 January the new Kevin Bisset enclosure was officially opened by Inverness Provost Bill Smith. The club had long promised terracing fans some shelter and finally the area behind the 'home' goal was enclosed. Before his illness Kevin worked for David Sutherland's company Tulloch Construction, and it was the chairman who suggested that the new structure be named after the former FIFA Grade One referee. Kevin is a very popular figure at Caledonian Stadium and all were delighted that he was fit enough to join Provost Smith as he declared the new enclosure open for business. In celebration the team went on to demolish Raith 5-0, in what turned out to be the highest league win of the season. A 3-0 defeat at Airdrie the next week was a major disappointment. All the goals came in the second half after Caley Thistle had the better of the first. In heavy rain, Airdrie took their chances well and deserved the points.

Hearts at Tynecastle

On 26 January the much-travelled Caley Thistle army headed south for the cup-tie against Hearts. The central belt brigade once more assembled and the Inverness support numbered a magnificent 4000. They were to be rewarded with another vintage cup performance on a dreadful pitch. The surface was due to be dug up straight after the match; heavy rain added to the difficulties. In addition there was a thick layer of sand on the pitch, leading one wit to remark 'for Tynecastle read Sandcastle.' Despite the handicaps it turned out to be a re-run of February 2000, with Hearts well beaten 3-1.

The team representing Inverness on this very special occasion was Nicky Walker, Ross Tokely, Roy McBain, Bobby Mann, Stuart McCaffrey, Grant

Munro, Russell Duncan, Dennis Wyness, Paul Ritchie, Charlie Christie and Barry Robson. Substitute David Bagan replaced Christie at half time, with Martin Bavidge, Stuart Golabek, Graeme Stewart and Jim Calder remaining on the bench.

Hearts showed little flair, and their star player Ricardo Fuller was well contained. Jambos' fan Tokely scored the first goal in 26 minutes with a 15-yard strike from his 'weaker' left foot. Gary Wales equalised right on half-time to set up a home revival. The Caley Thistle defence held firm and scored on the break through future Hearts player Wyness. Bagan secured the win with a goal later voted the 'Goal of the Day' on BBC Sportscene. A measured pass from McBain set Bagan on a run from the halfway line with Tommi Gronlund in close attendance pulling his shirt. Bagan collected the ball 20 yards out, turned Gronlund, took a touch into the box, then side-footed it past Antti Niemi. It was a goal fit to win any match. Hearts applied some late pressure to no avail. The whistle went and once more Caley Thistle went ballistic. One home player who had seen it all before was French defender Stephane Mahe. He was in the Celtic team famously beaten two years before. At the Celtic game in 2000 the club provided a bus to take staff, volunteers and players' families to Glasgow and the same happened for the Hearts match. The Celtic fans had been gracious in defeat, but the Edinburgh faithful were rather less friendly. To the great amusement of all, a Hearts fan chased the bus as it left Tynecastle and threw part of his fish supper at it!

Chairman David Sutherland praised the fans and the team: 'I reckon we had 4000 supporters at Tynecastle and the noise and encouragement was tremendous. To a man the team was colossal and Bobby Mann was our Mount Everest.' Steve Paterson compared this to the Celtic triumph: 'This certainly ranks alongside the Celtic result because it is two years on and we have seven new players in our squad. I thought there was a lot of quality about our play and we matched Hearts in determination and drive for another great cup performance.' Captain Bobby Mann added: 'You always have belief when you go into these games, especially when it is a one-off.' Hearts' keeper Antti Niemi admitted that the players had let the club down: 'It is an awful feeling at the moment but all credit to Inverness. They deserved their win.' Local MP David Stewart rewarded each goal-scorer with a bottle of House of Commons champagne. January's efforts earned Steve Paterson the 'Manager of the Month' award for leading the team to fourth in the league and a place in the Tennent's Scottish Cup quarter final against Partick Thistle. The Tynecastle crowd of 12,016 was the highest of the season.

On a cold and windy 2 February Ayr once more made the long journey to Inverness, but there was to be no repeat of previous free-scoring games. Both sides were coming back to earth from cup heroics and, in a rather low-key affair, a 1-1 draw was about right. Following some surprising results elsewhere, nine points now separated third from tenth, with Partick and Airdrie well ahead in the first two places. A week later high-flying Partick convincingly won the Scottish Cup dress rehearsal 4-1 at Firhill. Injuries led to Duncan Shearer coming out of retirement to take a place on the bench, and only Paul Ritchie's late consolation restored a little pride.

A 3-2 home win against Falkirk on the 16th ensured a climb back to fourth after a slip to sixth following the Partick defeat. The points should have been wrapped up by half-time but they only had Grant Munro's first senior goal to show for their superiority. Paul Ritchie missed a first-half penalty and Falkirk drew level just before the break. Dennis Wyness continued his fine form by scoring twice in the second period to clinch the points.

Partick in the Cup

February was dominated by the build up to the Scottish Cup quarter final tie away to Partick Thistle on the 23rd. It was 'Firhill for thrills' this time, after the team and 2000 fans battled through blizzards to a very white Glasgow. The team were joined on the bus south by a film crew from BBC Scotland and, in a similar vein, a supporters' club bus hosted *Herald* columnist Ian Black on a fact-finding mission. The Firhill terracing had to be cleared of snow to make it safe, but by kick-off the main problem was the bright sun. Caley Thistle dominated the first half but led only by Dennis Wyness's 6th-minute goal. The good work continued into the second half, but Partick fought back to equalise in 59 minutes. Wyness scored again two minutes later but 'Man of the Match' Scott Paterson netted a rare goal in 75 minutes to take the tie to a replay. The Inverness camp was happy still to be in the cup but disappointed not to turn early superiority into victory.

Steve Paterson was full of praise for Wyness: 'Dennis again showed his quality with a couple of goals and in all honesty I can't believe no-one has come in with an offer for him. I am a wee bit disappointed that the match is going to a replay but Partick are the form side in the Division and the fact that we almost beat them today is great credit to our performance.' The fans trekked back to the buses ready for the drive home, only to discover they had been moved. Apparently, a tannoy announcement had been drowned out. Then followed another long walk to find the elusive buses, a wait for the stragglers, then a police motorcycle escort for the convoy from Maryhill to the motorway.

A plan to raise money for players was unveiled on the club's unofficial website in February by webmaster Scott Mackenzie. He mooted a 'pay the players' scheme which would see supporters pledging regular donations to go directly to the manager for player purchases. Pledges were made and the plan was welcomed by the chairman as an innovative way to assist. The move was overtaken by the events that led to Tulloch's injection of £500,000 into the club later in the year. As February came to a close, the club's cost-saving continued with the release of two long-serving players – defender Mike Teasdale and goalkeeper Les Fridge. Teasdale moved on to combine playing with a commercial role at Elgin City and Fridge signed for Ross County. Bobby Williamson's departure from the hot-seat at Kilmarnock led once more to speculation about Steve Paterson's future. He was reported to be in the frame for the Killie post and was even receiving telephone calls congratulating him on his appointment: 'As well as being embarrassing it is unsettling. The Kilmarnock manager's job has never entered my head and will not until an official approach is made to the club.' The uncertainty did not last long. Jim Jefferies took the job a few days later.

Paul Ritchie scored his first hat-trick for the club in March's opening league game against St Mirren. The home 4-2 win was vital in the relegation fight and was achieved despite going behind to a 10th-minute penalty goal. David Bagan equalised in 38 minutes, but the rest of the game belonged to 'Man of the Match' Ritchie. Saints pulled another back but it was not enough.

The Partick cup replay took place on the evening of a very wet Tuesday 5 March with postponement a real possibility. Torrential rain in the afternoon had left large areas of surface water but after two inspections – the second just 45 minutes before kick-off – referee John Rowbotham allowed the match to go ahead. Over 5000 fans packed the stadium to see which of the 'Two Jags' would win the right to face Rangers in the semi-final at Hampden. Partick showed greater urgency in the opening stages, but Caley Thistle soon began to come more and more into the game. There were chances at both ends, and home fans were relieved when Scott Paterson netted in 55 minutes with a header, only for offside to be called. Paterson's goal at Firhill had been his first for the club and he chose Inverness to add his second. A free kick was awarded in the 67th minute just outside the Caley Thistle box and Paterson curled the ball brilliantly into the top corner for what proved to be the winner. Russell Duncan came close to an equaliser late on, but Kenny Arthur saved well. The cup dream was over for another season. Steve Paterson could not fault his players: 'It's a huge disappointment for everyone at the club. It took a wonder free kick to decide the outcome but, apart from that, there was nothing in the game. Both teams played with full commitment in what was a typical Scottish Cup-tie.' Bobby Mann thought neither team had been at its best: 'Both teams were scared to lose and it was always going to take just one goal to decide the outcome. Scott Paterson's goal was something special.'

Staving off relegation

It was back to the League and the fight against relegation. March was catch-up time, with six league games as well as the cup-tie. It was a hard struggle as, despite lying fourth, bottom side Raith were only seven points behind. Lack of resources and injuries led to three bench appearances by Duncan Shearer and matches with only three or four substitutes. The cup hangover hit at Arbroath on the ninth. The 1-0 defeat was a drab affair at a cold and windy Gayfield, and a goalless draw at Kirkcaldy against Raith Rovers a week later did nothing to excite. There was one incident during that game which most missed at the time but certainly caused amusement. Substitute keeper Jim Calder raced off the bench to protest when Neil MacDonald was fouled on the halfway line but managed, in his words, to be '... run over by a very big linesman.' Luckily for posterity, the incident was caught on the Scotsport camera. Calder has not been allowed to forget about it.

The third Highland derby of the season took place on 19 March (a mere two months late) and the fourth just four days later. A disappointing but frantic 0-0 draw in Dingwall was followed by a 1-1 draw in Inverness. The home side had played four matches without scoring, but Ross Tokely ended the drought. County went ahead through future ICT striker Steve Hislop, but Tokely headed an equaliser. Hislop was later shown yellow and red cards in succession after fouling Tokely. Steve Paterson's 300th game in charge the following week provided a welcome home win against Airdrie, with the only goal came from Martin Bavidge. The result stopped a slide down the league – there had been a slip from fourth to seventh in midweek, without kicking a ball, but a climb back to end the month in fifth place. The top league crowds of the season were for the two March matches against County – 4679 at Victoria Park on the 19th and 4685 at home on the 23rd.

On 6 April there was a long trip to Ayr, with two battle-weary sides needing a victory to be sure of avoiding relegation. It was a poor match, only decided when Ayr's Eddie Annand converted a penalty in the 65th minute after he had been brought down. This ensured Ayr's survival – but Caley Thistle still needed two points. On the following Saturday Clyde came to Inverness, having just made themselves mathematically safe. It was another uninspiring match, ending 1-1. The highlight was substitute Neil MacDonald's spectacular equaliser a minute from time. It was just enough: Falkirk were relegated along with Raith Rovers. Paterson was furious at his players' performance: 'My post-match feeling was utter disappointment in the team. Maybe the fact that we are safe will kick in later. There were certainly no celebrations in the dressing room afterwards.'

The creation of a Highland Football Academy was officially announced on 10 April by Dr Elaine Murray, Deputy Minister for Tourism, Culture and Sport. The Academy, one of a network planned throughout Scotland, was to be a joint venture by ICT, Ross County and Highland Council. £1.3m of funding was to come from Sportscotland (the renamed Scottish Sports Council), to support three campuses in Dingwall and Inverness. The first Academy was opened by Rangers in July 2001 and the aim of the national venture is to develop youth talent throughout Scotland – particularly those young players with the potential to progress to professional clubs.

Not surprisingly, there was a funereal atmosphere away to already-relegated Falkirk on 20 April. Roy McBain was injured in the warm-up and the already depleted squad was down to only 14. There were no goals but, despite the fact that there was nothing at stake, it was an entertaining game. Partick came north as champions for the last league game of the season. Jim Calder was captain for the day on his farewell appearance after eight seasons and 195 appearances. His place in the club's history was already assured, but he left the crowd with yet another memory when he cheekily cleared his lines in the 68th minute by backheeling to Stuart McCaffrey. This was also long-serving physio Ian Manning's final match in the dug-out. Caley Thistle put on a great show and won 3-0 with goals from Graeme Stewart, Paul Ritchie and Dennis Wyness, all in the first 21 minutes. Partick decided to party anyway and there was a good-natured pitch invasion at the end. This was not quite the end of the league season nationally, as the Ayr/Airdrie match had to be abandoned after 22 minutes when demonstrating Airdrie fans invaded the pitch in ugly mood and broke a set of goalposts. Airdrie's future was already in doubt, but strong SFA and Scottish League action was inevitable. Ayr were awarded a 1-0 win and the points.

New shareholding plan

As the season drew to a close David Sutherland announced his intention to stand down as chairman and finance director Ken Mackie was to be his successor. Ken Thomson had already decided to leave his vice chairman's post, and director of football Graeme Bennett was earmarked to take on this role. This was the plan but the club was thrown into disarray (and intense media spotlight) by a remarkable EGM of the PLC on 17 April. The board proposed a debenture issue and sought shareholder approval. The aim was to seek investment of £150,000 (in amounts as low as £250), repayable in three years (with 10% interest) or converted to shares. The share value would only be 25p and existing shareholders were concerned about the opportunity for new investors to buy in at 25% of the level which they paid. The vote went against the board because of the opposition of the members' club and major shareholders. This was taken as a vote of no confidence and most of the board intimated their resignations effective from the end of the season.

Director Roy McLennan was on holiday in Australia at the time of the EGM, so did not resign along with his colleagues. This proved vital, as he was able to act as mediator: 'The chairman was glad that I had decided to stay because it gave me the opportunity to bridge the gap between the board and the major shareholders.' A crucial meeting on 26 April (24 hours before the resignations were to take effect) led to a glimmer of hope. The following week it was announced that Tulloch were proposing to inject £500,000 cash into the club and take a 51% controlling interest. The major shareholders agreed in principle, but the fine print had to be seen and approval sought at a formal shareholders meeting. The board's resignation was rescinded and the close season was reached in better heart. The Tulloch plan would eventually come to fruition, although their interest in the club would remain below 30%.

In his last interview with the Matchday Programme in April 2002, outgoing chairman David Sutherland thanked all those who had helped the club during his term in office and summed up what he had aimed to achieve: 'I have tried to bring sound business principles and strategic thinking to the way this club has been run. It is not for me to judge whether or not this has worked. The perilous state of Scottish football suggests that we were ahead of the game in getting our finances right and hopefully I leave a good inheritance.' These words were written just as Motherwell went into administration, to be joined in 2003-4 by Dundee and Livingston. As other clubs such as Hearts also posted major losses, and Airdrie went out of business, it was clear that Sutherland's financial legacy was indeed a good one and would provide a sound base on which the new board could build.

Caley Thistle ended the season in sixth place with 48 points. In 46 league and cup games, the team had scored 79 goals and conceded 69. The goals were shared by 14 players with one own-goal. Dennis Wyness played in all 46 games, including two substitutions, and was top goalscorer with 22. Paul Ritchie was two goals behind on 20. Charlie Christie was still well ahead of the rest in the career appearance stakes, passing the 250 mark in October and reaching 279 by the end of the season. Mike Teasdale became the third player to pass the 200 mark in August, notching up 221 before he left for Elgin. Four players passed the 100 barrier during 2001-2 – Bobby Mann, Barry Robson, Martin Bavidge and Dennis Wyness. Wyness and Robson were both nominated by the Scottish Professional Footballers' Association for the First Division 'Player of the Year' award.

CHAPTER 12

TWO GOALS FROM ALBANIA
2002-3

INVERNESS CALEDONIAN THISTLE FC 2002-3   *(photo: Ken MacPherson)*

(*Back*) Roy McBain, Liam Keogh, Stuart Golabek, David Bagan, Richie Hart, Tony Low, Brian Gilfillan

(*Middle*) Duncan Shearer (assistant manager), Dennis Wyness, Graeme Stewart, Ally Ridgers, Mark Brown, Grant Munro, Paul Ritchie, Emily Goodlad (physio)

(*Front*) Ross Tokely, Stuart McCaffrey, Charlie Christie, Steve Paterson (manager), Bobby Mann (captain), Russell Duncan, Barry Robson

GOING BALLISTIC!

This was a season of high drama on and off the field. Financial turmoil behind the scenes dominated the build-up to the new season and there was little cash to strengthen the team. Financial security was eventually guaranteed in the medium term and the team surpassed all expectations. The change of management mid-season was a traumatic affair. Steve Paterson and Duncan Shearer were always going to be hard acts to follow when the seemingly inevitable parting of the ways came. However, John Robertson and Donald Park were soon into their stride and took the team to another dramatic victory over Celtic and a Scottish Cup semi-final at Hampden.

As planned, finance director Ken Mackie became the club's fourth chairman in its short history. Like his predecessor, Mackie came from a business, rather than a football, background. He had, however, been on the club board for over two years and had weathered the financial storms with David Sutherland. Mackie's steady hand was to see the club through to the end of its first decade. He retained the finance portfolio along with the chairmanship: his first major challenge was the former chairman's proposal that Tulloch take a major share in the club. Former player Graeme Bennett became vice chairman and Tulloch director Kenny Cameron took David Sutherland's place on the board. There was light at the end of the financial tunnel with the proposed cash injection from construction company Tulloch, who were to purchase a major block of shares at £1 each in return for boardroom control. This was all subject to another EGM. June saw the first steps in the possible creation of a Supporters' Trust. The Supporters' Club was represented at a meeting of Supporters Direct and Ken Mackie expressed his support for the initiative at a meeting with Lord Mike Watson, Sports and Culture Minister for the Scottish Executive.

The summer was dominated by Brazil's triumph in the South Korea/Japan World Cup, but much was happening in Scotland. Airdrie had lost their fight for survival in May and thus saved Falkirk from relegation. The vacant spot was taken by Gretna, who just beat off the challenge of paper consortium Airdrie United. The Airdrie United backers then purchased Clydebank and, once the deal had been ratified by the SFL and SFA, the new team took their place in Division Two – higher than they would have achieved had the earlier vote gone the other way. UEFA introduced two transfer windows, a close season window up to 31 August, then another during January.

TWO GOALS FROM ALBANIA

At the end of 2001-2 Martin Bavidge decided to revert to part-time football and use his geology degree to start a new career. He went to Forfar, then Neil MacDonald left for Clach. With the retirement of Jim Calder and Nicky Walker, plus the departures of Les Fridge and Mike Teasdale, there were plenty of vacant pegs in the dressing room. The first signing was midfielder Richie Hart from Brora Rangers, while the search continued for an experienced goalkeeper. Pre-season trialists were Neal Bennett and David Moran, but the position was eventually filled by ex-Rangers and Motherwell player Mark Brown. The Old Firm balance was completed by the signing of former Celtic reserve striker Liam Keogh. Just before the transfer window closed, defender Chris Miller arrived from Barnsley. Emily Goodlad took over trackside physio duties and doctors Ian Smith and Derek MacLeod continued to deputise for club doctor John MacAskill while he recovered from a lengthy illness.

Pre-season training started on 2 July and the team's first public outing was in Oban at the annual Keyline/Oban Saints tournament on the 13th. Six friendlies between 17 and 27 July produced mixed results, with the top matches being a home 1-0 defeat to an impressive Morton side and a 4-2 win at Montrose.

The league season opened on 3 August with a frustrating goalless draw against Alloa at home. Three days later it was a long midweek trip to Berwick in the Bell's Cup. A Neil Bennett penalty goal was enough to gain victory for the home side. On 10 August Caley Thistle travelled the relatively short distance to Perth to play St Johnstone for the first time, only to lose to a late own-goal from Stuart McCaffrey.

It was 17 August before the season's first senior goal arrived. Ross Tokely scored against Falkirk at home, but the concession of two late goals led to another defeat. The main frustration was that the team was playing well but gaining no breaks in front of goal. The tide turned on the 24th with a 2-0 home victory in the local derby with Ross County. A Dennis Wyness brace did the trick – to much relief. On the last day of the month came a well-deserved but amazing 4-0 away victory against promotion-fancied St Mirren. Two goals came from Barry Robson, Richie Hart scored his first for the club and Charlie Christie netted from a quickly-taken free kick. This result led to the sacking of St Mirren manager Tom Hendrie. The final of the Inverness Cup took place on 3 September against Ross County at Grant Street Park. The Dingwall side gained revenge for the league defeat with a narrow 1-0 victory. From ninth place after the Falkirk game, the two back-to-back wins earned a climb to fourth.

GOING BALLISTIC!

Tulloch investment

Financial events continued to dominate, and they came to a head in late August/early September. The fine print of Tulloch's proposed £500,000 investment nearly resulted in the plan being rejected and, in addition, many were suspicious that this was the first step to an enforced removal from East Longman and sale of the stadium site to Asda. The major stumbling block to Tulloch's investment was the insistence that a board of six should have three directors nominated by Tulloch. This was to include the chairman, who would have a casting vote. The arrangement would be open-ended and give effective control to the Inverness-based construction group. Their chairman David Sutherland's experience at the tail end of his tenure in charge of the football club convinced him that this move was essential to '... put an end to the situation where the Board's strategy can be held hostage by the blocking tactics of a small minority of people...Tulloch have been advised that it is a poor investment to inject £500,000 without safeguards which allow the Board to work without undue hindrance. Therefore this sum is only available under the proposals outlined by the Board.' The original proposal to take a 51% share in the club was altered because Stock Exchange rules would have forced an offer for the remaining shares if their share was more than 29.9%. New chairman Ken Mackie understood that Tulloch would have 'a light hand on the tiller'. Manager Steve Paterson backed the move: 'Like all the players I am right behind David Sutherland. I hope for the sake of the club and the city, his motion will be passed.'

The first significant vote came on 5 September when the Members' Club had to decide which way to pledge its 20% stake. This was important as the plan required a 75% positive vote at the PLC EGM to succeed and the Members' Club's 20% would make all the difference. Members' Club chairman Dougie McGilvray had been vocal in his opposition to the proposed control by Tulloch and suggested: 'Instead of perpetuity I would like to see control for just three to four years, but I am told this request has been rejected.' At the eleventh hour Tulloch chairman David Sutherland proposed that the period of effective control be reduced to five years and pledged that no stadium move would take place without both a referendum of supporters and an AGM of the PLC. This swung vital votes and the Members' Club came out 73-12 in favour of the proposal.

TWO GOALS FROM ALBANIA

A week later came the EGM of the PLC. There had been much bitterness and acrimony in advance of the meeting. There was relief all round when peace broke out and the Tulloch plan was accepted. Major shareholder Ian Fraser held the key to the vote and he abstained to allow smaller shareholders to decide the issue. Tulloch would now pay £480,000 to raise its share in the Club to 29.9% and make a further £20,000 available as an interest-free loan over 20 years. Worries about the club being forced to go part-time were now forgotten.

Steve Paterson said: 'We've had to live with insecurity in the club for the last two or three seasons but now we can settle down and concentrate on playing football.' Director of football Graeme Bennett looked forward to a period of calm in the boardroom: 'Now that the club is on a firmer footing, it will hopefully give other potential investors the confidence to come along and join us.' Dougie McGilvray said he was happy with the outcome: 'The main thing is that the club can now go forward without the hassle and the spin. Let's get back to where we were three years ago as a great community club.'

It was now possible for football rather than finance to dominate. On Tuesday 10 September Caley Thistle met Dumbarton at home in the CIS Cup. This first ever meeting of the clubs ended in a 2-0 victory for the Inverness side, with goals from Dennis Wyness and Paul Ritchie. The following Saturday it was off on another long trip to Dumfries. Bobby Mann set up a convincing 3-1 victory with an 8th minute headed goal and Dennis Wyness added a brace.

On 17 September Arbroath came to Inverness to defend in depth – and failed miserably. The 5-0 scoreline, including two goals from Ross Tokely, flattered the Lichties, and only goalkeeper Craig Hinchcliffe kept the score down. The victory resulted in a climb to third. Hart and Wyness combined to defeat St Mirren 3-1 the following Tuesday in the CIS Cup. It was 1-1 for a long time, but Wyness scored two late goals to confirm victory and earn a lucrative third-round tie against Celtic in Glasgow. With February 2000 in mind there was a race for tickets. A poor 3-0 defeat at Clyde on the 28th ended the good run and caused a drop back to fourth. Steve Paterson was named 'Manager of the Month' for September and Dennis Wyness was SFL 'Player of the Month'.

GOING BALLISTIC!

The first quarter of the league season was completed on 5 October with a 2-0 home win against an under-achieving Ayr side. The prolific strike force of Paul Ritchie and Dennis Wyness scored the goals which took Caley Thistle up to second. After a Saturday off while Scotland played Iceland, Alloa were hammered 6-0 at Recreation Park. This was to be the highest win of the season, with Ritchie and Wyness setting a new record when each scored three goals.

Celtic again...

Celtic manager Martin O'Neill was a spectator at Alloa in advance of the CIS Cup match on Wednesday 23 October. Caley Thistle were allocated 3000 tickets and most were snapped up. As in 2000, there was a major exodus from Inverness – but this time no repeat of the previous shock. The Caley Thistle starting eleven contained only four players from February 2000 – Bobby Mann, Stuart Golabek, Ross Tokely and Dennis Wyness – but Charlie Christie was on the bench on his return from injury. Sean Maloney's opener in the fourth minute seemed to be the start of a heavy defeat, but Paul Ritchie brought the away support to their feet with a 10th-minute equaliser from 20 yards. Ten minutes later John Hartson scored easily and it seemed all over when a deflected Alan Thompson free kick just before half-time made it 3-1. Hartson's second on the hour mark made it 4-1 and O'Neill fielded youngsters John Kennedy and Ross Wallace: he clearly thought it was all over. Wyness pulled one back in 71 minutes and Caley Thistle were right back in the game. Paterson sent on three substitutes, including Charlie Christie and Liam Keogh, two ex-Celts desperate to do well against their former team. The finish was exciting but ultimately unsuccessful for the visitors. In the dying minutes they were denied a penalty when Keogh went down in the box, and a Mann header was then cleared off the line by Jamie Smith.

It ended 4-2, but the Caley Thistle players deservedly left the field with heads held high. Paterson was upbeat: 'Celtic were too quick and had too much class in the last third of the park. But we kept our dignity and the supporters enjoyed the night.' O'Neill praised Caley Thistle's spirit and commented that some of their team would not look out of place in the SPL. He was to have another chance to see them at close hand before the end of the season. Local MP David Stewart had promised two bottles of House of Commons whisky to each Inverness goalscorer and he duly presented them to Ritchie and Wyness. The MP was proud of the team that he supports avidly: 'It was a tremendous barnstorming performance. In the closing 10 minutes they really put Celtic under strain and had a legitimate penalty claim turned down which, if allowed, would have put a different complexion on the match altogether.' The crowd of 32,122 was the highest of the season.

No doubt the next league opponents, St Johnstone, expected to benefit from a cup hangover when they came north three days later. They were to be disappointed – Dennis Wyness and Richie Hart scored in the 2-1 win. Wyness was named SFL 'Player of the Month' for October with Steve Paterson 'Manager of the Month'. This was the first time that the same pairing from the same club had won the honours in successive months.

Asda ended months of speculation on 2 October when they confirmed interest in the club's East Longman stadium site and said that it was the only one they were considering in the city. Caley Thistle chairman Ken Mackie met Asda representatives, but stressed that discussions were at a very early stage. Highland Council's Director of Planning John Rennilson was disappointed that Asda had made an announcement without discussing the matter with the Council, particularly as a supermarket development at East Longman was against the current local plan. Sandy Park, chairman of the Council committee responsible for planning, was equally surprised and added that the Council has entered into a 99-year lease, without breaks, with the club for recreational use: 'For the site to be used as a retail outlet requires Council consent either to renounce the lease or assign it to Asda. In either case it would be for the Council to decide the future rental or sale price.'

Speculation linking Steve Paterson with an SPL move resurfaced when Alex Smith was sacked as Dundee United manager on 7 October. Paul Hegarty was appointed as caretaker, Ian McCall turned down the chance to move from Falkirk, then Paterson was approached and accepted the job. The impact on his domestic situation weighed heavily and resulted in a quick change of mind. On 2 November Caledonian Stadium was buzzing with rumours that Paterson had already left and all eyes were on the dug-out before the league match against St Mirren. There was a palpable sense of relief when he took his usual place just before kick-off, and the team went on to win 4-1 including a brace from Dennis Wyness. This retained second place just two points behind Falkirk.

GOING BALLISTIC!

On 4 November it was announced that Paterson and Duncan Shearer had agreed five-year contracts to remain in Inverness but, in the event, nothing was ever concluded and the management team's days at the club were numbered. Dundee United chairman Eddie Thompson held a press conference the next day to announce that Paul Hegarty would continue in charge and took the public opportunity to deny that Paterson had ever been offered the job. The normally reticent Paterson was forced to make his own public statement to refute this. He gave his version of events at a press conference on 6 November and in a Matchday Programme interview: 'The problem was that they made the approach the wrong way and I was uncomfortable with that from day one, as I wanted them to make the approach officially to the club. They wouldn't because they didn't want to be publicly embarrassed with another First Division manager choosing to stay just like Ian McCall and Falkirk.' He expressed sadness at Thompson: 'The actions of the chairman pulling out my CV in a press conference which was basically called to announce a new manager was naïve at best but just downright insulting... it left me with no option but to come out with the true version and the true version is what everyone got, the fact that I had accepted the job and then had a change of heart on the Saturday.' McCall finally joined United in January 2003 and the managerial merry-go-round was to bring Alex Smith to Ross County.

It was back to the football, and on 9 November Ross County were beaten 2-0 in Dingwall. Barry Robson set things in motion with a record-breaking goal in only 40 seconds. The second was an own-goal from ex-Caley Thistle captain Mark McCulloch. County manager Neale Cooper had been through a torrid spell leading up to the game and this defeat proved the last straw. Two days later he resigned.

The week after the County success, Queen of the South were beaten at home in an amazing match. Red cards were shown to Queens' players either side of the break but despite the lack of numbers they put up a remarkable fight. It ended 5-3 for the home side with Paul Ritchie scoring a hat-trick and Barry Robson scoring two. For a while it seemed to be raining goals and it could just as easily have been 4-4. At 3-1 early in the second half, Queens looked beaten but suddenly it was 3-2, 4-2 then 4-3. Only Ritchie's tap-in a minute from time made victory a certainty. The 5-3 final score was the highest aggregate number of goals all season. A narrow 2-1 away win at Arbroath on the 23rd enabled Falkirk to be leapfrogged and top spot gained for the first time. November was completed with a 100% record on the 30th when Clyde were beaten 1-0 at home. Clyde's defence held firm until ten minutes from time, when Barry Robson scored direct from a free kick. Robson was rewarded for his spell of excellent form by being named SFL 'Player of the Month' for November. The run to the top of Division One earned Steve Paterson a third 'Manager of the Month' award in a row, but thrust him once more into the spotlight just as Aberdeen parted company with manager Ebbe Skovdahl. Speculation also continued to be rife about the futures of Dennis Wyness and Barry Robson.

Paterson and Shearer join Dons

The dramatic 3-3 away draw against Ayr United on 7 December was to be Steve Paterson and Duncan Shearer's last game in charge. With Ayr 3-0 ahead after 52 minutes it seemed all over. The history of Ayr matches should have taught otherwise. Bobby Mann headed a goal back in 54 minutes, then goals in quick succession from Paul Ritchie and Dennis Wyness made it 3-3. Both sides were reduced to ten men with 15 minutes left when James Grady and Russell Duncan were sent off. Two days later the Caley Thistle board reluctantly gave Aberdeen permission to speak to Paterson. Everything happened very quickly after that, and by 11 December Steve Paterson and Duncan Shearer were introduced at a press conference as the new Aberdeen management team. After the Dundee United saga, and the apparent agreement to sign long-term contracts, the Inverness fans were understandably stunned at their departure.

It emerged that Caley Thistle had offered Shearer the manager's job but the lure of his old team proved irresistible. Director of football Graeme Bennett said that they had tried hard to keep Shearer: 'We made Duncan a very good offer, a very attractive package. Aberdeen wanted him so greatly that they out-bid us in the end but not until after Duncan thought long and hard about leaving here.' Paterson summed up his reasons for leaving: 'It wasn't easy leaving Inverness after seven wonderful years, but I'm ambitious and want to show I can be a success at the top level. To me Aberdeen is Scotland's third-largest club and to have the chance to manage them is a huge opportunity for me.'

Chairman Ken Mackie said: 'This marks the end of a chapter in our club's history. We wish Steve and Duncan every success and look forward to a continued association with them.' Charlie Christie spoke for the players:

'Although the players are all tinged with sadness it was only a matter of time until Steve went to a bigger club. Everyone here wishes him and Duncan the very best success at Aberdeen because they've done a brilliant job here.'

Speculation about the succession started immediately. Graeme Bennett said that 'a young up-and-coming manager would fit the bill. We need someone with energy to drive us forward. This is a new step for us and I'm sure this job will appeal to many.' Early names linked to the post were Dundee United coach Maurice Malpas, Clyde manager Alan Kernaghan, Queen of the South boss John Connolly and Peterhead's Ian Wilson.

Until an appointment could be made, Bennett took interim charge with the assistance of John Docherty. Their first match on 14 December could not have been much harder – away to Falkirk. Caley Thistle took the lead after only one minute thanks to an own-goal, but John Hughes equalised in 17 minutes. Despite good football at both ends, there was no more scoring and Caley Thistle were happy to go home with a point. The visiting fans were satisfied with the result but less happy at being refused entry to the Brockville stand because of sporting team colours. All away fans, including the elderly and infirm, were forced to the terracing and official protests were made by the Supporters' Club to both Falkirk and the Scottish League. The reluctant management team took charge for one more game on 21 December – a poor 1-1 home draw with Alloa. Bobby Mann scored in five minutes direct from a free kick,but Gareth Hutchison equalised just before half-time. Referee Ian Frickleton was not a popular man in Inverness when he sent Grant Munro off in the 71st minute for two yellow cards. The first seemed very harsh. With Falkirk's game falling victim to a frozen Ayr pitch, a point was enough to make Caley Thistle the Christmas number one.

John Robertson arrives

Final interviews for the manager's post took place on 22/23 December. Livingston first-team coach John Robertson was unveiled as Steve Paterson's replacement on Boxing Day. His football credentials were impeccable – 631 competitive appearances and 271 goals in 18 seasons with Hearts, a short spell with Newcastle United in 1988 and 16 international caps. 'Robbo' had joined Livingston as player/coach in July 1998 and served under Ray Stewart, Jim Leishman and Davie Hay. Now he had achieved his ambition of becoming a manager. It had been an easy decision to accept the post: 'They are ambitious and they play attacking football. That's the way I like to see it played and that's what we will continue to do. I know I can coach and I will have to go out and see if I can manage. Normally when new managers come in teams are struggling, but Caley Thistle are at the top of the league so I don't think a lot of changes have to be made.'

Amidst much media hype Robertson made his debut against St Mirren at Paisley on 28 December. No assistant had been appointed, so coach John Docherty remained in the dug-out for one more game. It was dream start as Caley Thistle won 4-1. Saints' goalkeeper Ludo Roy kept the score blank for 14 minutes, but lost three goals before half-time from Dennis Wyness, Ross Tokely and Graeme Stewart. Paul Ritchie scored the fourth just after the break. The home side could only manage a late consolation. Falkirk beat Queen of the South 5-0, but Caley Thistle ended 2002 in the number one slot. Robertson was happy to get off to a winning start: 'I knew I had inherited a well-balanced squad, playing a style of football I like. I feel we have a duty to entertain and score goals – we certainly did that out there and I just hope we can keep it going.'

The transfer window re-opened on 1 January with much huffing and puffing. With a lack of money in the Scottish game, little actually happened. Inverness eyes were on Aberdeen and a player raid by Steve Paterson was expected. Prolific goalscorer Dennis Wyness was an obvious target but he elected to see out his contract. In a late move, Dundee United's new manager Ian McCall tabled a six-figure bid for Barry Robson but it was refused. Caley Thistle made one signing when striker Steve Hislop came from local rivals Ross County. Chris Miller left for East Fife. He had made only one substitute appearance and a desire for first-team football led to his release.

The start of January football was delayed as a hard frost led to the postponement of the derby match due to be played in Inverness on New Year's Day. This would have been Dennis Wyness's 100th game in a row, and many wondered whether he would be transferred before achieving this milestone. On 3 January former Caledonian, Hearts and Partick Thistle player Donald Park joined Robertson with the title of head coach but effectively assistant manager. Park had spent nine seasons at Hearts in two spells, broken by a period from September 1978 to May 1983 at Partick Thistle. He had also managed both Meadowbank Thistle and Arbroath. In

July 1994 he joined Hibs as a coach and spent two spells there under Alex Miller and Alex McLeish. For a very short spell he was assistant to Hibs manager Franck Sauzee and for a matter of days he was interim manager when Alex McLeish left for Rangers. When he joined Caley Thistle it was agreed that he would retain his role as Scotland Under-17 coach.

Park's debut should have been the next day at Dumfries, but the weather put paid to the whole of the First Division card that day. With the team already staying overnight near Glasgow, it proved to be an expensive and abortive trip. The supporters' bus was turned back at Kingussie. It was 18 January before the new management team made its debut. It was not a good start: the team went down 1-0 to Ayr at home and surrendered top spot in the league. Ayr scored in the third minute, holding out grimly to take the points. This game marked Dennis Wyness's delayed 100th consecutive match.

Cup run begins

Media coverage of the Scottish Cup is usually subtitled 'The Road to Hampden' and for Caley Thistle the run that started against Raith Rovers on 25 January really would lead to the cradle of Scottish football. This third-round tie was played at home in terrible conditions with the wind raging and the rain varying from light to torrential. In weather like this anything can happen but there was to be no upset as pre-match favourites Caley Thistle won 2-0. Amidst the January transfer window hype there was much speculation about promotion from Division One and who could meet the SPL criteria. St Mirren and St Johnstone had 10,000 seats, but only the Perth Saints were in the promotion race. The only other serious contenders were Falkirk and Caley Thistle, and both had grounds which failed the SPL test. This discussion was to last until the end of the season – and well beyond.

The heavy snow and frozen pitches continued into February – it was 8 February before the next match could be played. First played second as Falkirk came north in what it turned out to be a classic encounter. Caley Thistle were ahead for most of the game, but fell to an Owen Coyle hat-trick. His third goal just four minutes from the final whistle was the first time that Falkirk had been ahead in the game. This result opened up a seven-point gap at the top of the league and severely dented Caley Thistle's hopes of overtaking the leaders. A 2-0 defeat against St Johnstone in Perth the following week resulted in a slip to third spot. Charlie Christie was captain for the day to celebrate his 300th appearance. Saints were clearly the better side, but they only took the points with two very late Chris Hay goals.

Caley Thistle have a worldwide support including an amazing number of fans in England. Londoners Brian Wingrove and Ewan Clydesdale are among those who travel many thousands of miles each season following the team home and away. Both have become public transport timetable experts and strive to travel north, then home, as cheaply and efficiently as possible. Their dedication is a joy to behold – but for Ewan, the St Johnstone game was nearly a match too far. He flew to Edinburgh from Gatwick at 6.45 am on the day of the match after sleeping in the airport terminal, only to find that his bus to Perth was cancelled. The next bus was caught in a major traffic jam, but with the help of a fast taxi he only missed the first ten minutes. This allowed him to retain his 100% attendance record for the season. Ewan's return flight to Gatwick was delayed and he finally reached home at 1.30 am – a 26-hour day for 80 minutes of football (and a defeat)!

On 22 February there was another step on the way to Hampden, when Hamilton were beaten 6-1 at home in the fourth round of the Scottish Cup. The visitors were unlucky to be 2-1 down at half-time, especially as they had taken the lead through Martin Bonnar in the second minute. Caley Thistle totally dominated the second half and ran out easy winners. Dennis Wyness and Barry Robson each scored a brace, Paul Ritchie scored one and Stuart McCaffrey netted his first goal for the club. The quarter final draw two days later produced a mouth-watering home tie against Celtic. It was once again time for media hype – and a chance to relive February 2000.

On the following Tuesday the New Year derby match was finally played in Inverness. The form book was turned upside down as Alex Smith's revamped team ran out 5-1 winners. It was all over by half-time with relegation-threatened County 3-0 ahead. Just after the restart Mark Brown handled a pass-back and Caley Thistle faced a Hugh Robertson free kick a few yards out. With ten players on the line Robertson blasted goalwards and it rebounded into the net for 4-0. This bizarre goal summed up Caley Thistle's miserable evening. Three minutes from time Dennis Wyness scored a consolation goal, but Conor Gethins immediately replied to make it 5-1. County supporters were to throw this scoreline in the faces of home fans for some time to come.

March turned out to be an historic month despite the league title challenge faltering. It started brightly when on the 1ˢᵗ St Mirren visited Inverness and were beaten 3-1. Saints took an early lead, but Caley Thistle fought back to win convincingly – thanks to a Paul Ritchie hat-trick. The following midweek, also at home, a defensive Arbroath were beaten 2-0 with a goal from Richie Hart just before half-time and Tony Low's debut strike for the club in the dying seconds. It was with much trepidation that Caley Thistle went to Dingwall the following Saturday for the last derby match of the season, but there was revenge for the defeat eleven days earlier with a 2-0 victory. The pattern of Saturday/Tuesday games continued in an effort to catch up and it was off on the long road to meet Queen of the South in Dumfries. Despite good football from both sides it ended a goalless draw.

The second of three away matches in a row was on 15 March at a windy Gayfield Park, Arbroath. The home side took the lead just on half-time, but a brace from Dennis Wyness and a debut goal from Steve Hislop earned the points. It was quite a different story at Clyde the following Tuesday. The build-up to the cup-tie against Celtic had started, no matter how hard everyone tried to delay it, and Martin O'Neill was a very interested spectator at Broadwood. It turned out to be a disastrous night for the visitors. They lost a goal in 16 minutes and were three down after only 16 minutes. By the time O'Neill arrived, Clyde had already scored twice. Barry Robson pulled one back, but Clyde ran out 4-1 winners. Nothing would come off for Caley Thistle and O'Neill must have felt that his side had nothing to fear. Despite this defeat, Caley Thistle finished the March league programme in third place but Falkirk and St Johnstone had pulled away.

'His Royal Wyness'

It was now time to turn attention to the impending visit of Celtic. Live Sky television coverage ensured a Sunday fixture and a 6.15 pm kick-off. 23 March 2003 was set to go down in the history books of Scottish football alongside 8 February 2000. Tickets were like gold dust and 6050 spectators crammed into the stadium – the highest home crowd of the season. Celtic flew into Inverness on the back of a momentous UEFA Cup quarter-final victory against Liverpool, with most of their top players in the squad. In the event the manager rested some of the Liverpool heroes but still put out a high-quality side. New signing Slovakian defender Stanislav Varga was included and his debut for the club was to be a traumatic one. The most unlucky Caley Thistle player was Steve Hislop, who was cup-tied as a result of a ten-minute appearance for Ross County in round three. Charlie Christie came back from injury to take a place on the bench and Paul Ritchie replaced Hislop in the starting eleven.

The home line-up was Mark Brown, Stuart McCaffrey, Stuart Golabek, Bobby Mann, Grant Munro, Roy McBain, Ross Tokely, Dennis Wyness, Paul Ritchie, Richie Hart and Barry Robson. Graeme Stewart, Charlie Christie, David Bagan, Liam Keogh and Mike Fraser were on the bench. Keogh came on for Ritchie with ten minutes left and Christie replaced Robson for the last five minutes.

Caley Thistle played some excellent football in the first half, but rarely troubled Javier Broto. Mark Brown was in heroic form and was eventually named 'Man of the Match' as well as 'Player of the 5th Round'. Celtic rarely found a way through the home defence and, when they did, Brown was there. In first-half added time, Munro and Hart combined to set up Wyness and he slid the ball home to score the most valuable goal of his career. It was clear that Celtic would come out fighting in the second half and so it proved. Excellent defending, great goalkeeping and poor finishing kept the 1-0 score intact.

With less than 30 minutes to go, Celtic sent on John Hartson to partner captain Henrik Larsson up front, and this potentially lethal combination caused a few hearts to flutter. Brown was a hero in 52 minutes when Larsson was set up 12 yards out by David Fernandez. From close range the Swede is usually deadly, but an inspired Brown saved brilliantly. Larsson broke through into the box in 66 minutes, but McCaffrey's well-timed tackle ended the danger. Hartson then headed past and Tokely made two terrific blocks from Larsson and Jamie Smith. The last ten minutes plus three minutes of injury time seemed like an age to the home fans – but their team held out. The Celtic players trooped off in dejected mode,but once more the home players, officials and fans went ballistic!

The fact that some fringe players took the field was not used by O'Neill as an excuse. He rightly asserted that this was the mighty Celtic and these players should not have lost: 'It was a question of looking for balance and freshness in the side. But believe me I am bitterly disappointed about this.' It is hard to know where to place the 2003 triumph in comparison with 2000. An upset at home should be easier than away, but this was a revitalised Celtic on a high after success against Liverpool. In 2000 Celtic were in turmoil behind the scenes, but in 2003 there was stability. Whatever the viewpoint, this was a majestic victory which earned a semi-final place. Dennis Wyness's 27th goal of the season was seen by millions and the scramble for his signature in the summer was bound to intensify. Caley Thistle's 100% record against Celtic in the Scottish Cup was preserved – two played and two won.

The goalscorer made his usual low-key departure out the fire exit to avoid the limelight, but reporters descended on the rest of the heroes. Stuart McCaffrey summed up the feelings of the players: 'First of all there was disbelief. Even with a couple of minutes remaining Celtic kept piling on the pressure and we were all relieved to hear the final whistle. The dressing room was absolutely buzzing and it was just a brilliant end to a fantastic evening.' Captain Bobby Mann said: 'To beat Celtic once was something else but a second time is just unbelievable.' John Robertson reckoned that his side needed three ingredients to win the match: '... everyone to play well, Celtic not to be at their best and for us to have a slice of luck – and that's the way it turned out'.

An important feature of all matches is the printing and distribution of team lines and the Celtic listing produced a great deal of amusement. Team lists are given to the referee and exchanged 45 minutes before kick-off. A full set of team lines is then prepared for distribution to the press, officials, guests and sponsors. As the Celtic team list was being typed there was a realisation that only ten players had been named. Caley Thistle secretary Jim Falconer and referee Alan Freeland also noticed the error and an urgent call was made to Celtic for clarification. It emerged that Steve Guppy had been omitted in error. Someone suggested that Celtic would only need ten players while John Robertson wondered if this was Celtic giving themselves a handicap. In the end the joke was on Celtic!

As Inverness woke up to a collective hangover, a little of the gloss was taken from the victory when the timing of the semi-final was announced. The Easter weekend dates for the ties were Saturday 19 and Monday 21 April. It was likely that the Monday would be allocated for the Caley Thistle match with a 7.45 pm kick-off. Falkirk and Dundee had still to play their quarter-final match, but both agreed that the Monday was unacceptable. Eventually the SFA bowed to pressure and announced a change to Sunday 20 April at 3 pm. Chairman

Ken Mackie was relieved that common sense had prevailed: 'This means that more supporters will be able to get to the game. I don't think that people in the central belt appreciate the journeys we have to make every second week. We face a four-hour journey just to get to the game and it is much easier to be arriving back at a reasonable time instead of 2 am.'

While the publicity surrounding the Celtic victory did not reach 2000 levels, it did cause quite a stir nationally. It was even referred to in the Scottish Parliament when, during a debate on the SPL's seating requirements, local MSP Fergus Ewing addressed '... the Presiding Officer, fellow MSPs and His Royal Wyness'.

The SPL reacted to the promotion/relegation debate by announcing that the issue would not be decided until the identity of the First Division winners was known. If St Johnstone were to overtake Falkirk, then no decision would be required. With a free weekend at the end of March, John Robertson fulfilled a long-standing promise to take his players across the Minch to the Western Isles. Benbecula FC manager Iain MacDonald had been relishing the visit for months and even the 7-1 defeat did not take away from the occasion. As well as goals, the spectators were treated to cameo appearances from Robertson and director of football Graeme Bennett.

April started with a league match against Queen of the South on the 5th, but only 1656 turned up to watch despite the euphoria surrounding the Celtic victory. The home crowds continued to be a source of disappointment – especially with so much good football on show. The Queens' game turned out to be less than a classic but the three points were earned by a Ross Tokely headed goal. The home crowd against Clyde the following week was only 1682, although tickets for the cup semi-final were selling like hot cakes. Clyde arrived in Inverness several shirts short of a full kit following a break-in at Broadwood, and had to borrow the home side's change strip. The switch was certainly no handicap: Clyde won 2-1, despite Caley Thistle having most of the play. The defeat resulted in a slip to fourth.

Defeat at Hampden

Attention could now be turned to the big one – the Tennent's Scottish Cup semi-final against Dundee. The club produced T-shirts with the slogan 'SuperCaleyGoBallistic AllTheWayToHampden', merchandise sales increased dramatically, shops competed for the best ICT window display and every available bus for miles around was booked. Local coach operator Rapsons was overwhelmed by demand and had to turn to colleagues in Perthshire to satisfy demand. With an 11,000 allocation there was no shortage of Hampden tickets and the only competition was for the best seats. The weather in the days leading up to the match was Mediterranean and cup fever grew as the day approached.

John Robertson said his side were in the cup to win it: 'We are the last remaining First Division side in the Scottish Cup and we want to do the division proud. I'm a very positive person – even when the campaign started I believed we could go a long way.' Chairman Ken Mackie reflected on the economic side of it: 'The cup run will help stabilise the finances and keep us in reasonably good health. At the moment it all points to us managing to cover our costs for the season and hopefully we will have some funds left over.' He summed up the Inverness hopes: 'We would love to be in the final but we know it will be difficult. Dundee are a formidable obstacle but I believe we can do it.'

On Easter Sunday 20 April thousands of fans headed south for what they hoped would be another glory day. Cars and buses filled the A9 and a special 500-seater train ran to Glasgow. The team bus took players and officials to Glasgow the evening before the game for a tour of the national stadium then the team stayed overnight at the Westerwood Hotel in Cumbernauld. The most disappointed ICT player was Grant Munro, who missed the game due to illness, but otherwise John Robertson chose from a full squad. The line-up for the historic occasion was Mark Brown, Ross Tokely, Stuart Golabek, Bobby Mann, Stuart McCaffrey, Roy McBain, Russell Duncan, Dennis Wyness, Paul Ritchie, Richie Hart and Barry Robson. Charlie Christie and David Bagan came on for the last eight minutes, replacing McCaffrey and Duncan. Graeme Stewart, Liam Keogh and substitute goalkeeper Mike Fraser remained on the bench.

The cup fairytale was to end in tears as Dundee claimed victory with a solitary goal. The game was very tight – for a long time it looked as if a replay at Pittodrie would be required. There were two defining moments in the match – Julian Speroni's wonder save from Wyness, and Georgi Nemsadze's mis-hit shot which resulted in the winner. In between there was plenty of action but few shots on goal.

The Inverness side started well and Mann headed over a Hart cross in the first minute. In seven minutes Ritchie came close with a first-time effort but it flew over the bar. A goal looked like coming, and when Wyness let fly from 25 yards in the ninth minute the fans were on their feet thinking it had arrived. Somehow Dundee's Julian Speroni touched it onto the post. This was the closest the Inverness side were to come to scoring. Hart hit over in 15 minutes, then Dundee came back into the match. Brown touched a Steve Lovell shot for a corner, McCaffrey made a vital clearance and a Lee Wilkie header was hooked away by Tokely. Dundee should have scored when a Lovell cross from the right reached Steven Milne in space, he mis-hit and Mann headed clear. With five minutes of the first half left, Wyness was brought down by Wilkie just 19 yards out, but Mann's free kick came off the wall.

Dundee controlled the second half and Caballero missed a great chance in 59 minutes. A chip over the defence found him on the six-yard line with only Brown to beat. He tried to flick it over the advancing keeper but it cleared the bar. The winning goal came with 12 minutes left. Caballero worked hard down the left, then passed to Nemsadze on the 18-yard line. He failed to connect cleanly, but the ball deceived everybody and went in off the post. Dundee continued to surge forward and in 85 minutes Mann cleared a deflected Nemsadze dribbled pass off the line. In the two minutes of added time 'Man of the Match' Caballero hit low past the post, then Zurab Khizanishvili strode past two defenders before hitting over. The whistle went and Caley Thistle's cup adventure was over.

On the day Dundee were the better side – but this did not lessen the disappointment. John Robertson was upbeat about the team's performance and correctly pointed out how close Caley Thistle had been to matching an SPL team: 'Dennis hit a magnificent shot but the 'keeper managed to finger-tip it onto the post. Then Nemsadze didn't hit the ball well – it sclaffed off the post and into the corner. It's little things like that which make all the difference.' Dundee manager Jim Duffy praised his opponents: 'Our tactics were good but all credit to Caley Thistle for their tactical awareness and the way they approached the game.' Dundee eventually lost to Rangers in the final but earned an UEFA Cup place and a first-round draw against Albanian side KS Vllaznia. Caley Thistle had been only two goals away from a visit to Albania!

GOING BALLISTIC!

Falkirk clinched the First Division championship on the day before the cup semi-final so the rest of the season was about achieving the highest finish possible and planning for the future. The next game was an away match at relegation-threatened Alloa on the 26th. It was also important for Ross County as they were still not safe. Alloa were soundly beaten 5-1, with Paul Ritchie scoring his fourth hat-trick of the season.

The joy of victory soon turned to sadness when word came through that Dr John MacAskill had died that day after a long illness. John was a man of many parts and master of them all. His prime role was as a GP in Fort William, but he was also a world-renowned piper and composer. John was a football enthusiast whose love of the game started in the streets of Glasgow. As well as being the Caley Thistle doctor since 1994, he was part of the Scotland Youth and Under-21 backroom staff. The clinching of the Third Division championship in 1996-7 gave him particular pleasure, as it was the first time he had been involved with a side that had actually won something. During his nine-season service he was an integral part of the club and travelled many miles to indulge his football passion. When the team was at home he made the return drive from Fort William and for away trips he met the team bus at Newtonmore. Often he had to make a difficult return journey, and on at least one occasion his car had to be dug out of the snow by the players. At his funeral service in Fort William the club was represented by players and officials past and present and there was also a strong representation from the SFA. 'Doc' MacAskill was that rare man – truly irreplaceable.

A long midweek trip to Ayr on the 29th ended with a 1-0 defeat and on 3 May there was a disappointing home 2-1 defeat to St Johnstone. Paul Ritchie was named SFL 'Player of the Month' for April. The season ended on 10 May in front of a massive 7300 crowd at Falkirk, a new league record. Three years previously, Caley Thistle had been the opposition at what was meant to be Brockville's final game, but an 11th-hour reprieve was granted. This time it really was the end and Caley Thistle spoiled Falkirk's party by winning 3-2. Davie Nicholls did not help matters with an own-goal, Bobby Mann scored one and Charlie Christie's 82nd-minute winner proved to be the very last at Brockville. In Dingwall, Ross County beat Ayr 4-1 to avoid relegation on goal difference.

TWO GOALS FROM ALBANIA

The Falkirk game is one which Brian Wingrove will not easily forget. Our fan in Hertfordshire is used to 1000-mile round trips but when travel plans go wrong, they can go badly wrong. A 6 am departure from home and a drive to Stansted Airport is the norm, but on this occasion a lorry spill on the M25 led to the Edinburgh EasyJet flight being missed. At 10 am he managed to board a flight to Prestwick – which landed 45 minutes late. The only way to make the game was to take the train to Glasgow and a taxi to Falkirk. He arrived ten minutes before kick-off after travelling for nearly nine hours. Ninety minutes of football then back via Edinburgh to Stansted. That was the plan – but the return flight was delayed then eventually cancelled. At 2.45 am Brian finally left Edinburgh on a flight to Gatwick and reached home at 9.10 am. 27 hours in transit and his car still sitting in the short-stay car park at Stansted! Despite this experience Brian was back the next season for more of the same.

The 65 points gathered to take fourth place was a new First Division high for the club. In 44 league and cup games a record 90 goals were scored and 53 conceded. The goals were shared by 12 players with three own-goals. Dennis Wyness ended the season as club and division top scorer with 27 goals. He was also named First Division 'Player of the Year' by the Scottish Professional Footballers Association. Mark Brown started in all 44 games and Dennis Wyness also played 44 times – including one substitute appearance. The Falkirk match was Wyness's 119th in a row. On 15 February Charlie Christie passed the 300-appearance barrier and on 10 August Ross Tokely made his 200th appearance. During the season Bobby Mann, Barry Robson and Dennis Wyness completed 150 appearances and three players joined the century club – Roy McBain, Stuart Golabek and Stuart McCaffrey.

Stuart Golabek scooped the pool in the annual awards when he was named 'Player of the Year' by the Official Supporters Club, his fellow players and the Internet Supporters' Club. Dennis Wyness was named Supporters' 'Player of the Year' following a vote at the last home game. The Matchday Programme 'Player of the Year' was Richie Hart. Steve Paterson earned three 'Manager of the Month' titles, Dennis Wyness was SFL 'Player of the Month' twice and Barry Robson once.

CHAPTER 13

TREBLE CHANCE, DOUBLE TRIUMPH
2003-4

INVERNESS CALEDONIAN THISTLE FC 2003-4 *(photo: Ken MacPherson)*

(*Back*) Stuart Golabek, David MacRae, Darran Thomson, Paul Ritchie, David Proctor, Roy McBain, Tony Low

(*Middle*) Donald Park (head coach), John Docherty (coach), David Bingham, Ross Tokely, Mike Fraser, Mark Brown, Ally Ridgers, Steve Hislop, Grant Munro, Danny MacDonald (community and football development manager), Emily Goodlad (physio)

(*Front*) Craig MacMillan, Stuart McCaffrey, Barry Wilson, Charlie Christie, John Robertson (manager), Bobby Mann (captain), Russell Duncan, Liam Keogh, Richie Hart

The season – and the decade – ended in triumph. A full house at Caledonian Stadium saw John Robertson's side take the First Division championship on the final day. It would have been hard to script it any better. 2002-3 had been so successful that it looked to be the pinnacle of the decade but amazingly 2003-4 surpassed it. As the season drew to a close, Caley Thistle were in with the chance, albeit a slim one, of a unique domestic treble and European football. October's Bell's Cup win started the sequence – then the club reached the semi-final of the Tennent's Scottish Cup. As this went to a Pittodrie replay, the final opponents were known to be Celtic: if Dunfermline could be overcome, a UEFA cup spot was guaranteed. The league championship was a possibility but competition was fierce. The cup (and treble) dream ended at Pittodrie, but the league went to the wire. The SPL's entry requirements became a major issue as the season developed and came to a head after the championship win. The irony of the situation was that Caledonian Stadium could house a UEFA cup-tie but not an SPL match. The only possible solution was to groundshare 100 miles away in Aberdeen, hopefully for just one year. The prospect seemed unthinkable at first, but the lure of the SPL was irresistible.

Three weeks before the Bell's Cup win, Caley Thistle enjoyed a brief stint at the top of the league but, such was the competition, dropped to sixth a month later. Although hopes of the championship began to fade, by the end of November Caley Thistle were at the top once more. Caley Thistle were to stay in the top two for the rest of the season, although Clyde remained in the driving seat. Everything changed in a dramatic last two weeks.

After months of speculation the transfer window re-opened at the end of 2002-3 and two key players left. The first departure took place on 16 May when Barry Robson signed for Dundee United. The Tannadice side were always favourites to land Robson, despite Aberdeen coming in with a last-minute bid. Dennis Wyness had been the subject of much speculation for months, with interest from many clubs, including Hearts and Aberdeen – the Edinburgh side won the race and he was introduced to the Tynecastle faithful on 25 May. David Bagan left for Queen of the South, Brian Gilfillan signed for Cowdenbeath and Graeme Stewart joined the growing ex-Caley Thistle clan at Iain Stewart's Peterhead. Despite rumours to the contrary, Bobby Mann stayed. When pre-season training started on 1 July there were three new faces – striker David Bingham from Livingston and former Hibs' youngsters Darran Thomson and David Proctor. The squad was also strengthened by the signing of teenagers David MacRae and Craig MacMillan on professional contracts. Economics restricted further signings, but former Inverness favourite Barry Wilson returned to the club from Livingston just hours before the transfer window closed on 31 August.

The club's biggest-ever shirt sponsorship agreement was announced on 19 May. Major local employer Inverness Medical signed a one-year deal with the possibility of extensions. At the start of 2003-4 Doctors Ian Smith and Derek MacLeod took over jointly as club doctors with Donald McVicar supporting and deputising when required. Emily Goodlad continued with trackside and midweek physio duties, assisted on occasions by David Brandie. The board was reduced by one in May 2003 when Roy McLennan left, but he was replaced in October by Inverness Medical's operations director Nigel Spiller. On the commercial front Debbie Ross left mid-season and Les Kidger took over most of her duties with the title of business manager. He was assisted by Nicola Barclay, who joined the club as sales and marketing manager.

Youth and community

The whole youth and community set-up was revamped in July 2003 when Danny MacDonald rejoined the club as community and football development manager. The development team was expanded to four full-time members with the appointment of Mike Fridge as football development coordinator, Ronnie Duncan as football development officer and Fiona McWilliams as community development coordinator. Mike and Ronnie, along with a small army of volunteer coaches, now run teams at age 13, 14, 15 and 17 levels and all are part of the SFL's Youth Initiative Programme. Fiona, again with the assistance of volunteers, coaches four elite primary school squads drawn from Soccer Sevens' teams and is responsible for school visits, community liaison and projects involving Inverness College and Highland Disability Sport. During school holidays the club runs the Highland Hotshots for boys and girls aged 5 to 12 years. This comprises football and fitness in a fun environment and it is always heavily subscribed. It involves all the coaching staff with the assistance of first-team squad players. During term-time, work with the 5- to12-year-old group continues with evening sessions at Inverness College games hall.

GOING BALLISTIC!

The opening of the new Highland Football Academy in January 2004 gave all teams access to indoor facilities, and this is now used two nights a week and on Sunday. Outdoors, the teams have the use of pitches at Bught Park and Culloden Academy. All the hard work on the youth and community side has the aim of eventually providing players for the first team but also expanding interest in the club throughout the local area. While only a tiny number of players can make it through to the top level, it is always hoped that the others will retain an interest in the club and become supporters. Links created between the community and the club will also hopefully reap the reward of a greater fan base.

A young ICT side took part in Oban's annual Keyline tournament on 12 July, then the pre-season friendlies started with a run of away victories against Clach, Forres and Brora. Over the three matches a total of 30 players were used including numerous youngsters, a trialist and a brief appearance by the manager. To add to the usual mix of Highland League opposition, three high-profile home friendlies were arranged and again there was 100% success. Steve Paterson's Aberdeen came west on 19 July and were beaten 1-0 thanks to a Bobby Mann penalty. On the 21st, Roy McBain earned a 1-0 win over John Robertson's former club Livingston and, on the 28th, it was 2-1 against Hearts. Paul Ritchie scored a brace and Dennis Wyness netted for Hearts – as he left the field Wyness was given a standing ovation by the home fans. Sandwiched between the Livingston and Hearts matches were 3-1 away wins at Lossiemouth and Forfar. The highlight of the Forfar match on the 26th was David Bingham's record-breaking 29-second opening goal.

A hectic start

August was hectic, with three Bell's Cup-ties and four league matches. There was complete success in the cup and mixed fortunes in the league. The cup run started on the second with a long trip to Gretna and a first-ever meeting with the league's newest side. The result was an emphatic 5-0 win, including two from Richie Hart. 2 August was also the start of a regular series of friendlies against Highland League opposition. With 15 clubs in the league, one was free each Saturday and agreement was reached to play the idle side. The first game, against Nairn at home, ended with a 5-2 win. This arrangement was designed to keep the club's youngsters active against quality opposition. In the event, the matches were not always played as planned on the 'free' Saturday, but the link was established and it proved advantageous to both sides. The opening league match away to Falkirk (with the Bairns ground-sharing at Stenhousemuir's Ochilview) on 9 August was a traumatic affair, especially for Stuart McCaffrey. He scored the first goal, Falkirk equalised, then in 78 minutes McCaffrey was red-carded. The offence was alleged stamping, but television footage proved his innocence and the card was rescinded. Caley Thistle still had to play for 12 minutes with ten men and Falkirk snatched a winner. The referee's error was a costly one.

The following Tuesday the team headed east to Peterhead in the second round of the Bell's Cup. It ended in a narrow 2-1 win with both goals coming from Steve Hislop. Peterhead followed the lead of many clubs and issued no programme for the Bell's Cup-tie. On 16 August there was a dour 0-0 home draw with Clyde, while in the following week St Johnstone were beaten on their own ground for the first time. David Bingham ran the show and scored the opener early in the second half. Saints equalised but Steve Hislop grabbed a deserved winner.

Hislop was also the hero on the 26th when he scored the only goal to knock his former club Ross County out of the Bell's Cup, the first meeting of the clubs in a national cup. The teams played again the following Saturday in the league at Victoria Park. County scored with a penalty in only two minutes but Bobby Mann equalised direct from a free kick. John Robertson was disappointed to come away with just one point: 'We dominated most of the game but to lose a goal so early in the game was a set-back. It was a really good entertaining derby match with many chances, good open football and a few crunching tackles.' ICT finished August in seventh place. Goalkeeper Mark Brown joined the Scotland Under-21 squad for a match in Norway on 19 August but, in the event, he was a spectator.

On 2 September Caley Thistle were firm favourites against Queen's Park in round one of the CIS Insurance Cup, particularly with home advantage, but the match did not go according to the script. The Spiders achieved a 2-1 giant-killing victory, despite Caley Thistle taking the lead. After a break for internationals, the next match was at home in the league against Ayr on the 13th. The 1-0 victory came thanks to Paul Ritchie but chances were squandered and the crowd were restless. The semi-final of the Bell's Cup the following Tuesday, away to Raith Rovers, saw a vastly improved performance. Raith pressurised the defence over the first 20 minutes but the tide turned and it ended with a decisive 4-0 win. This earned a final spot against Airdrie United with St Johnstone's McDiarmid Park chosen as the venue. Barry Wilson and Paul Ritchie each scored a brace and Ritchie thought it was a great result: 'I'm always delighted to score but to get two goals tonight was really special. The showdown with Airdrie may not quite be the Scottish Cup final but we want to win.' Manager John Robertson was full of praise for his team's performance: 'It was terrific and everyone gave their all. The crowd were very vocal and it was good for us to give them something to shout about. I hope they will come down and enjoy the final.'

On the 20th it was off to Brechin's Glebe Park for the first time in over five years. Roy McBain and Paul Ritchie scored in the 2-0 victory but it was not much of a game. The result did push ICT up to joint first place in the league, third on goal difference. The last game of September was at home to St Mirren. Goals from Paul Ritchie and Stuart McCaffrey earned three points and resulted in a September finish joint top with Ross County. County demolished Raith Rovers 7-1 so remained ahead on goal difference. John Robertson earned his first SFL First Division 'Manager of the Month' award for September's exploits and Mark Brown was named SFL 'Player of the Month'.

On 4 October Raith Rovers visited Inverness, still recovering from their heavy defeat the previous week against Ross County. Goals from Ross Tokely and Stuart McCaffrey should have made the points safe, but John Sutton's late strike led to a nervous last few minutes. With County dropping a point at Clyde, Caley Thistle sat proudly alone at the top of Division One. The stint as top-dog lasted two weeks. There was a week's break for Scotland against Lithuania and then defeat at Dumfries on the 18th. Queen of the South were unexpectedly lying second and their exploits attracted a remarkable crowd of over 3500. Paul Ritchie scored first and David Bingham netted in the final minute, but three Queens goals in-between did the damage. Earlier in the week, speculation on John Robertson's future started when Livingston manager Marcio Maximo resigned. David Hay was quickly named interim manager and the heat was off – at least temporarily.

Bell's Cup final

There was one game left in October – the long-awaited Bell's Cup final against Airdrie United. This took place on Sunday 26 October at McDiarmid Park and, despite early worries about ticket sales, close on 3000 northern fans made the relatively short trip to Perth. They were not to be disappointed. Originally there were to be no tickets available at the ground, but Caley Thistle set up a mobile club shop to resolve this contentious issue and capitalise on the demand for merchandise. The Inverness side were favourites but Airdrie, as expected, put up a good show.

The team for this landmark match was Mark Brown, Ross Tokely, Stuart Golabek, Bobby Mann, Stuart McCaffrey, Russell Duncan, Barry Wilson, Richie Hart, Paul Ritchie, Roy McBain and David Bingham. Steve Hislop came on for Ritchie, Liam Keogh replaced Hart near the end and Darran Thomson took over from Bingham with a minute left. Grant Munro and Mike Fraser were unused substitutes.

Airdrie soaked up early pressure, pushing hard in the latter stages of the first half. The goals were a long time coming but 'Man of the Match' David Bingham finally made the breakthrough in 79 minutes when he headed home. Airdrie hung on, but the game was finally put beyond their reach a minute from time when substitute Steve Hislop scored a superb solo goal – his fifth of the tournament. Bobby Mann proudly collected the club's first senior cup and the ghost of the 1999 defeat was finally laid. It was a satisfying moment for the new management team – exactly ten months after John Robertson's appointment as manager. 'Robbo' paid tribute to his team and to assistant Donald Park: 'As a player it's great to win a cup final but it's fantastic to win my first trophy as manager. It's also great for the club because I think there is great potential here and I want to use this cup win as a springboard. Donald Park has been magnificent for me and a great foil. His experience has really helped me along.' Both goalscorers had extra reasons to enjoy being on the winning side. David Bingham had experienced defeat in a Bell's Cup final: 'When I was at Livingston we lost on penalties and that really hurt.' Steve Hislop was disappointed not to start the game: 'That gave me extra motivation when I finally did get on. I wanted to turn a negative into a positive and I'm pleased to finish as the leading goalscorer in the tournament.' Inverness Provost Bill Smith was there to witness the cup win: 'It was really an exciting day, very enjoyable. A little bit tense in the first half but the better team won on the day.' Local MP David Stewart was thrilled: 'It was a tremendous feather in the cap for John Robertson, Donald Park and the team. It was also fitting that they scooped silverware in the 10th anniversary season.'

GOING BALLISTIC!

The optimism at the club continued at the AGM three days later, when the first ever operating profit was revealed. To be in the black to the tune of £129,000 for the year to 31 May 2003 contrasted sharply with a loss of £272,000 for the previous year. A plan for temporary seating to meet SPL requirements, should promotion be achieved, was also unveiled.

November was busy, and ultimately successful, with six league games. The start was disappointing, with a 2-1 home defeat to Falkirk then a midweek 1-0 loss to Clyde at Broadwood. Things picked up after that, with Ayr soundly beaten 3-0 at Somerset Park on the 8th. Scotland were playing Holland the following Saturday, so the home derby against Ross County was brought forward to the Friday evening. It turned out to be a night of drama. Between the 30th and 33rd minutes goals from David Bingham, Steve Hislop and Barry Wilson seemed to set up a comprehensive win, but things turned out rather differently. County quickly made it 3-1 then, with 20 minutes to go, it was 3-2. With two minutes of added time already played, Steve McGarry volleyed a shock equaliser from 20 yards and for Caley Thistle it felt like a defeat. The 4-0 win away to St Mirren on the 22nd was a repeat of the match in August 2002 which led to the end of Tom Hendrie's reign as manager – this time John Coughlin fell on his sword. The damage was inflicted by two goals each from Roy McBain and David Bingham.

The talk of Scottish football a few days later was Dundee's slide into administration with debts of £20 million. The spectre of liquidation loomed large: 15 players were immediately sacked to ease the wage bill. In the same week, Hearts announced debts of over £17 million and a desire to sell Tynecastle. Everyone asked who would be next. The answer was Livingston. Caley Thistle's book-balancing over the previous two years had clearly been a crucial step in the face of a decline in football's fortunes.

The final game of November was at home to bottom club Brechin who were coming in on the back of a mini-revival. It was not to continue – they were demolished 5-0 in heavy rain. Steve Hislop's goal in only 56 seconds started the rout, Ross Tokely scored two, Barry Wilson added another and Liam Keogh netted his first for the club after a superb solo run which brought the normally subdued crowd to its feet. This took Caley Thistle to the top of the league on goal difference. Amazingly, the first six teams were only separated by two points.

Early December wins against Queen of the South and Raith gained top spot outright but this was surrendered on 20 December when the away Falkirk match was postponed due to a waterlogged pitch. Clyde took advantage by beating Ayr 2-1 to go top by one point. The final game of 2003 was a six-pointer at home against early title-favourites St Johnstone. Despite ICT dominance, Saints held out until very late. Ross Tokely was up-ended in the box, culprit Paul Bernard was red-carded and a penalty awarded. As he stepped up to take the kick Barry Wilson asked referee Gary Mitchell how long there was to go. Mitchell replied 'Ten minutes – one goal will win it.' Wilson thanked the referee for adding to the pressure then promptly wrong-footed Craig Nelson to score the winner. December's 100% record deservedly won John Robertson his second 'Manager of the Month' award.

caleythistleonline.com

In calendar year 2003 the club's website notched up a remarkable 2 million hits. It was started in late 1994 by Scott McKenzie on an unofficial basis, but with the blessing of the club. When David Sutherland took over as chairman in January 2000 he gave it the full backing of the club and in December 2001 an official site was launched. The unofficial site remained dominant and in late 2002 it was agreed that the sites should be combined. Site 'hits' are between 150,000 and 200,000 each month, recording an all-time high of 300,000 in two days after the first Celtic cup win in February 2000. The success of the site is put down by Scott partly to the close ties with the club: 'When the club agreed that this would be the official site it gave it a bit of an edge. A number of sites dedicated to the club have come and gone but this one has been around as long as the club and has developed and grown over the years.' The site is accessed at www. caleythistleonline.com and is carefully split into official and unofficial sections. This allows fans to have their say in an environment divorced from club influence or responsibility. The message forum has become a popular place for exchange of views and extracts are published each week in the *Inverness Courier*. On the official side, the club promotes commercial activities, advertises merchandise and publicises future games and events. Under the heading of 'Boardroom Banter', the directors use the website as a direct means of communicating with fans on a monthly basis. This covers current and future events, personnel changes and responses to points raised on the site. The days when fans could complain that they were kept in the dark are long gone. After each match two reports are posted – one rather irreverent unofficial one by fans and a more subdued factual effort by the author. Thus all bases are covered. The site also includes the contact e-mail addresses for a wide range of club activities. Scott continues to run the website on a voluntary basis despite a move to Toronto in May 2003.

The new year begins

The opening of the January transfer window led to one player out and one in – Darren Mackie came on loan from Aberdeen and reserve keeper Ally Ridgers left for Clach and regular football. Ridgers had made his first squad appearance on 8 August 2000, but after 48 bench appearances had never played for the first team. For the last two seasons he had alternated on the bench with Mike Fraser, but the form and fitness of Mark Brown had prevented either being called into action.

The first New Year's derby at Dingwall for nine years went County's way. Stuart Golabek's unfortunate own-goal was enough to give them the points. A week later it was the start of the Scottish Cup and a home tie against First Division bottom club Brechin City. On paper this was a banker and Caley Thistle duly won 5-1 including a Paul Ritchie hat-trick. Ayr were the next visitors on the 17th, their young side struggling in the league. First half dominance resulted in just one Paul Ritchie goal and it was all very tense when Ayr equalised. David Bingham continued his fine form with a late winner. William Hill took this as a sign and made Caley Thistle 11/8 favourites for the league title. The away league game at Brechin on the 24th ended 4-2, but it was tight until Russell Duncan's contender for 'Goal of the Season' seven minutes from time. It had looked comfortable at 3-1 but it went to 3-2 before Duncan sent in a curling shot from the edge of the box to secure the win. January's last game was a day of milestones at home to St Mirren and a dress rehearsal for the Scottish Cup. This was John Robertson's 50th game in charge and both Stuart Golabek and Roy McBain reached the 150-appearance mark. St Mirren had appointed Gus MacPherson as manager in December and were now a vastly improved side. It was 1-0 to Saints for most of the match until David Bingham popped up two minutes from time to save the day with a close-range goal. With Clyde's game at Dumfries postponed, one point was enough to regain top spot on goal difference.

In February former Brora Rangers' manager Rod Houston was appointed development manager of the newly-opened £2.1m Highland Football

Academy in Dingwall. Despite its location, the Academy is a region-wide resource funded by a partnership involving sportscotland (formerly known as the Scottish Sports Council), Highlands and Islands Enterprise and Highland Council. Both Ross County and Caley Thistle were deeply involved with the project from its inception and quickly began to make full use of its facilities. The indoor pitch is used by players of all ages from throughout the Highland area. The Academy concept includes not only the Dingwall indoor facilities but also high-specification floodlit outdoor pitches at Charleston, Inverness. Two outdoor pitches have been laid close to the main Academy building. Rangers opened the first Scottish training complex of its kind in 2001 at Milngavie near Glasgow, the Dingwall development was second and Hearts' joint venture with Heriot-Watt University was opened on 31 May 2004. Rod Houston has a dream – in his retirement he wants to watch a match between Caley Thistle and Ross County with half of the squads having come through the Academy: 'Then we will have done our job. If kids realise their potential and the game has been sustained in the Highlands then the Academy will have succeeded.'

Prior to the Tennent's Scottish Cup fourth-round draw, fans were invited to enter a competition with the prize of picking the teams live on TV at McDiarmid Park. One of the winners was Caley Thistle fan Liz Macrae, who took part in the programme wearing her club shirt. She drew out St Mirren and her fellow prize-winner (a St Mirren fan) selected Caley Thistle. The tie took place on 7 February and it was not a match to relish. To play a team from your own division away from home raised the prospect of defeat and little financial return. With such a close result in the league, a long injury list and the Saints' revival, there was little optimism.

It turned out to be a busy day for the Caley Thistle defence, in weather which David Bingham later described as 'four seasons in one day'. In turn there was hail, sleet, rain and driven snow. Caley Thistle spent most of the match pinned back and Mark Brown performed heroics in goal. With 12 minutes left, Ross Tokely took a throw-in on the right while the Saints' players protested that it had been given the wrong way – TV evidence later lent strength to this claim. A neat turn and pass by David Bingham set up youngster Darran Thomson, who calmly scored with a low shot from just outside the box. Paul Ritchie nearly made it two a few minutes later, but one was enough. The home fans were stunned: even the Caley Thistle fans conceded that the 1-0 result was a steal. John Robertson said: 'It was a real battle out there so we're delighted to get through'. Saints' assistant manager Andy Millen was 'devastated'. The only thing that mattered to ICT was that the quarter-final had been reached for the fourth time in ten years. The draw threw up another away tie – SPL side Motherwell at Fir Park.

Back to the league and a home match against a much-changed Raith Rovers side. A new Spanish-dominated foreign legion had arrived at the club and they held Caley Thistle to a single-goal lead until two late strikes made it a comfortable 3-0. It was not so good at Dumfries the following week. Queens were now only on the fringes of the promotion race, but they recorded a 2-1 win. Clyde took advantage of this slip by beating Raith Rovers to regain top spot. The final Saturday of February was to be the big showdown. Clyde were due in Inverness and sitting three points ahead with a game in hand. A win for either side would have been crucial. All went flat as snow and frost wiped out the First Division card.

The weather relented enough to allow the away game against Falkirk to go ahead on 2 March. Ochilview was only just playable and the pitch was bone-hard in the shade of the main stand. It was a terrific end-to-end match which stood 1-1 at half-time, poised to go either way. There was a major blow in 27 minutes when David Bingham limped off, adding to the club's injury woes. Falkirk controlled the second half, scoring a controversial winner. A free kick taken from the wrong spot led to substitute Kieran McAnespie scoring with an unstoppable 30-yard rocket. Despite protests, the goal stood.

The Motherwell cup-tie on the 6th was another great day out for Inverness fans, supplemented by a legion of south-based supporters. Sponsors Tennent came up trumps with five free supporters' buses, the fleet augmented by the usual contingents from pubs and clubs throughout the north. The build-up to the game was strange. Motherwell were going through a good spell in the SPL and this, combined with a spate of ICT injuries, led to a high degree of pessimism. The pitch at Fir Park was known to be poor, but this was more of a leveller than a handicap. John Robertson vowed to play attacking football, but in the end it was four at the back supplemented by a backtracking midfield and Paul Ritchie alone up front. Former Motherwell player Mark Brown – a victim of their financial troubles – was one player with a special reason to put in a good performance, but he was rarely troubled. His defence stood firm and spent most of the game repelling high balls with ease. What proved to be the winning goal came in 10 minutes when Barry Wilson took a neat pass from Russell Duncan then spotted Gordon Marshall off his line. He decided to try his luck with a 30-yard lob, which came off in spectacular style. With the bright sun Marshall's only defence, the ball dropped behind him and into the net. It was backs-to-the-wall after that, with only occasional breaks upfield. The Caley Thistle defence handled everything thrown at them and, in a rare attack, Russell Duncan came close to scoring a second goal with a minute left. The whistle went. Caley Thistle had reached the Scottish Cup semi-final stage for the second year in a row.

The semi-final

The build-up to the semi-final draw was nearly as tense as for the quarter-final match. With Celtic and Dunfermline in the hat, as well as the winners of the Aberdeen/Livingston replay, the permutations were many. In the event, Caley Thistle came out first and Dunfermline second – a tricky draw against the team lying fourth in the SPL. Having just beaten fifth team Motherwell, the task was not impossible. A headline after the draw on BBC Ceefax demonstrated how far Caley Thistle had come in ten seasons: 'Celtic avoid Inverness in Cup semis'. Confident Inverness fans looked forward to meeting Celtic in the final. There was no repeat of the previous year's wrangle about timing of the semi-final. Both ties were pencilled in for Easter weekend 10/11 April and the Celtic match was chosen for live Sunday TV coverage. This left Caley Thistle and Dunfermline with the prime Saturday 3pm slot.

Many games were being labelled crucial at this time, but playing St Johnstone and Clyde on March 13th and 16th respectively certainly fell into this category. While Caley Thistle were at Motherwell, St Johnstone beat Clyde 3-2 then, in midweek, both teams picked up three points in rearranged matches. This gave Clyde a six-point lead at the top over Caley Thistle, with Saints a further three points behind. Falkirk lay just one point adrift of Saints, with an extra game played. It was far from being a two-horse race.

At Perth on the 13th St Johnstone took a 2-0 lead, but a brace from Paul Ritchie in the second half set up a dramatic finish. A Barry Wilson late 'winner' was chalked off for offside – TV evidence later supported the claim that a defender was playing Wilson onside – then, in injury time, Saints' Keigan Parker scored a spectacular goal to make it 3-2. It was one fit to win any match, but for Caley Thistle it meant three league defeats in a row and a major setback to the league challenge. Clyde only took a point against Brechin but still had a seven-point lead over both Caley Thistle and St Johnstone. The home Clyde match on the 16th would certainly be crucial.

It was quite a night. Paul Ritchie scored in 35 minutes to give ICT the lead: a long ball from well into the Clyde half 40 seconds later looked harmless. It carried on the strong wind, however, and bounced over Mark Brown before finishing up in the net. This freak goal stunned the home camp, but the lead was regained when David Bingham latched onto a clearance held up in the wind and headed the second goal. Although Roy McBain's red card for hand-ball was a blow, Clyde could not take advantage. With two minutes left, Liam Keogh was brought down and Barry Wilson scored from the penalty spot to secure the points – a vital win which reduced the deficit to four points. A 1-1 draw at a windy Ayr the following Saturday was disappointing, but the conditions made it a lottery. Clyde soundly beat St Johnstone 3-1 and extended their lead to six points.

Caley Thistle's home league derby win the following week came thanks to a goal by Barry Wilson on the hour mark. It was an exciting match in front of a large crowd, although a rather smaller number turned up three days later for the meeting of the clubs in the North Cup semi-final. It was 1-1 after extra time but Caley Thistle won on penalties. After every league match Clyde and St Johnstone's results were eagerly awaited and the gaps calculated. At the end of March, Clyde were just four points ahead and Saints three points behind Caley Thistle. The visit to relegation-threatened St Mirren on 3 April was not a match to remember. Enough chances were created to win, but it ended goalless. Minds could now turn back to the cup.

On Saturday 10 April Inverness emptied for the day as fans headed for the Scottish Cup semi-final at Hampden. To reach this stage two seasons in a row was remarkable – and this time the players vowed to make up for 'freezing' last year against Dundee. There was no argument about the date this time, but there was some discussion about the venue. Pittodrie was mooted, but the dream is always to go to Hampden: Pittodrie stayed in reserve for a possible replay.

As in 2003, the squad stayed on the Friday night at the Westerwood Hotel in Cumbernauld, then it was off to Hampden. With a full squad back in training,

TREBLE CHANCE, DOUBLE TRIUMPH

John Robertson had very pleasant selection problems. Injuries in previous rounds had necessitated the blooding of youngsters, but this time the manager could turn to more experience. His choices were limited by the SFA rule that at least two outfield squad members must be under 21. The starting eleven was Mark Brown, Ross Tokely, Stuart Golabek, Bobby Mann, Stuart McCaffrey, Russell Duncan, Barry Wilson, Roy McBain, Paul Ritchie, Liam Keogh and David Bingham. The Under-21 qualifiers were substitutes Darran Thomson and David Proctor. The other substitutes were Grant Munro, Steve Hislop and goalkeeper Mike Fraser. The disappointed members of the travelling squad were Richie Hart, Darren Mackie, Craig MacMillan and David MacRae.

The crowd of 13,255 was slightly down on the previous season and the Inverness fans were outnumbered. The South Stand was, however, awash with the club colours and there was plenty of excitement in the air. Scarves, flags, hats and replica shirts by the hundred were on view and the face-painters had been busy. The match turned out to be less than a classic, but the team gave everything and at the end were running on empty. Over the piece Dunfermline had the upper hand, but the ICT defence held firm against the twin threats of Stevie Crawford and Craig Brewster for most of the match.

In 13 minutes Brewster closed in on 'Man of the Match' Mark Brown, but Stuart McCaffrey stepped in to take the ball off his feet. Stuart Golabek did the same in 21 minutes as Brewster hesitated and Brown dived to tip away a goal-bound shot from Derek Young. As the clock ticked over 45 minutes, Paul Ritchie netted his 20th goal of the season to give Caley Thistle a half-time lead. The creators were Roy McBain and David Bingham, but it was Ritchie's well-struck header that sent the fans wild. Just after the break Ritchie nearly made it 2-0 but his powerful header flew past the post. Brown made the save of the match in 57 minutes from a Crawford header which looked a certain goal. Ritchie made way for the fresh legs of Steve Hislop on the hour mark, but it was the Pars who grabbed a goal. Their sustained pressure finally paid off in 67 minutes when Brewster headed in a Darren Young cross. It was now all about holding on and substitutes David Proctor and Liam Keogh were introduced. There were a few chances on the break, but the main theme was survival. In the last period the heavy Hampden pitch finally took its toll and fatigue set in all round. It ended 1-1 and the tie went to a Pittodrie replay on 20 April. Emotions had run high amongst the Inverness fans throughout the game – from elation at the opening goal, disappointment at the equaliser and finally relief that their team held out for a replay.

Dunfermline manager Jimmy Calderwood was livid with his side's 'poor' performance: 'We are the luckiest team still to be in the competition.' John Robertson was disappointed not to have held on to the lead: 'The dream is still alive. Once we got in front we were hoping one goal was going to be enough to take us into the final. Dunfermline are a quality side and we knew they would come back at us. We defended deeper and deeper and, ultimately, their equaliser was deserved. We're happy with how we played for 60 minutes or so and we live to fight another day.'

Celtic's victory against Livingston ensured UEFA Cup qualification for the other cup finalist and thus the replay took on even more significance. Dunfermline faced a fixture pile-up and asked the SFA if the replay could be delayed by a day. The possibility of a change to Perth was also mooted. Caley Thistle would have agreed to a change of date and venue but in the end Sky TV's decision to screen the match live ended the argument. Pittodrie on the 20th was confirmed.

Before the cup replay there were two important league matches. The home game against basement club Brechin had to be postponed to the following Tuesday because of the Hampden appearance. A Barry Wilson penalty goal earned the points, but it was a poor performance. The following Saturday Queen of the South made the long trip north. Pre-match, all the talk was of John Robertson being linked to the manager's job at Hibernian. Bobby Williamson was still in post, but it was clear that he was about to leave for Plymouth. Robertson expressed interest in the position, despite his legendary status at Hearts, but it was all theoretical. While Williamson did go to Plymouth, Hibs opted to make a temporary appointment from within the club until the close season. Queens were duly dispatched 4-1, with Steve Hislop netting two goals. Clyde matched the score against Raith Rovers and the gap remained four points.

Ticket sales for the Pittodrie replay were slow for a match of this magnitude, but it was live on Sky TV and the venue and timing were not ideal. The Dunfermline fans were the ones who took real umbrage at going to Aberdeen and Inverness supporters comprised the majority of the 5728 crowd. Barry Wilson missed out with a hamstring injury and Steve Hislop took his place. Hislop's bench spot was taken by Darren Mackie. Otherwise the team matched that from Hampden. Three substitutes were used – Darran Thomson replaced the injured Russell Duncan early in the second half, Darren Mackie came on for Paul Ritchie with 15 minutes left, then David Proctor took Ross Tokely's place for the last five minutes. It turned out to be a great night. The team put on a superb performance and the supporters sang and cheered for the whole game – the only thing wrong was the final score. It all started so well when, in only the seventh minute, Ritchie gave the ICT fans something to sing about with the opening goal. Darren Young equalised for the Pars midway through the half then the match turned on three moments around the hour mark. A Hislop shot crashed off the bar, Derek Stillie somehow saved a net-bound Ritchie header. then Dunfermline took the lead through Craig Brewster. Barry Nicholson scored a captain's goal to make it 3-1 and it seemed all over. Into injury time and Mackie was brought down in the box. David Bingham scored from the penalty spot, but with no time left for any more heroics it ended 3-2. The twin dreams of a Scottish Cup final and European football were over but it was very close. John Robertson paid tribute to his team: 'Everyone to a man was magnificent. We played very well and so did they.' Dunfermline's Lee Bullen was amazed by the Inverness fans: 'Even when they were 3-1 down they went berserk.' The BBC report talked about a 'five goal thriller'.

A thrilling finale

Despite the disappointment at Pittodrie, there was a positive atmosphere at the club and a determination to fight Clyde all the way for the league title. There was no cup hangover away to Raith Rovers the following Saturday, although the good performance only earned a narrow 1-0 victory. It was enough to put real pressure on Clyde as they only managed a point at Dingwall – there were now only two points in it. It was becoming clear that the meeting of the top two clubs on 8 May would be decisive. The next day it was the final of the North Cup at Forres against Elgin City. For the first time ever, this was a battle between two SFL teams and Elgin narrowly won 1-0. The following Wednesday a high-profile advert for BT was filmed at Caledonian Stadium with 250 fans as extras and the team playing their part on the pitch. On May Day, Caley Thistle entertained Falkirk and Clyde made the difficult trip to relegation-threatened Ayr. Caley Thistle did everything but score, despite Falkirk playing for the last half-hour with ten men. The gloom was lifted somewhat when news of the 1-1 score at Ayr came through.

The trip to Broadwood on 8 May had all the atmosphere of another cup semi-final rather than a league match. A win for Clyde and they would take the title, while an Inverness victory would ensure the battle continued until the last day of the season. Crowd predictions were for an 8000 full house, including an expected influx of Partick Thistle fans anxious to see arch-rivals Clyde fail. Partick were lying bottom of the SPL and Clyde had a potential groundshare arrangement with Kilmarnock in place, should they achieve promotion. Later events were to lead to severe complications but, at the time, Partick's only chance of survival seemed to be an ICT title win and no promotion. In the event, 1500 ICT fans made a stirring spectacle in the away stand, joined by a handful from Partick. The Scottish Football League organisation was ready if matters were settled at Broadwood and Lord Macfarlane, honorary life president of Bell's parent company Diageo, was on hand to present the trophy. The important cup was in the boot of Lord Macfarlane's car. At the end of the day, there it stayed.

The atmosphere was electric and the first half was played at a frantic pace. Despite much huffing and puffing, it was goalless at half time, then Caley Thistle began to dominate. Liam Keogh gave them a valuable lead in 54 minutes from 18 yards, then a soft penalty award and an Ian Harty conversion in 72 minutes brought Clyde right back into it. The home crowd's optimism was shattered seven minutes later when ICT substitute Steve Hislop rose high to head in from a Keogh chip. Clyde produced little after that and left the field in dejected mode. The visitors were quite rightly triumphant as they moved to the top of the First Division by one point. John Robertson was very surprised at the penalty award but proud of his players: 'We asked the players before the game to be brave and positive and they've given me everything once again.' Clyde player/manager Alan Kernaghan was naturally very disappointed: 'In the cold light of day we just had too many players who didn't play to their potential and Inverness did.'

A day to remember for all Caley Thistle fans, but a job only half completed. If this was the semi-final of the First Division championship, the following week's St Johnstone match was the final. For Caley Thistle, a win was the only realistic option. Clyde were odds-on to win at Brechin – that would mean a draw would not be enough for ICT. Liam Keogh summed up the position with a classic understatement: 'We know that all we need now is to win against St Johnstone and we've won the league!' The manager said that they had come too far now not to win it: 'We have to go out and do that and I know we can. It will be very tough, but we'll be looking for the same kind of performance that we had against Clyde.' Advantage Inverness.

The climax to the season – and the decade – came on 15 May at Caledonian Stadium. At first only the stand was to be all-ticket but, as demand grew, terracing tickets were also put on sale. The interest in the game was so great that Caledonian Macbrayne altered the Ullapool/Stornoway ferry departure from 5.30 pm to 7 pm to allow Western Isles' fans time to get to Caledonian Stadium and back in one day. By 1.30 pm on the Saturday all tickets for the home end were gone and people were being turned away. The sun shone, the ground was packed, there was tension in the air and the First Division trophy was waiting in a helicopter at Braemar. It just remained for the team to make one last major effort – and they did just that. John Robertson was adamant that there was no pressure on his players: 'Pressure is what you get when you're fighting for your lives at the other end. The good thing is that we have kept it in our own hands.'

Clyde were leading Brechin 1-0 before the Inverness match even started, but this changed nothing as it had always been clear that a win was essential. It took a while to break the deadlock, but on the half-hour mark a David Bingham overhead kick fooled Saints' keeper Craig Nelson and it was 1-0. Close to half-time Keigan Parker hammered the ball past Mark Brown from long range to equalise. Seconds later, a Barry Wilson goal was chalked off for offside. In 56 minutes Wilson powered into the Saints' penalty area and was brought down by Nelson – a stonewall penalty. Despite the pressure, Wilson sent Nelson the wrong way. The title was a little closer. A male streaker joined the celebrations on the pitch and was promptly evicted with a policeman's hat strategically in place. By this time Clyde were 4-0 ahead at Brechin, but their fans were silenced as the 2-1 score reached them from the Highland capital. Any lingering worries amongst the Inverness fans disappeared when Paul Ritchie headed goal number three with 14 minutes left. Tannoy announcer Glen Campbell asked that fans stay off the pitch at the end, but it was an impossible request. The final whistle went – and once more the Inverness fans went ballistic.

The players were swamped by supporters, but it was all good humoured and the stewards gave up trying to stem the tide. The SFL helicopter landed at Culloden House Hotel and the official party was brought to the stadium in double-quick time for the presentation. The pitch was cleared, a table set up and Lord Macfarlane presented the trophy to Bobby Mann. A magic moment for the crowd and everyone involved with the club. The noise was deafening and some were moved to tears. The management team and players went off on a lap of honour and it was a long time before the stadium party ended.

An emotional John Robertson stated that 'everything fell in place. We're the top goalscorers in the league with the best defensive record and we never lost a game by more than one goal. We knew that Clyde had gone ahead before we started but that only helped us. The honesty we get from this team is remarkable. We held our nerve and it was a fitting way to claim the title.' Proud chairman Ken Mackie took a turn holding the trophy aloft and praised the management team: 'John Robertson and Donald Park took over from Steve Paterson and to have taken us to this level in the short period of time they have been here is fantastic. You can see they have done a great job. It is the greatest thing ever for Caley Thistle and it is a marvellous occasion for the city of Inverness.' Steve Paterson and Duncan Shearer sent a message of congratulations: 'We are both delighted that Caley Thistle won the championship. We still have lots of friends at Caledonian Stadium and the players, along with John and Donald, deserve full credit for taking the Club, hopefully, into the SPL.' Inverness Provost Bill Smith watched the game and was full of praise for the team's achievement. He confirmed that the city would mark the occasion with some form of civic recognition. The cup and the players moved on to the Supporters' Club end-of-season party at the Chieftain Hotel – the celebrations continued well into the night.

The only sad note was the certainty of losing three key players. Charlie Christie had announced his retirement from the playing side some weeks earlier but is to remain behind-the-scenes at the club. Paul Ritchie let it be known that he would not be seeking a new contract as he wanted to go part-time and concentrate on an accountancy career. With 63 goals in three seasons, he will be a hard act to follow – Caley Thistle's loss is Brechin's gain. Ritchie said that he could not ask for more: 'To score the clinching goal capped a remarkable season for me and the Club. The players deserve to be in the Premier League and they're good enough to be.' The third departure was captain Bobby Mann, who had concluded a pre-contract agreement with his home-town team Dundee. It was an offer he could not refuse. His strength and excellent timing had played a crucial part in the club's rise to the top and he will also be very difficult to replace. Mann reflected on the day's events: 'I've had five great years here with the Celtic games, two Scottish Cup semi-finals and now this. Getting to the SPL was the big target. We have shown we are the best team in the league during the season and we can take great pride.'

When Caledonian Stadium opened in November 1996, then chairman Dougie McGilvray was convinced that the club would win promotion to the Premier League within 10 years. During a radio interview he struck a bet with BBC Scotland 'Off the Ball' presenter Tam Cowan – £500 to a pie. McGilvray promised to double the money and donate it to charity. It was now time to collect.

Winning the First Division title was by far the greatest achievement in the club's league history and the 70 points gathered beat the previous record by five. The championship success earned John Robertson the Bell's First Division 'Manager of the Year' title. 92 goals were scored in 47 games and 41 conceded. The goals were shared by 14 players with one own-goal. Paul Ritchie was top scorer with 23 goals and was named Bell's 'Player of the Year'. Mark Brown played in all 47 games and was the only ever-present. Brown was voted both Supporters' 'Player of the Year' and 'Players' Player of the Year'. He also shared the 'Matchday Programme Player of the Year' award with Stuart McCaffrey.

Now a major decision had to be made. It had always been known that Caledonian Stadium could not be brought up to SPL standards without massive investment. The only possibility was a groundshare and Pittodrie was the nearest SPL ground. At first this was thought to be totally impractical, but the euphoria of the championship victory forced a rethink. The talking and financial projections started in earnest. *The Daily Record* headline said it all: 'Caley at the Crossroads.'

CHAPTER 14

SPL – TO BE OR NOT TO BE?

(photo courtesy of the Press & Journal)

Chairman Ken Mackie celebrates the groundshare agreement with Aberdeen

In August 1994, the road to the top was clear. Scottish Football was in the hands of two organisations – the SFA governed the game and the SFL ran the league system. The league had just been revamped into four divisions of 10 – the Premier, First, Second and Third Divisions – and, as a new entrant, Caley Thistle started in the Third. Given success on the field it was possible to progress directly up the league ladder to the Premier Division. A new stadium was essential and its capacity would need to be increased if, as was hoped, crowds increased over the years. The creation of the breakaway Scottish Premier League in 1998, and the arrival of a new rulebook, changed all that. Potential difficulties over seating capacity seemed remote as ICT were in the Second Division at the time, but they were to loom large in 2004. As the seasons passed, economic assessments prevented expansion at Caledonian Stadium to meet the SPL's 10,000-seat requirement. When the First Division title was won on the final day of the 2003-4 season the only way to gain promotion to the Bank of Scotland Premierleague was a groundshare with an SPL club. Initial discussions had taken place with Aberdeen FC before the end of the season and a legally binding agreement was reached with Aberdeen by late May. Promotion then hinged on a vote by the 12 SPL clubs at their General Meeting on 1 June. SPL criteria had been fully met and there appeared to be no further obstacles in the way – but it was not to prove that simple. Eight positive votes were required, but 'No' votes or abstentions by five clubs denied ICT promotion. The result of the ballot started a furious backlash against the obvious unfairness. Relegation candidates Partick Thistle threatened legal action if the decision was reversed and the media-dubbed 'Thistlegate' row dominated the sporting press for weeks. For a while things changed on a daily basis and the whole messy affair only ended after a second ballot at an SPL General Meeting held on 22 June and the subsequent dismissal of a Partick Thistle appeal by the SFA on 8 July.

The SPL was formed on 1 August 1998 as a result of a split from the SFL by the ten Premier Division clubs and Scottish football now had three governing bodies – the SFA, SPL and SFL. In January 1990, the report by Lord Justice Taylor into the April 1989 Hillsborough disaster was published. It recommended all-seater stadia at 'all matches at grounds in the first and second divisions of the Football League, the Premier Division of the Scottish League, and at national stadia, subject to a reasonable extension of time in the case of a club promoted to the second division of the Football League or the Premier Division of the Scottish Football League.' Until June 2004, SPL rules stated that grounds should be all-seated and have a minimum of 10,000 covered seats. This figure came from the Safety of Sports Grounds Act 1975 which followed the Wheatley inquiry into the 1971 Ibrox disaster. The connection in the Taylor Report between the all-seater requirement and the 10,000 minimum is one for the lawyers, but Taylor did not appear to preclude smaller all-seater stadia. It is interesting to note Taylor's recommendation of 'a reasonable extension of time in the case of a club promoted to the second division of the Football League or the Premier Division of the Scottish Football League' – if the SPL had adopted this, then many of the future arguments could have been avoided. Taylor's reference to groundsharing is also of interest in the light of future events.

A glass ceiling

The SPL's seating requirement became a glass ceiling for SFL clubs, with Falkirk the first victims. In 1999-2000 they came third in the First Division and, with the SPL about to be increased to twelve, Falkirk should have played bottom-club Aberdeen in a play-off. Brockville was sub-standard and Aberdeen were spared possible embarrassment. It was a similar story at the end of 2002-3 when, after winning the championship (and commissioning a new stadium), Falkirk agreed a groundshare at Airdrie with the prospective owners of the Shyberry Excelsior Stadium. The future of SPL basement team Motherwell was bound up in these events: the SFL had to issue a provisional fixture list with nine teams plus 'Team X'. The SPL rejected Falkirk's application, and an appeal to the SFA Appeals Committee also failed. Falkirk conceded defeat on 2 July but announced that a complaint would be made to the Office of Fair Trading. They had considered further formal legal action, but felt it better to remove the uncertainty with the new season rapidly approaching.

The provision of a 10,000-seat stadium in Inverness has been the subject of much discussion over the years with the best hope always having been seen as supermarket giant Walmart-Asda's interest in the East Longman site. Speculation began seriously in December 2001 and eventually Asda confirmed an interest in moving to Inverness, but emphasised that they were looking at various options. Even if the club did want to move, and compensation was sufficient to provide a new stadium, a suitable alternative location was a major problem. There was also the fact that the East Longman site is held on a long-term lease from the Inverness Common Good Fund, and thus the Highland Council would be a major player in any discussions.

The possible sale of the supermarket chain Safeway led to a cooling of Asda's interest in the Longman site. Asda were one possible purchaser of the Safeway brand, and this would have given them a two-store presence in Inverness. In late September 2003 a Competition Commission ruling led to the English company Morrisons winning the battle for the acquisition of Safeway and thus expanding into Scotland. Asda almost immediately revived their plans for the Caledonian Stadium site but, with no obvious alternative, it was still all academic. In the run up to Xmas 2003, the Asda saga took a new turn when they approached Highland Council with a £17.6m offer to buy land between the stadium and the nearby Kessock Bridge. The football club would have gained a new stand as compensation for the loss of car parking, but the council rejected the offer, citing the major problem of traffic flow. The existing roundabout at the south side of the bridge could not have coped with the massive increase in traffic, and expensive diversions would have been required.

The issue of SPL criteria became a major topic of discussion during 2003-4 once promotion became a distinct possibility. At the AGM on 29 October chairman Ken Mackie announced that steps were being taken to erect temporary stands should promotion to the SPL be achieved. He told shareholders that costings had been carried out and it would be financially viable: 'We're proposing to put forward a planning application to find out the council's view. It's the same type of seating used at the Open golf championship and the Edinburgh Tattoo. We did look at this last season and had discussions with the SPL – the outcome was that they did not mind if it was permanent or temporary provided there was a safety certificate for 10,000 seats.'

A new hurdle

The seating requirement was well known but in December 2003 the SPL added a new hurdle. They announced that any team seeking promotion must have undersoil heating installed before their application could be accepted. Although SPL chairman Lex Gold stated that this requirement had been passed at an SPL meeting in July, SFL clubs claimed that this was the first they had heard of it. Caley Thistle's solution to the seating problem seemed to pave the way for possible promotion, but further investment would now be required. With the First Division set to go to the wire, no club could realistically go to this expense in time. Potentially the pitches of all those in contention would need to be dug up weeks before the end of the season. The fact that three out of twelve SPL clubs – Dundee and Motherwell (two clubs in administration) and Dunfermline – did not have undersoil heating was apparently irrelevant. The Fife side were taking part in a UEFA experiment utilising an artificial surface and, as John Robertson correctly pointed out, they did not have soil to heat! Inverness East, Nairn and Lochaber MP David Stewart (a loyal Caley Thistle supporter) reported the SPL to the Office of Fair Trading: 'It is difficult not to suspect this as another device aimed at ensuring no SPL side is relegated, yet again.' In late January it emerged that, if promotion was achieved, one option being considered by the board was a groundshare at Perth or Aberdeen. Ken Mackie confirmed that it was the subject of discussion but far down the line of possibilities. The economic viability was doubted by many and the travelling involved was seen as impractical. Fans used the website's message boards to make their disapproval known and the issue seemed to be dead. A few months later it would be resurrected and lead to a national debate.

Each of the promotion contenders had their own agenda. St Johnstone's McDiarmid Park was already SPL-friendly and Falkirk's new stadium at Westfield was well under way. Clyde's Broadwood Stadium needed a fourth stand, and now undersoil heating, to meet the SPL's entry requirements. Work on the new fourth stand at Broadwood began in the spring, but quickly stopped because of a dispute over non-payment of rent to their North Lanarkshire Council landlords. Caley Thistle's preferred solution was still temporary stands. Plans were well under way, with a projected completion date of mid July. A planning application for three structures was submitted and the SPL had already indicated that this type of seating would be acceptable. Timing was now the vital issue, but the deadline for SPL compliance was an impossible one. It was clearly not prudent financial management to put stands and undersoil heating in place before the league was settled, but SPL rules insisted that this had to be completed before 31 March. Catch 22! The club's solution was to ask the SPL for a time extension until matters were clearer – this was submitted to an SPL meeting on 30 March. Clyde sought a similar extension, but both were refused. Nobody in Scottish football was surprised to see the exclusive club close ranks to repel intruders – things could have been so different if Taylor's recommendation of 'a reasonable extension of time' had been adopted. Caley Thistle had a plan that was perfectly acceptable in every way but time. It is hard to understand why a short delay could not have been approved.

At the eleventh hour Clyde came up with an alternative plan to groundshare at Kilmarnock which took everyone by surprise. The SPL meeting had also to consider a Dundee/Dundee United proposal to share a new ground, Hearts' suggested move to Murrayfield and a Falkirk plan to temporarily decamp to Dunfermline. All these possibilities were approved and this set the scene for Caley Thistle to consider something similar. At the time groundshare was not thought to be a practical solution and thus they were left empty-handed and angry. The SPL did have a sting in the tail for Clyde and Falkirk – they must only register one ground per season, so, even if their new/upgraded homes were available earlier, they could not be used!

Chairman Ken Mackie voiced the club's dismay at the SPL's refusal: 'This is pure economics. There is little point in us having a 10,000 seat stadium in this tight league and not being promoted.' MP David Stewart voiced the feelings of many supporters: 'The bureaucrats have managed to do what many opposing teams have failed to do – beat Caley Thistle. I am very disappointed that these artificial rules have been so strongly applied. The irony is that if they win the semi-final of the Scottish Cup they could be in the UEFA Cup so it would be quite in order to play Barcelona but not Partick Thistle.' Fans made their views known with a chant of 'SPL you're having a laugh' – not the first time this had been heard, but it was definitely growing louder. The letters SPL were irreverently said by many to stand for the 'Self-Preservation League'.

The groundshare debate

The focus in Inverness was now about winning the league rather than stepping up to the SPL, but the board felt it prudent to hold a straw poll on the question of a groundshare at Aberdeen. Voting forms were issued via the web site and to the majority of fans purchasing Scottish Cup semi-final tickets, with a closing date of 17 April. On 26 April it was announced that the poll had resulted in a 56%/44% vote in favour. Many claimed that the vote was not truly representative. The board made it clear that they had only been looking for an indication of opinion.

With Clyde in top spot for most of 2004, promotion plans seemed academic – but all that changed on 8 May. The win at Clyde opened the door to the championship and started an intense debate on the practicalities of a temporary move to Pittodrie. A week later the title was won on a day of high drama and excitement at Caledonian Stadium. The dilemma was now real. With the SPL having already sanctioned other share proposals, the principle had been established. Twenty-four hours after the promotion party, SPL chairman Lex Gold made an unexpected statement. Much criticism had been levelled at his organisation for its strict entry criteria, but he always argued that it was the Taylor report that set the standards. Others argued that the SPL were being selective in their interpretation of Taylor's recommendations. Gold announced that a meeting would take place the next day with representatives of the SFA and SFL specifically to discuss a relaxation of the much-maligned criteria. Any change would not, however, affect the current situation – it would come in at the beginning of 2005-6.

To ensure that matters were aired properly, the board quickly arranged three consultative meetings for the following Monday, Tuesday and Wednesday. The club's preferred groundshare partner had to be intimated to the SPL by Monday 17th, so Aberdeen was selected by the board in advance of the first meeting. Dundee United and Dundee emerged later as options, but too late for consideration. Shareholders met first, followed by those in the Members' and Supporters' Clubs. The final meeting was open to all fans. The views of the players and management team were already known – the vote from the dressing room was for SPL football. There was one unexpected issue to consider. It had been thought that cup-ties could be played in Inverness but the SFA stated that, if Pittodrie was registered as the club's official ground for a season, then all competitive matches had to be played there. A dispensation was later granted to allow cup matches to be played in Inverness. There was also the threat of a legal challenge by First Division-bound Partick Thistle. They felt that Caley Thistle should not be allowed to consider a groundshare as they had not intimated their intention before the meeting on 30 March.

The Kingsmills Suite at the stadium was packed every night as the chairman set out the board's position. He first set out the problem: 'Groundshare in Aberdeen: to be, or not to be: that is the question.' Five main issues were highlighted, although it was recognised that there were many more: stay and stagnate; move and reduce the fan base; sponsorship losses;

travel costs; and plan for next year. The board had calculated best and worst scenarios, ranging from a loss for the year of £350,000 to a profit of £300,000. Television money was a great unknown, as the SPL had signed a new deal with Irish company Setanta and full information was hard to obtain. The board made this proposal: 'We the Board propose that the long term viability of the Club would be best served with a move to Aberdeen for one season and trust you will support us in this momentous decision for Inverness and all connected with the Club.'

In an important statement, former chairman David Sutherland pledged the weight of major shareholders Tulloch behind the move and gave assurances that permanent modular seating could be put in place in time for the start of 2005-6. The proposal to open negotiations with Aberdeen met with almost unanimous approval. The message to the Board was 'go for it!' As negotiations began it was clear that the true cost would be more than first estimated. Time was of the essence, as a deal had to be completed by 28 May in advance of the vital SPL meeting on 1 June. For a week the board burned the midnight oil to prepare financial projections, negotiate with Aberdeen and discuss all aspects of a season in transit.

Finally all was ready and, at a press conference on Thursday 27 May, Ken Mackie announced that a deal with Aberdeen had been concluded: 'This is an historic step and we're very pleased that a great deal of work behind the scenes has achieved a solution acceptable to both ourselves and Aberdeen FC. We look forward to the SPL meeting on Tuesday now being able to formally admit us to play at the highest level in August, only 10 years from the formation of our club. Our supporters, shareholders and sponsors have been virtually unanimous in their call for us to take up our SPL place. We did not leap in to this, we held our consultations, we let people know the position. The people who matter most to this club wanted us to do this – and now that we have taken this major step, we look for their continued support next season. Our financial projections have been made but much will hinge on the level of attendances at ICT home games at Pittodrie. We need our fans next season more than ever. Without decent income at the turnstiles, we would be stretched financially.'

'The board is unanimous in its decision to sign the agreement and I'm grateful to those who have worked tirelessly in the past two weeks to make this happen. Our lawyers have worked overnight to put in place an arrangement for which there is no precedent at this level. Aberdeen FC, while naturally representing their own interests, have been extremely cordial and constructive and we hope that our one year's tenancy may reinforce a relationship which can be of ongoing mutual benefit in the years ahead.'

The chairman was under no illusions about the way ahead: 'There will be all sorts of logistical difficulties for us over the 2004-5 season. We are taking a leap of faith in groundsharing to play SPL football. We dearly wish we could have been playing at home, but we accept the rules. It is crucially important that our Aberdeen adventure does not leave the club with a level of debt that is unsustainable. We have put in phenomenal work on the costings and we think that our budget is sustainable, given the support in match attendances.'

Director of football Graeme Bennett admitted that a minority on the club's six-man board had their doubts, but he believed it to be worth the gamble as they might never get another chance of promotion: 'It has been a difficult time for the club, but I know the support of the fans will be vital to us next season should the SPL approve the groundshare agreement at the monthly meeting on 1 June.' Aberdeen chief executive Keith Wyness said: 'We believe this agreement assists both clubs whilst protecting the position of Aberdeen Football Club. This agreement is a first for Scottish football and we look forward to a season of collaboration which will benefit both clubs.' The arrangement was notified to the SPL the next day and their decision was awaited with bated breath. As soon as the groundshare was confirmed, Partick renewed their threat to take legal action. Chairman Tom Hughes vowed that they would remain in the SPL and Caley Thistle would not be promoted. The vote on 1 June would apparently decide the matter: eight votes in favour were needed for SPL football to be a reality.

The SPL vote

Nothing was being taken for granted, but it seemed inconceivable that SPL entry could be denied. A binding groundshare agreement was in force, the SPL executive had seen the documentation (and assisted in its preparation) and all was in place in advance of the 1 June meeting at Hampden. The main fear was that Partick would go to court if ICT won the day. Many could not understand why a vote was even required and assumed it was just a formality. There were major concerns about going to Aberdeen, but the only alternative was to stay in the SFL – to make progress, a year of pain was necessary. The scene was set for admission to the SPL.

GOING BALLISTIC!

To say that the result of the vote was a complete surprise would be a massive understatement – there was absolute shock. Seven votes were cast in favour of the motion to admit Caley Thistle, one short of the required eight. There had been rumours leading up to the vote that Partick's behind-the-scenes lobbying had met with some success but it seemed unlikely that four clubs (as well as Partick) would vote 'No'. As it turned out there were three 'No' votes and two abstentions – by a twist of the rules the abstentions were effectively 'No' votes.

The events of 1 June amazed the football world and the story dominated the media for days – the sympathies of most observers were with the Inverness side and the perceived injustice. In a statement to the BBC Ken Mackie said: 'We will be appealing. I don't know the composition of the voting at all - all I know is that there were seven positive votes and I would like to say thank you to the clubs who voted in our favour. It is disappointing because we felt we had a good case and met all the criteria the SPL was asking for, so we thought we would move forward. But we were only one vote away, so we have to be positive and say it was close.' Partick co-manager Gerry Britton was understandably pleased: 'We'll see what happens, I wouldn't be surprised if there were a few more twists and turns but it is obviously great news so far for everyone involved with the club.'

A major campaign began in the press to determine who voted which way – the ballot was a secret one but gradually the truth emerged. The result was at first thought to have been decided by the central belt teams voting with Partick, but Rangers and Celtic both confirmed they had voted 'Yes', after taking legal advice, and the other positive votes turned out to be Aberdeen, Hibs, Hearts, Motherwell and Kilmarnock. Partick, Dundee and Dunfermline voted against and the abstentions were Dundee United and Livingston. Dundee United chairman Eddie Thompson claimed later that he understood 31 March was the deadline for intimating a groundshare but crucially he was to change this view a week later. Livingston's ownership was about to change hands and the administrator apparently felt he could not commit the new owners either way.

Reaction to the ongoing farce came from many directions. The *Scotsman* editorial on 2 June said: 'At the end of the day, as they say in football, you get what you deserve... at the end of this particular day, it is the SPL members who have got what they deserve – ridicule, and a competition with neither credibility nor respect.' Local MP David Stewart described it as a 'sad day for Scottish football. This decision by the SPL is a slap in the face not just to north football, but to Scottish football. It makes a mockery of the game to have no promotion or relegation for the second year running. The First Division is harder to escape from than Alcatraz.' John Robertson was devastated: 'It is a very, very sad day for Scottish football. We are a young club coming through and could have brought so much to the game at the top level.' Aberdeen Chief Executive Keith Wyness said: 'You really have to shake your head at the SPL sometimes.' Hearts' Chairman Chris Robinson was equally surprised: 'You would need to ask the clubs why they voted like that, but it's fair to speculate that they voted in self interest.'

The SPL's letter confirming the ballot result reached the Club on 3 June. Ken Mackie said: 'We have this morning received the SPL's letter and responded by notifying the SFA that we are appealing. We have been greatly encouraged by the tremendous national support we're receiving from ordinary fans, by calls, letters and e-mails. There is clearly a massive perception of injustice.' On 3 June, during First Minister's Questions in the Scottish Parliament, Jack McConnell was asked by Ross, Skye and Inverness West MSP John Farquhar Munro: 'Does the First Minister consider it appropriate that existing members of the SPL should have control of the promotion of teams from the lower divisions and will he be prepared to make representations to the Scottish Football Association to rectify this absurd and unfair situation?' Mr McConnell said the rules were a matter for the SPL as a private sporting association and added 'Where I come from, and in the football that I have always watched, the team that wins the league goes up and the team that loses the league goes down. Somehow, somewhere, somebody has to start to recognise that.'

On the evening of 3 June news broke that Hibs and Hearts had jointly agreed to seek a further General Meeting of the SPL to revisit the matter. The rules state that any two clubs can call such a meeting with 14 days notice, and it was arranged for 22 June. Caley Thistle's appeal against the original decision was also due to be heard by the SFA Appeals Committee around the same time. After the new poll was announced Partick objected and stated their intention to seek legal advice. With the 2004-5 fixture list due to be issued on 24 June, there was a very real prospect of Scottish football being thrown into complete disarray. Partick did, however, offer to accept relegation if the SPL reimbursed the £1m cost of the stand they had completed in 2002. They also suggested that ICT be granted a waiver to allow Caledonian Stadium to be used for SPL matches. Later they withdrew the £1m demand but offered to vote in favour of a 13-team SPL as long as they were not relegated.

Any doubts regarding ICT's compliance with SPL rules were dispelled in a BBC Radio Scotland interview with SPL Secretary Iain Blair on Sunday 6 June. He stated that: 'If their agreement with Aberdeen to share at Pittodrie is acceptable to the clubs then they meet the necessary criteria.' He was asked by interviewer Kenny Macintyre about the 31 March deadline: 'The 31st of March deadline applies to the stadium and Inverness Caledonian Thistle are proposing a groundshare at Pittodrie. Now at the 31st March Pittodrie clearly met the SPL criteria and continues to meet the SPL criteria... What then becomes important is whether the agreement between Inverness and Aberdeen is acceptable to the clubs in General Meeting... I certainly wrote to the clubs in the First Division and I made it clear to them that in terms of the stadium the 31st of March deadline did apply and that any request for any waiver or period of grace in terms of the stadium would have to be able to be considered by the clubs before the 31st March. That isn't the case for a groundsharing agreement. There is no specific deadline for a groundsharing agreement.'

Partick object

Iain Blair's decisive comments seemed to settle the legality of ICT's actions once and for all but, not surprisingly, Partick did not accept that. After taking legal advice they decided to attempt to stop the second vote taking place. The Inverness side entered into talks with SPL clubs: it quickly became clear that attitudes were changing. The imminent takeover of Livingston by Pearse Flynn led to a pledge by the new owner that he would vote in favour of ICT at the second vote. Flynn was not due to take control of football matters until 1 July so the club's representative at the 22 June vote would be the administrator – despite this complication, their vote was pledged to Inverness. Dundee United's Eddie Thompson met with Ken Mackie on 8 June and pledged to vote 'Yes' at the second vote on 22 June. Thompson also sportingly proposed another vote to allow a dispensation for the club to stay in Inverness, subject to speedy ground improvements, and Dunfermline agreed to support this proposal. Thompson was firmly of the view that ICT's 'community role is severely undermined by supporters having to travel a 200-mile round trip to support their club'.

The 1 June SPL meeting had agreed to reduce the seating requirement to 6,000 from the start of 2005-6, but this change went almost unnoticed amidst the fury created by the promotion vote. Dundee United and Dunfermline proposed that this change be brought forward to the start of 2004-5 and ICT be given reasonable time to comply. Thompson's about-turn was explained in a statement on the United website: 'We have received confirmation from the SPL lawyer that the deadline of March 31 does not apply to groundsharing where the ground to be shared is already compliant with the SPL stadium criteria. This could be construed by some people as "flying in the face" of precedents already set but we have no wish to return any further to that question. Instead we would like to move on... it was clear from the meeting [with Ken Mackie] that ICT have done everything in good faith and have carried out all the requirements as set down to them by the SPL authorities.' Dundee chief executive Peter Marr expressed his club's belief that the groundshare did not sufficiently look after the welfare of the fans.

The doubts surrounding SPL entry were causing havoc with planning on all fronts. Players could not be signed, season tickets could not be sold, hospitality packages could not be marketed and the entire club organisation was in limbo. If the Aberdeen groundshare was to go ahead there would be hundreds of issues to be resolved – and the start of the new season was looming. Clyde stepped into the picture on 9 June with a bold proposal to solve the dispute – expand the SPL immediately to 14 or 16 clubs. This met with little support and was not pursued. On 11 June the SPL held a press conference to defend their handling of the affair and to confirm what they had advised the clubs. It was pointed out that a letter sent to SFL clubs requested groundsharing proposals by 31 March but this was not a deadline. SPL chairman Lex Gold also denied that there had been ambiguity over the 1 June vote. Hamilton secretary Scott Struthers came up with his solution to the wrangle – an SPL of thirteen teams. Not surprisingly, this suggestion was immediately rejected.

There was a brief lull in hostilities as everybody awaited the new vote on 22 June and the SFA appeal on the first vote which was due to take place shortly thereafter. Euro 2004 took over the football headlines, but 'Thistlegate' returned to prominence on 17 June, when Partick announced their intention to seek an interim interdict to prevent the second SPL vote. On the same day ICT chairman Ken Mackie announced that £1m funding was in place to provide 6000 seats at Caledonian Stadium and install undersoil heating, thanks to a proposed £400,000 loan from Highland Council, matching funding from Tulloch and a contribution from the football club. Installation could be achieved in 12 weeks if Dundee United's new proposal found favour.

The Partick court case took place the next day when David Sellar QC appeared at the Court of Session on their behalf seeking an interim interdict from Lord Brodie. The hearing was continued to Monday 21 June – one day before the second vote was due to take place. Representations were made to Lord Brodie on behalf of ICT and the SPL, and the matter was held over until the next morning. Everything happened very quickly on 22 June as, shortly before the Hampden meeting, Lord Brodie refused the interdict, the second vote took place and the Hearts/Hibs motion was approved 10 to 2. It was confirmed later that Dundee and Partick had voted against. Caley Thistle had won the day: the end of the whole sorry affair was finally in sight. The champagne flowed in Inverness and Partick chairman Tom Hughes indicated that his club would accept the decision: 'Realistically we must now attempt to bring some certainty to the club in football terms. I will discuss the position with Gerry (Britton), Derek (Whyte) and the Board but it seems sensible now to prepare for the First Division.' There was no need for the appeal to the SFA on the 1 June vote and SPL planning could start in earnest and with great speed. The 22 June SPL meeting also formally ratified the change in stadia criteria from 10,000 to 6000 covered seats and announced that, in future, a new five-man board would make decisions regarding the application of membership criteria rules. Lex Gold said: 'This has been a truly difficult time for Scottish football. These new rules aim to ensure that we do not have a repeat of these events. A huge step forward has been taken.'

This seemed to draw a line under the matter – but Partick had other ideas. Their board did not share the views of Tom Hughes, and a meeting two days later resulted in a statement that 'The Board of Partick Thistle FC Ltd, having given the matter further detailed consideration, unanimously decided to exercise its right of appeal to the Scottish Football Association... PTFC has consistently argued that this matter ought to be determined by the SFA, the ultimate arbiter in the Scottish game, and it would, therefore, have been illogical to take any other decision.' This was obviously a further unwanted twist in the saga but, with time marching on, the SPL and Caley Thistle proceeded as if the matter was over.

On 24 June (the same day that Partick announced their intention to appeal), the SPL fixture list was issued with Inverness Caledonian Thistle's name firmly in place. There were problems with both Aberdeen and ICT listed at home on three Saturdays, but the SPL insisted that this was deliberate and it was up to the clubs to agree alternative dates. Ken Mackie announced on the same day that, after talks with Eddie Thompson, the Dundee United/Dunfermline motion for a stadium dispensation would not be pursued and the club would go ahead with its Aberdeen plans. Soundings from other SPL clubs had revealed little support for the idea and it seemed best to move on.

Partick duly submitted their appeal on 29 June. A meeting of the SFA Appeals Committee was scheduled for 8 July. In the interim, Caley Thistle were technically not in the SPL but had to prepare as if they were – to wait until after 8 July would have been meant an impossible timetable on both the playing and administrative fronts. The official position was noted on Partick's website: '... In the meantime the SFA have "Set Aside" the original decision taken on 22nd June, which means that, as of now, Partick Thistle are back in the SPL.'

The three-man SFA Appeals Committee met at Hampden on the evening of 8 July under the chairmanship of Lord McLean and, after over three hours, found against Partick. SFA Chief Executive David Taylor revealed the decision: 'The Appeals Committee has decided that Partick Thistle have no grounds of appeal in terms of their submissions under Article 133.1 of the SFA Constitution. The appeal therefore fails.' Article 133.1 states that 'A player, official, referee, club, league or association has the right to appeal to the Appeals Committee against such a decision of a club or any recognised football body which is imposed upon such a person or body.' The Committee concluded that the decision of 22 June was not a decision 'imposed' on Partick. After contemplation overnight, a Partick press release put an end to the long drawn-out affair: 'The legal steps taken by this Club were always with a tacit acceptance that the Scottish Football Association was the ultimate authority in Scottish football and with the aim of achieving an independent interpretation of Rule A2.3.1 of the Rules of the Scottish Premier League. The Board now accepts that this will not be possible. Although there are other legal options available these would be time consuming and incur further expense. First and foremost we are a football club and all our energies will now be channelled in that direction.' So, on 9 July, the curtain came down on Partick's hopes and removed all doubts surrounding Caley Thistle's SPL membership. The saga could now pass into history and the lessons learned would hopefully ensure that, with SPL rules amended, nothing similar ever happened again. Finally everyone could move on with some certainty.

The story of Inverness Caledonian Thistle started with a vote to admit two new clubs to the Scottish Football League and the trauma of a fraught merger. The first decade came to a close with two SPL ballots and high drama which eventually took them into the Scottish Premier League. It has been an amazing adventure and a tribute to all those who made it possible. The directors and supporters of Caledonian and Thistle took a major step to unite their resources and create something special. Sponsors, shareholders and volunteers invested their time and money to further the cause. Four chairmen of the unified club carried the burden of merger battles, financial challenges and courageous decisions to ensure survival and lead the way into the SPL. Three managers gathered together players capable of taking on the best in Scotland and winning. Legions of supporters took the team to their hearts and were rewarded with progress through the ranks that few would have believed possible. At the top of the list must go the 100 squad players who have worn the club badge with pride and passion – others provided the framework, but the players worked their socks and boots off to take Inverness Caledonian Thistle to the First Division championship and the SPL.

With the trauma of 'Thistlegate' positively resolved, it was time to move forward. The immediate future was secure, but there was a great deal of work ahead. John Robertson's attempts to strengthen the squad had been hampered by uncertainty but now he could offer potential new players top-level football. The long delay had taken its toll on everyone and arguably there had been no real close season – just 24 hours after the conclusion of the promotion saga, the second decade of football started with an away friendly at Brora. The new season and the SPL adventure was only a month away. The prime aim of 2004-5 would be SPL survival whilst Caledonian Stadium was being upgraded in time for the start of 2005-6. The pain of the Thistle and Caledonian merger led to the long-term gain of reaching the Scottish Football League. Membership of the SPL was finally achieved after ten years of success on the field and eight weeks of political drama. Hopefully, the short-term pain of a season's travel on the A96 can lead to the long-term gain of a secure place in the Scottish Premier League. Inverness and the Highlands deserve nothing less.

APPENDIX A MATCH RESULTS
1994-5

DATE	OPPONENTS	H/A	MATCH TYPE	LGE DIV	CUP RD	SCORE	SCORERS & NOTES
20-Jul-94	Combined Services XI	Kin	Friendly			2-0	Hercher & Hardie
22-Jul-94	Golspie Sutherland	A	Friendly			5-1	
30-Jul-94	St Mirren	H	Friendly			0-3	
3-Aug-94	Bolton	H	Friendly			0-2	
6-Aug-94	Brechin City	H	Friendly			0-0	
9-Aug-94	East Stirling	A	CCC		I	2-0	Robertson, Hercher
13-Aug-94	Arbroath	H	League	3		5-2	Hercher 3, McKenzie, Robertson
17-Aug-94	Dundee	A	CCC		2	0-3	
20-Aug-94	Queen's Park	H	League	3		0-4	
27-Aug-94	Ross County	A	League	3		3-1	MacLeod og, Somerville og, Robertson
3-Sep-94	Albion Rovers	A	League	3		1-0	MacMillan
10-Sep-94	Forfar Athletic	H	League	3		3-1	Bennett 2, McKenzie
17-Sep-94	Celtic	H	Friendly			1-4	Smart
24-Sep-94	Alloa Athletic	A	League	3		1-1	Scott
28-Sep-94	Dundee	H	B & Q Cup		2	1-1 aet	DMacDonald - Dundee 4-3 penalties
1-Oct-94	East Stirling	H	League	3		3-3	Noble pen, McAllister, Robertson
8-Oct-94	Cowdenbeath	H	League	3		0-3	
15-Oct-94	Montrose	A	League	3		1-3	MacMillan
19-Oct-94	Fort William	H	Inverness Cup		I	2-0	McCraw, Bennett
22-Oct-94	Arbroath	A	League	3		2-1	McCraw 2
26-Oct-94	Ross County	A	Inverness Cup		SF	2-0	MacMillan 2
29-Oct-94	Ross County	H	League	3		0-0	
5-Nov-94	Queen's Park	A	League	3		2-0	Robertson, McKenzie pen
9-Nov-94	Brora Rangers	H	Inverness Cup		Final	0-1	
12-Nov-94	Forfar Athletic	A	League	3		1-2	McAllister
19-Nov-94	Albion Rovers	H	League	3		2-1	Christie 2
26-Nov-94	Alloa Athletic	H	League	3		2-2	Christie, Andrew pen
3-Dec-94	East Stirling	A	League	3		0-2	
17-Dec-94	Q of the South	H	TSC		I	1-2	McAllister
26-Dec-94	Cowdenbeath	A	League	3		1-1	Andrew pen
2-Jan-95	Ross County	A	League	3		1-3	Andrew pen
14-Jan-95	Elgin City	A	North Cup		I	0-0	
14-Jan-95	Arbroath	H	League	3		1-1	Brennan
21-Jan-95	Queen's Park	A	League	3		1-4	John MacDonald
4-Feb-95	Elgin City	A	North Cup		I Replay	4-2	Hercher 2, Buchanan, Urquhart
4-Feb-95	Forfar Athletic	H	League	3		1-1	Scott
11-Feb-95	Fort William	A	North Cup		2	0-2	
11-Feb-95	Albion Rovers	A	League	3		2-1	MacMillan, Lisle
14-Feb-95	Montrose	H	League	3		0-4	
18-Feb-95	Alloa Athletic	A	League	3		0-1	
25-Feb-95	East Stirling	H	League	3		3-3	Christie 2, McKenzie
4-Mar-95	Cowdenbeath	H	League	3		3-1	McAllister, MacMillan, Mitchell
11-Mar-95	Montrose	A	League	3		1-0	Robertson
18-Mar-95	Forfar Athletic	A	League	3		1-4	Scott pen
1-Apr-95	East Stirling	A	League	3		0-1	
8-Apr-95	Alloa Athletic	H	League	3		0-1	
11-Apr-95	Albion Rovers	H	League	3		0-2	
15-Apr-95	Cowdenbeath	A	League	3		3-1	Bennett, Scott, Hercher
17-Apr-95	Clachnacuddin	A	ICCC			3-1 aet	Lisle, Bennett & MacMillan
22-Apr-95	Montrose	H	League	3		0-3	
29-Apr-95	Arbroath	A	League	3		0-2	
6-May-95	Ross County	H	League	3		3-0	MacMillan, Hercher, Christie
9-May-95	Highland Lge Select	Hun	Challenge Match			2-2	MacMillan, McCraw
13-May-95	Queen's Park	H	League	3		1-1	Hercher

Hun: Huntly; Kin: RAF Kinloss; TSC: Tennent's Scottish Cup; ICCC: Inverness Courier Challenge Cup; CCC: Coca-Cola Cup;

1995-6

DATE	OPPONENTS	H/A	MATCH TYPE	LGE DIV	CUP RD	SCORE	SCORERS & NOTES
23-Jul-95	Lossiemouth	A	Friendly			2-3	Bennett, Green
26-Jul-95	Buckie Thistle	A	Friendly			5-1	Hercher 2, Green, Scott, Stewart
28-Jul-95	Motherwell	H	Friendly			2-0	Green, Lisle
29-Jul-95	Inverurie	A	Locos Tournament			1-2	Green
30-Jul-95	Huntly	Inv	Locos Tournament			0-2	
5-Aug-95	Berwick Rangers	A	CCC		1	1-1 aet	OG by Graham - Berwick 5-3 penalties
12-Aug-95	Livingston	H	League	3		0-3	
22-Aug-95	Alloa Athletic	H	LCC		1	1-2	MacMillan
26-Aug-95	Brechin City	H	League	3		1-2	Stewart
2-Sep-95	Albion Rovers	A	League	3		2-2	Hercher 2
9-Sep-95	Queen's Park	H	League	3		3-1	Stewart pen, Green, Hercher
16-Sep-95	Arbroath	A	League	3		1-2	Stewart
23-Sep-95	Alloa Athletic	A	League	3		5-0	Christie 3, Stewart 2
30-Sep-95	Ross County	H	League	3		1-1	Hercher
7-Oct-95	East Stirling	A	League	3		5-0	Brennan, Ross, Stewart 2, Mitchell
14-Oct-95	Cowdenbeath	H	League	3		3-2	Hercher, Hastings, Stewart
21-Oct-95	Albion Rovers	H	League	3		6-1	Stewart 3 (1 pen), Ross, Mitchell 2
28-Oct-95	Brechin City	A	League	3		0-0	
31-Oct-95	Nairn County	H	Inverness Cup		1	4-1	Christie 2, Hercher, OG by Rudkin
4-Nov-95	Arbroath	H	League	3		5-1	Hastings, Stewart 2, Christie 2
7-Nov-95	Forres Mechanics	A	Inverness Cup		SF	3-1	Green, Stewart, Hercher
11-Nov-95	Queen's Park	A	League	3		3-0	Stewart 2, Hercher
18-Nov-95	Ross County	A	League	3		0-2	
25-Nov-95	Alloa Athletic	H	League	3		1-1	Christie
2-Dec-95	East Stirling	H	League	3		1-1	Ross
9-Dec-95	Ross County	Gra	Inverness Cup		Final	5-2	Stewart 3, Christie, Teasdale
16-Dec-95	Cowdenbeath	A	League	3		0-0	
6-Jan-96	Livingston	H	TSC		2	3-2	Ross, Teasdale, Hercher
10-Jan-96	Elgin City	A	Friendly			1-3	
13-Jan-96	Alloa Athletic	A	League	3		2-0	Thomson, Christie
13-Jan-96	Forres Mechanics	H	North Cup		1	1-2	Lisle
17-Jan-96	Livingston	A	League	3		2-0	Christie, Teasdale
20-Jan-96	East Stirling	A	League	3		5-1	Scott, Stewart 3, Ross
23-Jan-96	Ross County	H	League	3		1-1	Stewart
27-Jan-96	East Fife	H	TSC		3	1-1	Stewart
3-Feb-96	Cowdenbeath	A	League	3		1-2	Christie
12-Feb-96	East Fife	A	TSC		3 Replay	1-1 aet	Hercher - CT 3-1 penalties
17-Feb-96	Stenhousemuir	A	TSC		4	1-0	Thomson
21-Feb-96	Arbroath	A	League	3		2-1	Stewart, Scott
24-Feb-96	Brechin City	H	League	3		0-1	
28-Feb-96	Albion Rovers	A	League	3		2-0	Stewart pen, Hercher
2-Mar-96	Livingston	A	League	3		2-2	Sinclair og, Teasdale
5-Mar-96	Queen's Park	H	League	3		1-1	Hercher
9-Mar-96	Rangers	Tan	TSC		QF	0-3	"Home" match
12-Mar-96	Alloa Athletic	H	League	3		0-0	
16-Mar-96	Ross County	A	League	3		1-2	McAllister
23-Mar-96	Arbroath	H	League	3		1-1	Hercher
30-Mar-96	Queen's Park	A	League	3		2-1	Stewart, Christie
6-Apr-96	East Stirling	H	League	3		0-3	
13-Apr-96	Cowdenbeath	H	League	3		2-0	Christie, Thomson
20-Apr-96	Albion Rovers	H	League	3		1-1	Christie
27-Apr-96	Brechin City	A	League	3		1-0	Hercher
4-May-96	Livingston	H	League	3		1-2	Stewart
8-May-96	Clachnacuddin	H	ICCC			3-1	Green 2, Hercher

Inv:Inverurie; Gra: Grant Street, Inverness; Tan: Tannadice, Dundee; CCC: Coca-Cola Cup; LCC: League Challenge Cup; TSC: Tennent's Scottish Cup; ICCC:Inverness Courier Challenge Cup

1996-7

DATE	OPPONENTS	H/A	MATCH TYPE	LGE DIV	CUP RD	SCORE	SCORERS & NOTES
20-Jul-96	Fraserburgh	Pet	Buchan Cup			3-2	Thomson 2, McLean
21-Jul-96	St Johnstone	Pet	Buchan Cup		Final	0-1	
26-Jul-96	Q of the South	H	Friendly			2-0	Thomson, Stewart
29-Jul-96	Hamilton	H	Friendly			0-0	
3-Aug-96	Clyde	A	CCC		1	0-1 aet	
10-Aug-96	Livingston	A	LCC		1	2-1	Thomson, Cherry
17-Aug-96	Cowdenbeath	H	League	3		1-3	Thomson pen
24-Aug-96	Forfar Athletic	A	League	3		1-3	Thomson pen
27-Aug-96	Stirling Albion	A	LCC		2	1-3	Stewart
31-Aug-96	Alloa Athletic	H	League	3		1-0	Teasdale
7-Sep-96	Albion Rovers	A	League	3		0-0	
14-Sep-96	East Stirling	H	League	3		2-0	Hercher, Noble
21-Sep-96	Queen's Park	H	League	3		2-2	Stewart, Christie
28-Sep-96	Ross County	A	League	3		3-1	Stewart 2, Thomson
5-Oct-96	Arbroath	H	League	3		2-0	Thomson, Stewart
12-Oct-96	Montrose	A	League	3		2-2	Stewart, Ross
19-Oct-96	Cowdenbeath	A	League	3		4-3	Thomson 2 (1 pen), Hercher, Stewart
20-Oct-96	Highland Lge Select	H	Challenge match			0-3	
26-Oct-96	Forfar Athletic	A	League	3		0-2	
2-Nov-96	East Stirling	A	League	3		0-0	
6-Nov-96	Inverness & Dist Select	H	Friendly			6-2	McLean 4, Stewart, Cherry
9-Nov-96	Albion Rovers	H	League	3		1-1	Stewart
12-Nov-96	Lossiemouth	H	Inverness Cup		1	4-2	McLean 2, Hercher, Wilson
16-Nov-96	Ross County	H	League	3		2-0	Stewart 2
23-Nov-96	Queen's Park	A	League	3		3-2	McLean, Wilson, Christie
27-Nov-96	Forres Mechanics	A	Inverness Cup		SF	3-0	Hercher 2, Addicoat
30-Nov-96	Arbroath	A	League	3		4-1	Addicoat, Wilson, Stewart, Christie
14-Dec-96	Montrose	H	League	3		2-0	Stewart, McLean
21-Dec-96	Cowdenbeath	H	League	3		2-1	Stewart 2 (1 pen)
13-Jan-97	Stranraer	A	TSC		2	1-1	McLean
15-Jan-97	Stranraer	H	TSC		2 Replay	0-0 aet	ICT won 4-3 on penalties
18-Jan-97	Arbroath	H	League	3		4-1	Hercher 2, McLean, Ross
18-Jan-97	Elgin City	A	North Cup		1	0-3	
22-Jan-97	Queen's Park	H	League	3		1-0	Stewart pen
25-Jan-97	Hamilton	H	TSC		3	1-3	Stewart
1-Feb-97	Montrose	A	League	3		2-0	McLean, Stewart pen
8-Feb-97	East Stirling	H	League	3		3-2	Stewart, Wilson, McLean
12-Feb-97	Ross County	A	League	3		3-0	McLean 2, Wilson
15-Feb-97	Albion Rovers	A	League	3		3-0	Teasdale, Tokely, Stewart
22-Feb-97	Forfar Athletic	H	League	3		1-1	Stewart
1-Mar-97	Alloa Athletic	H	League	3		3-1	Stewart 2 (1 pen), Ross
8-Mar-97	Queen's Park	A	League	3		2-1	Stewart, Tokely
11-Mar-97	Alloa Athletic	A	League	3		2-0	McLean, Noble
15-Mar-97	Ross County	H	League	3		3-0	Stewart 2, Thomson
22-Mar-97	Arbroath	A	League	3		0-0	
5-Apr-97	Montrose	H	League	3		3-2	Stewart 3
12-Apr-97	Albion Rovers	H	League	3		4-1	Thomson 2, Wilson, De-Barros
19-Apr-97	East Stirling	A	League	3		3-0	Stewart, Ross, Thomson
26-Apr-97	Cowdenbeath	A	League	3		1-2	Cherry
3-May-97	Forfar Athletic	H	League	3		0-4	
10-May-97	Alloa Athletic	A	League	3		0-1	
14-May-97	Aberdeen	H	Friendly			3-2	Stewart 3

Pet: Peterhead; CCC: Coca-Cola Cup; LCC: League Challenge Cup; TSC: Tennent's Scottish Cup

1997-8

DATE	OPPONENTS	H/A	MATCH TYPE	LGE DIV	CUP RD	SCORE	SCORERS & NOTES
19-Jul-97	Wick Academy	A	Friendly			5-0	De-Barros, Addicoat, Tokely, Wilson, Christie
20-Jul-97	Dunfermline	H	Friendly			1-3	Tokely
21-Jul-97	Lewis/Harris Select B	A	Friendly			4-0	Stewart 3, De-Barros -
22-Jul-97	Lewis/Harris Select A	A	Friendly			7-1	Teasdale 2, Stewart 2, Cherry 2, Wilson
23-Jul-97	Deveronvale	A	Friendly			2-2	Hercher, Black
25-Jul-97	Huntly	H	Friendly			3-1	Stewart, Hercher, Thomson
28-Jul-97	St Johnstone	H	A Hercher Test.			1-3	Ross
2-Aug-97	Stenhousemuir	H	CCC		1	5-1	Thomson 3 (1 pen), Christie, Wilson
6-Aug-97	Livingston	H	League	2		1-1	Thomson
9-Aug-97	Motherwell	A	CCC		2	2-2 aet	Thomson pen, Addicoat - Motherwell 4-1 penalties
13-Aug-97	Q of the South	H	LCC		1	0-2	
16-Aug-97	Brechin City	A	League	2		2-2	Thomson, Stewart
23-Aug-97	East Fife	H	League	2		0-1	
30-Aug-97	Stenhousemuir	A	League	2		2-3	Thomson pen, Addicoat
13-Sep-97	Stranraer	H	League	2		2-2	Shearer, Stewart
20-Sep-97	Q of the South	A	League	2		1-2	Wilson
27-Sep-97	Clyde	H	League	2		1-2	McCulloch
4-Oct-97	Forfar Athletic	A	League	2		1-2	Stewart
7-Oct-97	Rangers	H	Friendly			3-4	McCulloch, Stewart, Shearer
14-Oct-97	Ross County	H	Inverness Cup		Final	2-0	Cherry, Shearer - Final of 1996/97 Cup
18-Oct-97	Clydebank	H	League	2		0-0	
25-Oct-97	East Fife	A	League	2		5-1	Stewart 3, Shearer, Cherry
1-Nov-97	Brechin City	H	League	2		0-0	
8-Nov-97	Stenhousemuir	H	League	2		4-1	Thomson, Wilson, Addicoat, Stewart
15-Nov-97	Stranraer	A	League	2		1-2	Thomson pen
18-Nov-97	Lossiemouth	H	Inverness Cup		1	7-2	Stewart 2, Tokely, Andersen, Shearer, Thomson pen, Addicoat
22-Nov-97	Clyde	A	League	2		3-4	Thomson, Cherry, Stewart
29-Nov-97	Q of the South	H	League	2		2-1	Stewart 2 (1 pen)
6-Dec-97	Whitehill Welfare	H	TSC		1	3-1	Stewart 2 (1 pen), Wilson
9-Dec-97	Forres Mechanics	A	Inverness Cup		SF	6-1	Stewart 2, Ross, Addicoat, Teasdale, Wilson
13-Dec-97	Clydebank	A	League	2		1-1	Ross - played at Boghead, Dumbarton
20-Dec-97	Forfar Athletic	H	League	2		2-2	Cherry 2
27-Dec-97	East Fife	H	League	2		4-0	Cherry, Robson, Teasdale, Wilson
3-Jan-98	Queen's Park	H	TSC		2	2-0	Robson, Stewart
6-Jan-98	Clachnacuddin	H	Inverness Cup		Final	2-1	Shearer, Robson
17-Jan-98	Clyde	H	League	2		5-1	Stewart 2, Thomson, Wilson, Robertson
24-Jan-98	Annan Athletic	H	TSC		3	8-1	Wilson 2, Stewart, Thomson 2, Robson, Leslie og, Shearer
31-Jan-98	Q of the South	A	League	2		0-1	
7-Feb-98	Clydebank	H	League	2		3-2	Thomson pen, Shearer 2
14-Feb-98	Dundee United	A	TSC		4	1-1	Sheerin
18-Feb-98	Dundee United	H	TSC		4 Replay	2-3 aet	Thomson, McCulloch
21-Feb-98	Livingston	H	League	2		2-2	Shearer, McCulloch
25-Feb-98	Brechin City	A	League	2		1-3	Cherry
28-Feb-98	Stenhousemuir	A	League	2		3-0	Robson, Thomson, Cherry
3-Mar-98	Livingston	A	League	2		2-2	Robson, Wilson
7-Mar-98	Stranraer	H	League	2		1-2	Cherry
10-Mar-98	Forfar Athletic	A	League	2		2-1	Sheerin 2
14-Mar-98	Clyde	A	League	2		6-1	Thomson 2, Wilson, Sheerin, McLean, Stewart
14-Mar-98	Forres Mechanics	H	North Cup		1	1-1	Cherry - switched to Forres
21-Mar-98	Forres Mechanics	A	North Cup		1 Replay	2-1	Shearer 2
21-Mar-98	Q of the South	H	League	2		0-2	

DATE	OPPONENTS	H/A	MATCH TYPE	LGE DIV	CUP RD	SCORE	SCORERS & NOTES
28-Mar-98	Clydebank	A	League	2		0-1	Played at Boghead, Dumbarton
28-Mar-98	Clachnacuddin	H	North Cup		2	2-1	Cherry, Huband
4-Apr-98	Forfar Athletic	H	League	2		0-0	
4-Apr-98	Wick Academy	A	North Cup		SF	0-0	
7-Apr-98	Celtic	H	C Christie Test.			3-3	Stewart 2, Cherry
11-Apr-98	Stenhousemuir	H	League	2		2-1	Teasdale 2
11-Apr-98	Wick Academy	Gra	North Cup		SF Replay	2-1	Huband & McLean
18-Apr-98	Stranraer	A	League	2		1-3	Stewart
25-Apr-98	East Fife	A	League	2		1-0	Thomson
25-Apr-98	Elgin City	Cal	North Cup		Final	1-3	Tokely
2-May-98	Brechin City	H	League	2		2-1	Thomson, Stewart
9-May-98	Livingston	A	League	2		2-1	Stewart, Sheerin

Cal: Caledonian Stadium; Gra: Grant Street, Inverness; CCC: Coca-Cola Cup; LCC: League Challenge Cup; TSC: Tennent's Scottish Cup

1998-9

DATE	OPPONENTS	H/A	MATCH TYPE	LGE DIV	CUP RD	SCORE	SCORERS & NOTES
18-Jul-98	Cove Rangers	A	Friendly			2-2	Sheerin, Cherry - The Barracks, Bridge of Don
18-Jul-98	Thurso Academicals	A	Centenary Match			4-1	
19-Jul-98	Keith	A	Friendly			7-0	Christie, McLean, Cherry, Robson, Shearer, Farquhar, Bavidge
21-Jul-98	Rothes	A	Friendly			2-3	Sheerin, Robson
22-Jul-98	Aberdeen	H	Friendly			2-2	Sheerin, McLean
25-Jul-98	Hamilton	H	Friendly			2-0	Shearer, McLean
27-Jul-98	Lossiemouth	A	Friendly			5-0	Sheerin, McLean, Bavidge, Shearer 2
1-Aug-98	Q of the South	A	League Cup		1	4-1	Sheerin, McLean, Shearer, Cherry
4-Aug-98	Partick Thistle	A	League	2		1-0	Wilson
7-Aug-98	Nairn County	A	North Cup		1	0-1	
8-Aug-98	Aberdeen	H	League Cup		2	0-3	
15-Aug-98	Livingston	H	League	2		2-1	Shearer, Wilson
22-Aug-98	Alloa Athletic	A	League	2		1-1	Tokely
29-Aug-98	East Fife	A	League	2		5-1	Teasdale, Cherry, Shearer, Sheerin pen, Bavidge
5-Sep-98	Arbroath	H	League	2		2-1	Crawford og, Shearer
12-Sep-98	Q of the South	H	League	2		3-2	Sheerin, McLean, Wilson
19-Sep-98	Stirling Albion	A	League	2		1-0	Shearer
26-Sep-98	Clyde	A	League	2		1-4	Cherry
3-Oct-98	Forfar Athletic	H	League	2		2-2	McLean, Wilson
10-Oct-98	Livingston	A	League	2		1-2	McLean
11-Oct-98	Alford Amateur FC	A	Friendly			5-0	
17-Oct-98	Partick Thistle	H	League	2		3-2	McLean 2, Sheerin
24-Oct-98	East Fife	H	League	2		4-2	Shearer, Christie, Sheerin, McLean
27-Oct-98	Elgin City	A	Inverness Cup		1	6-1	Shearer 2, McLean 2, Robson, Sheerin pen
31-Oct-98	Arbroath	A	League	2		1-0	Cherry
7-Nov-98	Stirling Albion	H	League	2		3-1	McLean 2, Wilson
14-Nov-98	Q of the South	A	League	2		2-2	Sheerin, McLean
17-Nov-98	Clachnacuddin	H	Inverness Cup		SF	2-0 aet	Farquhar, McLean
21-Nov-98	Clyde	H	League	2		1-1	Wilson
28-Nov-98	Forfar Athletic	A	League	2		2-2	Shearer, McLean
8-Dec-98	Wick Academy	A	Friendly			6-1	McLean 3, McCulloch, Shearer, Robson
16-Dec-98	Alloa Athletic	H	League	2		3-2	Robertson, McCulloch, McLean
19-Dec-98	Partick Thistle	A	League	2		1-2	Wilson pen
27-Dec-98	East Fife	A	League	2		2-3	Teasdale, McLean
2-Jan-99	Livingston	H	TSC		2	1-2	OG by Alan McManus

221

Date	Opponents	H/A	Match Type	LGE DIV	CUP RD	Score	Scorers & Notes
9-Jan-99	Arbroath	H	League	2		2-0	Sheerin pen, Wilson
16-Jan-99	Clyde	A	League	2		1-1	Glancy
30-Jan-99	Forfar Athletic	H	League	2		2-0	Wilson, Christie
6-Feb-99	Stirling Albion	A	League	2		5-1	Sheerin pen, McCulloch, Teasdale, Glancy 2
13-Feb-99	Q of the South	H	League	2		1-0	Rowe og
20-Feb-99	Alloa Athletic	A	League	2		4-1	Shearer 2, Wilson, Christie
27-Feb-99	Livingston	H	League	2		3-1	McLean, Wilson, Shearer
6-Mar-99	Arbroath	A	League	2		1-3	McLean
9-Mar-99	Hibernian	H	Jim Calder Test.			2-1	Glancy, Robson
13-Mar-99	East Fife	H	League	2		4-0	McLean, Wilson, Sheerin, Teasdale
20-Mar-99	Forfar Athletic	A	League	2		3-0	McLean 2, Sheerin
26-Mar-99	Ross County	H	Inverness Cup		Final	1-0	Tokely
3-Apr-99	Clyde	H	League	2		3-0	Wilson, Sheerin pen, Shearer
10-Apr-99	Stirling Albion	H	League	2		2-2	Shearer 2
11-Apr-99	Fraserburgh	A	John Thomson Test.			3-3	Robson, Shearer, Stewart
17-Apr-99	Q of the South	A	League	2		1-1	Wilson
24-Apr-99	Partick Thistle	H	League	2		3-2	McLean 2, McCulloch
1-May-99	Livingston	A	League	2		3-4	McCulloch, Christie, Stewart
8-May-99	Alloa Athletic	H	League	2		1-1	Stewart

TSC: Tennent's Scottish Cup

1999-2000

Date	Opponents	H/A	Match Type	LGE DIV	CUP RD	Score	Scorers & Notes
13-Jul-99	Fort William	A	Friendly			4-1	G Stewart 2, Hind, Craig
13-Jul-99	Clachnacuddin	A	Friendly			6-1	Glancy 3, McCulloch, Wilson, Sheerin
16-Jul-99	Cove Rangers	A	Friendly			5-1	McCulloch 2, Bavidge, Anthony, Wilson pen
17-Jul-99	Forfar Athletic	A	Friendly			2-2	Cherry, Sheerin pen
18-Jul-99	Keith	A	Friendly			4-2	McLean 3, Golabek
21-Jul-99	Lossiemouth	A	Andy Fiske Test.			5-1	I Stewart 3, Mann, Golabek
21-Jul-99	Forres Mechanics	A	Friendly			2-0	Shearer, Bavidge
24-Jul-99	Dundee	H	Friendly			1-2	I Stewart
27-Jul-99	Rothes	A	Friendly			3-1	Glancy 2, Christie
31-Jul-99	Stenhousemuir	A	CIS		1	3-1	McLean 2, Wilson
7-Aug-99	Dunfermline	A	League	1		0-4	A Allan sent off
10-Aug-99	St Mirren	H	BCC		1	1-0	Teasdale
14-Aug-99	Falkirk	H	League	1		2-3	Sheerin, Tokely
14-Aug-99	Wick Academy	A	North Cup		2	2-0	Bavidge, Jordan MacDonald
17-Aug-99	St Mirren	H	CIS		2	2-0 aet	Sheerin pen, Byers
21-Aug-99	St Mirren	A	League	1		2-3	Sheerin pen, Teasdale
21-Aug-99	Forres Mechanics	A	North Cup		SF	2-1	I Stewart, Shearer
24-Aug-99	Hamilton	A	BCC		2	3-0	I Stewart 2, McLean - played at Firhill
28-Aug-99	Ayr United	A	League	1		0-1	
4-Sep-99	Greenock Morton	H	League	1		1-1	Glancy
11-Sep-99	Clydebank	H	League	1		1-0	Sheerin pen
12-Sep-99	Lossiemouth	For	North Cup		Final	3-0	Glancy, Kellacher & Robson
14-Sep-99	Clydebank	H	BCC		QF	2-0	Glancy, Robson
18-Sep-99	Livingston	A	League	1		2-2	Bavidge, Sheerin pen
25-Sep-99	Raith Rovers	H	League	1		0-2	
28-Sep-99	Livingston	H	BCC		SF	1-0	Sheerin
2-Oct-99	Airdrie	A	League	1		1-1	Glancy
12-Oct-99	Motherwell	H	CIS		3	0-1	
16-Oct-99	Falkirk	A	League	1		2-0	Crabbe og, McLean

23-Oct-99	Dunfermline	H	League	I		1-1	Bavidge
27-Oct-99	Brora Rangers	A	Inverness Cup		I	12-0	Kellacher, Christie 4, Stewart, Tokely 3, McLean 2, Craig
30-Oct-99	Clydebank	A	League	I		3-0	Sheerin pen, Teasdale, Wilson - played at Cappielow
6-Nov-99	Livingston	H	League	I		2-0	Golabek, McLean
9-Nov-99	Clachnacuddin	H	Inverness Cup		SF	4-1	Xausa 2, Mann, Wilson
12-Nov-99	Greenock Morton	A	League	I		1-5	Tokely
21-Nov-99	Alloa Athletic	Air	BCC		Final	4-4 aet	Wilson, Sheerin 3 incl 2 penalties - Alloa 5-4 penalties
24-Nov-99	Forres Mechanics	A	Inverness Cup		Final	6-0	Bavidge 2, Glancy, Tokely, Byers, Teasdale
27-Nov-99	Airdrie	H	League	I		2-0	Wilson, Xausa
30-Nov-99	Ayr United	H	League	I		1-1	Christie
4-Dec-99	Raith Rovers	A	League	I		2-4	Sheerin pen, Bavidge
11-Dec-99	St Mirren	H	League	I		1-1	Wilson
18-Dec-99	Dunfermline	A	League	I		0-1	
27-Dec-99	Clydebank	H	League	I		4-1	Sheerin 2, Wilson 2
3-Jan-00	Livingston	A	League	I		1-1	Wilson
8-Jan-00	Greenock Morton	H	League	I		6-2	Byers, Bavidge, Wilson 2, Sheerin, Tokely
22-Jan-00	Raith Rovers	H	League	I		1-1	Glancy
5-Feb-00	Airdrie	A	League	I		4-1	Wyness, Sheerin pen, Xausa, Wilson
8-Feb-00	Celtic	A	TSC		3	3-1	Wilson, Moravcik og, Sheerin pen
12-Feb-00	St Mirren	A	League	I		0-2	
20-Feb-00	Aberdeen	H	TSC		4	1-1	Mann
26-Feb-00	Falkirk	H	League	I		0-3	
29-Feb-00	Aberdeen	A	TSC		4 Replay	0-1	
4-Mar-00	Clydebank	A	League	I		1-0	Wyness - played at Cappielow, Greenock
7-Mar-00	Ayr United	A	League	I		3-1	Wilson, Sheerin, Xausa
18-Mar-00	Livingston	H	League	I		4-1	Xausa 3, Wyness
25-Mar-00	Ayr United	H	League	I		1-1	Wilson
1-Apr-00	Greenock Morton	A	League	I		2-0	Wyness, Xausa
4-Apr-00	St Johnstone	H	Mike Noble Test.			2-0	Craig, Noble pen
8-Apr-00	Raith Rovers	A	League	I		0-2	
15-Apr-00	Airdrie	H	League	I		1-5	Wyness
22-Apr-00	Dunfermline	H	League	I		1-2	Xausa
29-Apr-00	Falkirk	A	League	I		2-2	Xausa, Wilson
6-May-00	St Mirren	H	League	I		5-0	Xausa, McCulloch 2, Wilson, Bavidge

Air: Airdrie; For: Forres; CIS: CIS Insurance Cup; BCC: Bells Challenge Cup; TSC: Tennents Scottish Cup

2000-I

DATE	OPPONENTS	H/A	MATCH TYPE	LGE DIV	CUP RD	SCORE	SCORERS & NOTES
18-Jul-00	Lossiemouth	A	Friendly			2-1	Tokely pen, McBain
20-Jul-00	Mansfield	H	Friendly			5-2	Bavidge 2, Craig, Sheerin 2
21-Jul-00	Peterhead	A	Friendly			4-2	Munro 2, McBain, Shearer
22-Jul-00	Aberdeen	H	Friendly			1-0	I Stewart
25-Jul-00	Fort William	A	Friendly			6-1	Wyness 3, I Stewart 2, Bavidge
29-Jul-00	Huntly	A	Friendly			9-1	I Stewart 3, Christie 2, Bagan, Bavidge, Wyness, Tokely pen
1-Aug-00	Rothes	A	Friendly			5-0	I Stewart 3, Craig, Low
5-Aug-00	Airdrie	H	League	I		2-0	Tokely, Xausa
8-Aug-00	Peterhead	A	CIS		I	3-2	I Stewart, Xausa, Mann
12-Aug-00	Livingston	A	League	I		1-3	I Stewart
15-Aug-00	Alloa Athletic	A	BCC		I	3-2	I Stewart 2, Bavidge
18-Aug-00	Nairn County	H	North Cup		I	7-2 aet	Allan pen, N MacDonald 2, Bavidge 3, Byers

19-Aug-00	Falkirk	H	League	I		2-3	Bavidge 2
22-Aug-00	Airdrie	H	CIS		2	0-2	
26-Aug-00	Raith Rovers	A	League	I		1-4	I Stewart
30-Aug-00	Golspie Sutherland	H	North Cup		2	4-1	Glancy 2, Low, N MacDonald
2-Sep-00	Stranraer	H	BCC		2	1-2	Bavidge
2-Sep-00	Forres Mechanics	A	North Cup		SF	2-4	G Stewart & Farquhar pen
9-Sep-00	Clyde	H	League	I		1-2	Bagan
16-Sep-00	Ross County	H	League	I		0-1	
23-Sep-00	Alloa Athletic	A	League	I		4-1	Robson, Sheerin, Xausa & Bavidge
30-Sep-00	Ayr United	A	League	I		3-3	Xausa, Sheerin & Mann
3-Oct-00	Ross County	H	Inverness Cup		I	2-4	Christie & N MacDonald
7-Oct-00	Greenock Morton	H	League	I		4-0	Bavidge 2, McBain & Bagan
14-Oct-00	Airdrie	A	League	I		2-1	Sheerin & Xausa
21-Oct-00	Livingston	H	League	I		2-2	McBain & Sheerin
28-Oct-00	Raith Rovers	H	League	I		1-2	Sheerin
4-Nov-00	Clyde	A	League	I		1-1	Wyness
11-Nov-00	Alloa Athletic	H	League	I		2-1	Teasdale, Sheerin
18-Nov-00	Ross County	A	League	I		3-0	Wyness 2 & Teasdale
25-Nov-00	Greenock Morton	A	League	I		0-2	
2-Dec-00	Ayr United	H	League	I		7-3	Wyness 3, Bagan 2, Teasdale & Sheerin pen
9-Dec-00	Falkirk	A	League	I		2-2	Wyness & Sheerin
16-Dec-00	Airdrie	H	League	I		4-0	Bagan, Christie, Xausa & Wyness
23-Dec-00	Clyde	H	League	I		2-2	Bagan & Xausa
2-Jan-01	Ross County	H	League	I		3-3	Sheerin, Wyness 2
6-Jan-01	Alloa Athletic	A	League	I		1-1	Xausa
13-Jan-01	Ayr United	A	League	I		1-1	Wyness
27-Jan-01	Ayr United	H	TSC		3	4-3	Sheerin, Mann, Xausa & Wyness
3-Feb-01	Falkirk	H	League	I		1-1	Wyness
17-Feb-01	Kilmarnock	H	TSC		4	1-1	Robson
28-Feb-01	Kilmarnock	A	TSC		4 Replay	0-0	Abandoned after 27 mins - frozen pitch
6-Mar-01	Kilmarnock	A	TSC		4 Replay	1-2	Xausa
10-Mar-01	Raith Rovers	A	League	I		1-1	Wyness
13-Mar-01	Greenock Morton	H	League	I		4-2	Wyness 3, Bagan
17-Mar-01	Alloa Athletic	H	League	I		2-0	Wyness & Robson
23-Mar-01	Raith Rovers	H	League	I		2-0	Wyness 2
27-Mar-01	Clyde	A	League	I		2-2	Bagan & Wyness
31-Mar-01	Ross County	A	League	I		1-0	McBain
3-Apr-01	Livingston	A	League	I		1-4	Wyness
7-Apr-01	Greenock Morton	A	League	I		3-0	Christie, Wyness, N MacDonald
14-Apr-01	Ayr United	H	League	I		1-0	Wyness
21-Apr-01	Airdrie	A	League	I		1-1	Wyness
28-Apr-01	Livingston	H	League	I		2-3	Sheerin - 2 penalties
5-May-01	Falkirk	A	League	I		1-2	Wyness

CIS:CIS Insurance Cup; BCC: Bells Challenge Cup; TSC: Tennents Scottish Cup

2001-2

DATE	OPPONENTS	H/A	MATCH TYPE	LGE DIV	CUP RD	SCORE	SCORERS & NOTES
20-Jul-01	Huntly	A	Friendly			2-0	Bavidge & McBain
21-Jul-01	Forfar Athletic	A	Friendly			1-2	Christie
24-Jul-01	Lossiemouth	A	Friendly			3-0	Robson, Bavidge, Mann pen
27-Jul-01	Celtic XI	H	Friendly			2-0	Bavidge, Wyness
28-Jul-01	Peterhead	A	Friendly			1-1	Wyness
31-Jul-01	Elgin City	A	Friendly			4-0	McBain, D Craig og, Bavidge, Ritchie
4-Aug-01	Clyde	A	League	I		1-1	Mann pen

Date	Opposition	H/A	Competition	Round	Round2	Score	Scorers
7-Aug-01	Forfar Athletic	H	BCC		1	3-2 aet	Christie, Bavidge, Ritchie
11-Aug-01	Falkirk	H	League	1		1-2	Mann pen
11-Aug-01	Golspie Sutherland	A	North Cup		1	2-0	N MacDonald, Robson
14-Aug-01	Alloa Athletic	A	BCC		2	2-3 aet	Ritchie & Wyness
18-Aug-01	Partick Thistle	A	League	1		0-1	
18-Aug-01	Ross County	H	North Cup		2	1-0	MacRae
25-Aug-01	St Mirren	A	League	1		1-1	Mann
25-Aug-01	Fort William	A	North Cup		SF	1-1 aet	N MacDonald - 9-8 on penalties
29-Aug-01	Buckie Thistle	A	Challenge Match			4-0	Teasdale, Wyness, Low & Bavidge
4-Sep-01	Orkney	A	Friendly			9-0	Wyness 4, Ritchie 2, Tokely, Robson, Mann.
8-Sep-01	Arbroath	H	League	1		5-1	Wyness 3, Mann & McBain
11-Sep-01	Albion Rovers	A	CIS		1	2-0	Ritchie 2
15-Sep-01	Ross County	A	League	1		1-2	Robson
19-Sep-01	Raith Rovers	H	League	1		5-2	Wyness 4, Ritchie.
22-Sep-01	Airdrie	A	League	1		0-6	Record defeat
22-Sep-01	Clachnacuddin	A	North Cup		Final	0-2	
26-Sep-01	Partick Thistle	H	CIS		2	3-3 aet	Robson 2 & Teasdale. 4-2 on penalties.
29-Sep-01	Ayr United	H	League	1		3-1	Ritchie 2 & Christie
9-Oct-01	Dunfermline	A	CIS		3	1-1 aet	Bavidge. 4-1 on penalties.
13-Oct-01	Clyde	H	League	1		5-1	Wyness 2, Ritchie, Bavidge, Duncan
20-Oct-01	Falkirk	A	League	1		2-1	Mann & Ritchie
27-Oct-01	Arbroath	A	League	1		2-3	Ritchie 2
3-Nov-01	St Mirren	H	League	1		1-2	Wyness
6-Nov-01	Forres Mechanics	H	Inverness Cup		1	8-1	Bavidge 3, G Stewart, Tokely, N MacDonald, MacRae, N Calder
10-Nov-01	Raith Rovers	A	League	1		5-1	Mann pen, Christie, Ritchie, Tokely, Robson
17-Nov-01	Ross County	H	League	1		3-0	McCormick og, Wyness 2
20-Nov-01	Elgin City	H	Inverness Cup		SF	7-1	Ritchie 3, G Stewart, Bavidge, McCaffrey pen, Wyness
24-Nov-01	Ayr United	A	League	1		0-3	
28-Nov-01	Ayr United	A	CIS		QF	1-5	Tokely
1-Dec-01	Airdrie	H	League	1		1-2	Ritchie
8-Dec-01	Partick Thistle	H	League	1		1-2	Wyness
11-Dec-01	Ross County	H	Inverness Cup		Final	3-2	Bavidge, Munro & N MacDonald
15-Dec-01	Clyde	A	League	1		0-1	
22-Dec-01	Arbroath	H	League	1		3-2	Ritchie, Wyness & Bavidge
29-Dec-01	St Mirren	A	League	1		0-0	
8-Jan-02	Arbroath	A	TSC		3	2-0	Robson & Ritchie
12-Jan-02	Raith Rovers	H	League	1		5-0	Tokely, McBain, Bavidge, Mann & Bagan
19-Jan-02	Airdrie	A	League	1		0-3	
26-Jan-02	Hearts	A	TSC		4	3-1	Tokely, Wyness & Bagan
2-Feb-02	Ayr United	H	League	1		1-1	Wyness
9-Feb-02	Partick Thistle	A	League	1		1-4	Ritchie
16-Feb-02	Falkirk	H	League	1		3-2	Munro, Wyness 2
23-Feb-02	Partick Thistle	A	TSC		QF	2-2	Wyness 2
2-Mar-02	St Mirren	H	League	1		4-2	Ritchie 3, Bagan
5-Mar-02	Partick Thistle	H	TSC		QF Replay	0-1	
9-Mar-02	Arbroath	A	League	1		0-1	
16-Mar-02	Raith Rovers	A	League	1		0-0	
19-Mar-02	Ross County	A	League	1		0-0	
23-Mar-02	Ross County	H	League	1		1-1	Tokely
30-Mar-02	Airdrie	H	League	1		1-0	Bavidge
6-Apr-02	Ayr United	A	League	1		0-1	
13-Apr-02	Clyde	H	League	1		1-1	MacDonald
20-Apr-02	Falkirk	A	League	1		0-0	
27-Apr-02	Partick Thistle	H	League	1		3-0	Stewart, Ritchie & Wyness

CIS:CIS Insurance Cup; :BCC:Bells Challenge Cup; TSC:Tennents Scottish Cup

2002-3

DATE	OPPONENTS	H/A	MATCH TYPE	LGE DIV	CUP RD	SCORE	SCORERS & NOTES
17-Jul-02	Greenock Morton	H	Friendly			0-1	
20-Jul-02	Montrose	A	Friendly			4-2	Ritchie 2, Tokely, Hart
21-Jul-02	Peterhead	A	Friendly			5-1	Wyness 3, Hart 2
23-Jul-02	Lossiemouth	A	Friendly			0-2	
25-Jul-02	Huntly	A	Friendly			2-2	Wyness & Robson
27-Jul-02	Elgin City	H	Friendly			1-0	Mann
3-Aug-02	Alloa Athletic		League	1		0-0	
6-Aug-02	Berwick Rangers	A	Bell's Cup		1	0-1	
10-Aug-02	St Johnstone	A	League	1		0-1	
14-Aug-02	Nairn County	A	Inverness Cup		SF	2-0 aet	Keogh & Robson pen
17-Aug-02	Falkirk	H	League	1		1-2	Tokely
24-Aug-02	Ross County	H	League	1		2-0	Wyness 2
31-Aug-02	St Mirren	A	League	1		4-0	Robson 2, Hart & Christie
3-Sep-02	Ross County	Gra	Inverness Cup		Final	0-1	
10-Sep-02	Dumbarton	H	CIS		1	2-0	Wyness & Ritchie
14-Sep-02	Q of the South	A	League	1		3-1	Wyness 2 & Mann
21-Sep-02	Arbroath	H	League	1		5-0	Tokely 2, Hart, Wyness & Ritchie
24-Sep-02	St Mirren	H	CIS		2	3-1	Wyness 2 & Hart
28-Sep-02	Clyde	A	League	1		0-3	
5-Oct-02	Ayr United	H	League	1		2-0	Ritchie & Wyness
19-Oct-02	Alloa Athletic	A	League	1		6-0	Wyness 3, Ritchie 3
23-Oct-02	Celtic	A	CIS		3	2-4	Ritchie & Wyness
26-Oct-02	St Johnstone	H	League	1		2-1	Wyness & Hart
2-Nov-02	St Mirren	H	League	1		4-1	Wyness 2, Hart, Robson pen
9-Nov-02	Ross County	A	League	1		2-0	Robson, McCulloch og
16-Nov-02	Q of the South	H	League	1		5-3	Ritchie 3, Robson 2 (incl 1 pen)
23-Nov-02	Arbroath	A	League	1		2-1	Wyness & Hart
30-Nov-02	Clyde	H	League	1		1-0	Robson
7-Dec-02	Ayr United	A	League	1		3-3	Mann, Ritchie & Wyness
14-Dec-02	Falkirk	A	League	1		1-1	OG by Scott Mackenzie
17-Dec-02	Deveronvale	A	Testimonial			3-4	Keogh, Bagan & Munro
21-Dec-02	Alloa Athletic	H	League	1		1-1	Mann
28-Dec-02	St Mirren	A	League	1		4-1	Wyness, Tokely, Stewart & Ritchie
18-Jan-03	Ayr United	H	League	1		0-1	
25-Jan-03	Raith Rovers	H	TSC		3	2-0	Robson pen & Wyness
8-Feb-03	Falkirk	H	League	1		3-4	Robson, Wyness & Ritchie
15-Feb-03	St Johnstone	A	League	1		0-2	
22-Feb-03	Hamilton	H	TSC		4	6-1	Wyness 2, Robson 2, Ritchie, McCaffrey
25-Feb-03	Ross County	H	League	1		1-5	Wyness
1-Mar-03	St Mirren	H	League	1		3-1	Ritchie 3
4-Mar-03	Arbroath	H	League	1		2-0	Hart & Low
8-Mar-03	Ross County	A	League	1		2-0	Hart & Robson
11-Mar-03	Q of the South	A	League	1		0-0	
15-Mar-03	Arbroath	A	League	1		3-1	Wyness 2 & Hislop
18-Mar-03	Clyde	A	League	1		1-4	Robson
23-Mar-03	Celtic	H	TSC		QF	1-0	Wyness
28-Mar-03	Benbecula	A	Friendly			7-1	Keogh 3, Hislop 2, Robson 2 (1 pen)
5-Apr-03	Q of the South	H	League	1		1-0	Tokely
12-Apr-03	Clyde	H	League	1		1-2	Hislop
14-Apr-03	Deveronvale	A	Friendly			1-1	Low
20-Apr-03	Dundee	Ham	TSC		SF	0-1	
26-Apr-03	Alloa Athletic	A	League	1		5-1	Ritchie 3, Mann, Golabek
29-Apr-03	Ayr United	A	League	1		0-1	
3-May-03	St Johnstone	H	League	1		1-2	Hart
10-May-03	Falkirk	A	League	1		3-2	Nicholls og, Mann, Christie

Gra: Grant Street, Inverness; Ham: Hampden; CIS: CIS Insurance Cup; TSC: Tennents Scottish Cup

2003-4

DATE	OPPONENTS	H/A	MATCH TYPE	LGE DIV	CUP RD	SCORE	SCORERS & NOTES
14-Jul-03	Clachnacuddin	A	Friendly			4-1	Bingham 2, Tokely, MacKinnon
15-Jul-03	Forres Mechanics	A	Friendly			2-0	Hart, MacKinnon
16-Jul-03	Brora Rangers	A	Friendly			2-0	A Christie, Low
19-Jul-03	Aberdeen	H	Friendly			1-0	Mann pen
21-Jul-03	Livingston	H	Friendly			1-0	McBain
23-Jul-03	Lossiemouth	A	Friendly			3-1	Proctor, MacKinnon & Low
26-Jul-03	Forfar Athletic	A	Friendly			3-1	Bingham, Tokely & Ritchie
28-Jul-03	Hearts	H	Friendly			2-1	Ritchie 2
2-Aug-03	Gretna	A	Bell's Cup		1	5-0	Bingham, Hislop, Ritchie, Hart 2
9-Aug-03	Falkirk	A	League	1		1-2	McCaffrey - played at Ochilview
12-Aug-03	Peterhead	A	Bell's Cup		2	2-1	Hislop 2
16-Aug-03	Clyde	H	League	1		0-0	
19-Aug-03	Ross County	A	Inverness Cup		SF	1-3 aet	Proctor
23-Aug-03	St Johnstone	A	League	1		2-1	Bingham & Hislop
26-Aug-03	Ross County	H	Bell's Cup		3	1-0	Hislop
30-Aug-03	Ross County	A	League	1		1-1	Mann
2-Sep-03	Queen's Park	H	CIS		1	1-2	Ritchie
13-Sep-03	Ayr United	H	League	1		1-0	Ritchie
16-Sep-03	Raith Rovers	A	Bell's Cup		SF	4-0	Wilson 2, Ritchie 2
20-Sep-03	Brechin City	A	League	1		2-0	McBain & Ritchie
27-Sep-03	St Mirren	H	League	1		2-0	Ritchie & McCaffrey
4-Oct-03	Raith Rovers	H	League	1		2-1	Tokely & McCaffrey
18-Oct-03	Q of the South	A	League	1		2-3	Ritchie & Bingham
26-Oct-03	Airdrie United	Per	Bell's Cup		Final	2-0	Bingham & Hislop
1-Nov-03	Falkirk	H	League	1		1-2	John Hughes own goal
5-Nov-03	Clyde	A	League	1		0-1	
8-Nov-03	Ayr United	A	League	1		3-0	Golabek, Hart, Hislop
14-Nov-03	Ross County	H	League	1		3-3	Bingham, Hislop & Wilson
22-Nov-03	St Mirren	A	League	1		4-0	Bingham 2, McBain 2
29-Nov-03	Brechin City	H	League	1		5-0	Tokely 2, Hislop, Keogh & Wilson
6-Dec-03	Q of the South	H	League	1		4-1	Hislop 2, McCaffrey, Wilson
13-Dec-03	Raith Rovers	A	League	1		3-1	Munro, Bingham, Ritchie
27-Dec-03	St Johnstone	H	League	1		1-0	Wilson pen
3-Jan-04	Ross County	A	League	1		0-1	
10-Jan-04	Brechin City	H	TSC		3	5-1	Ritchie 3, Bingham, McBain
17-Jan-04	Ayr United	H	League	1		2-1	Ritchie & Bingham
24-Jan-04	Brechin City	A	League	1		4-2	Thomson, Ritchie, Bingham & Duncan
31-Jan-04	St Mirren	H	League	1		1-1	Bingham
7-Feb-04	St Mirren	A	TSC		4	1-0	Thomson
14-Feb-04	Raith Rovers	H	League	1		3-0	Bingham, Keogh & Wilson
21-Feb-04	Q of the South	A	League	1		1-2	Ritchie
2-Mar-04	Falkirk	A	League	1		1-2	Ritchie
6-Mar-04	Motherwell	A	TSC		QF	1-0	Wilson
13-Mar-04	St Johnstone	A	League	1		2-3	Ritchie 2
16-Mar-04	Clyde	H	League	1		3-1	Ritchie, Bingham & Wilson pen
17-Mar-04	Nairn County	A	North Cup		Group	4-1	Finnigan, C Christie, MacMillan, Thomson
20-Mar-04	Ayr United	A	League	1		1-1	Wilson pen
24-Mar-04	Forres Mech	H	North Cup		Group	5-0	Finnigan 2, MacMillan 2, Hart
27-Mar-04	Ross County	H	League	1		1-0	Wilson
30-Mar-04	Ross County	H	North Cup		SF	1-1 aet	Hart - 4-2 on penalties
3-Apr-04	St Mirren	A	League	1		0-0	
10-Apr-04	Dunfermline	Ham	TSC		SF	1-1	Ritchie
13-Apr-04	Brechin City	H	League	1		1-0	Wilson pen
17-Apr-04	Q of the South	H	League	1		4-1	Hislop 2, Bingham & Wilson
20-Apr-04	Dunfermline	Abe	TSC		SF Replay	2-3	Ritchie & Bingham pen
24-Apr-04	Raith Rovers	A	League	1		1-0	Ritchie
25-Apr-04	Elgin City	For	North Cup		Final	0-1	
1-May-04	Falkirk	H	League	1		0-0	
8-May-04	Clyde	A	League	1		2-1	Keogh & Hislop
15-May-04	St Johnstone	H	League	1		3-1	Bingham, Wilson pen, Ritchie

For:Forres; Ham:Hampden; Per:Perth; Abe:Aberdeen; CIS:CIS Insurance Cup; TSC:Tennents Scottish Cup

227

ICTFC STATISTICS - ALL MATCHES

SEASON	Home Played	Away Played	Total Played	Total Wins	Win %	Total Draws	Total Losses	Total Goals For	Total Goals Against
1994-5	20	20	40	13	33%	9	18	52	67
1995-6	22	21	43	18	42%	13	12	72	48
1996-7	20	22	42	25	60%	8	9	75	46
1997-8	24	20	44	17	39%	11	16	88	62
1998-9	20	19	39	22	56%	9	8	85	54
1999-2000	24	23	47	20	43%	11	16	80	64
2000-1	22	21	43	17	40%	13	13	84	68
2001-2	21	25	46	19	41%	10	17	79	69
2002-3	23	21	44	25	57%	5	14	90	53
2003-4	21	26	47	29	62%	8	10	92	41
TOTAL	*217*	*218*	*435*	*205*	*47%*	*97*	*133*	*797*	*572*

ICTFC STATISTICS - LEAGUE MATCHES

SEASON	Home Played	Away Played	Total Played	Total Wins	Win %	Total Draws	Total Losses	Total Goals For	Total Goals Against
1994-5	18	18	36	12	33%	9	15	48	61
1995-6	18	18	36	15	42%	12	9	64	38
1996-7	18	18	36	23	64%	7	6	70	37
1997-8	18	18	36	13	36%	10	13	65	51
1998-99	18	18	36	21	58%	9	6	80	48
1999-2000	18	18	36	13	36%	10	13	60	55
2000-1	18	18	36	14	39%	12	10	71	54
2001-2	18	18	36	13	36%	9	14	60	51
2002-3	18	18	36	20	56%	5	11	74	45
2003-4	18	18	36	21	58%	7	8	67	33
TOTAL	*180*	*180*	*360*	*165*	*46%*	*90*	*105*	*659*	*473*

ICTFC STATISTICS - ALL CUP MATCHES

SEASON	Home Played	Away Played	Total Played	Total Wins	Win %	Total Draws	Total Losses	Total Goals For	Total Goals Against
1994-5	2	2	4	1	25%	0	3	4	6
1995-6	4	3	7	3	43%	1	3	8	10
1996-7	2	4	6	2	33%	1	3	5	9
1997-8	6	2	8	4	50%	1	3	23	11
1998-9	2	1	3	1	33%	0	2	5	6
1999-2000	6	5	11	7	64%	1	3	20	9
2000-1	4	3	7	3	43%	1	3	13	14
2001-2	3	7	10	6	60%	1	3	19	18
2002-3	5	3	8	5	63%	0	3	16	8
2003-4	3	8	11	8	73%	1	2	25	8
TOTAL	*37*	*38*	*75*	*40*	*53%*	*7*	*28*	*138*	*99*

MATCH STATISTICS

Home Wins	Home Draws	Home Losses	Home Goals For	Home Goals Against	Away Wins	Away Draws	Away Losses	Away Goals For	Away Goals Against
5	7	8	29	36	8	2	10	23	31
6	9	7	33	31	12	4	5	39	17
14	3	3	38	22	11	5	6	37	24
11	7	6	51	29	6	4	10	37	33
14	4	2	45	25	8	5	6	40	29
11	7	6	41	27	9	4	10	39	37
10	5	7	48	33	7	8	6	36	35
13	3	5	53	28	6	7	12	26	41
15	2	6	49	25	10	3	8	41	28
15	4	2	44	15	14	4	8	48	26
114	51	52	431	271	91	46	81	366	301

Home Wins	Home Draws	Home Losses	Home Goals For	Home Goals Against	Away Wins	Away Draws	Away Losses	Away Goals For	Away Goals Against
5	7	6	27	33	7	2	9	21	28
5	8	5	28	23	10	4	4	36	15
13	3	2	37	19	10	4	4	33	18
7	7	4	31	21	6	3	9	34	30
14	4	0	44	20	7	5	6	36	28
7	6	5	34	25	6	4	8	26	30
9	4	5	42	25	5	8	5	29	29
11	3	4	47	22	2	6	10	13	29
10	2	6	35	23	10	3	5	39	22
13	4	1	37	12	8	3	7	30	21
94	48	38	362	223	71	42	67	297	250

Home Wins	Home Draws	Home Losses	Home Goals For	Home Goals Against	Away Wins	Away Draws	Away Losses	Away Goals For	Away Goals Against
0	0	2	2	3	1	0	1	2	3
1	1	2	5	8	2	0	1	3	2
1	0	1	1	3	1	1	2	4	6
4	0	2	20	8	0	1	1	3	3
0	0	2	1	5	1	0	0	4	1
4	1	1	7	2	3	0	2	13	7
1	1	2	6	8	2	0	1	7	6
2	0	1	6	6	4	1	2	13	12
5	0	0	14	2	0	0	3	2	6
2	0	1	7	3	6	1	1	18	5
20	3	14	69	48	20	4	14	69	51

APPENDIX C

1994-5 DIVISION 3	P	W	D	L	F	A	PTS
FORFAR ATHLETIC	36	25	5	6	67	33	80
MONTROSE	36	20	7	9	69	32	67
ROSS COUNTY	36	18	6	12	59	44	60
EAST STIRLING	36	18	5	13	61	50	59
ALLOA ATHLETIC	36	15	9	12	50	45	54
CALEDONIAN THISTLE	36	12	9	15	48	61	45
ARBROATH	36	13	5	18	51	62	44
QUEEN'S PARK	36	12	6	18	46	57	42
COWDENBEATH	36	11	7	18	48	60	40
ALBION ROVERS	36	5	3	28	27	82	18

1995-6 DIVISION 3	P	W	D	L	F	A	PTS
LIVINGSTON	36	21	9	6	51	24	72
BRECHIN CITY	36	18	9	9	41	21	63
CALEDONIAN THISTLE	36	15	12	9	64	38	57
ROSS COUNTY	36	12	17	7	56	39	53
ARBROATH	36	13	13	10	41	41	52
QUEEN'S PARK	36	12	12	12	40	43	48
EAST STIRLING	36	11	11	14	58	62	44
COWDENBEATH	36	10	8	18	45	59	38
ALLOA ATHLETIC	36	6	11	19	26	58	29
ALBION ROVERS	36	7	8	21	37	74	29

1996-7 DIVISION 3	P	W	D	L	F	A	PTS
INVERNESS CALEDONIAN THISTLE	36	23	7	6	70	37	76
FORFAR ATHLETIC	36	19	10	7	74	45	67
ROSS COUNTY	36	20	7	9	58	41	67
ALLOA ATHLETIC	36	16	7	13	50	47	55
ALBION ROVERS	36	13	10	13	50	47	49
MONTROSE	36	12	7	17	46	62	43
COWDENBEATH	36	10	9	17	38	51	39
QUEEN'S PARK	36	9	9	18	46	59	36
EAST STIRLING	36	8	9	19	36	58	33
ARBROATH	36	6	13	17	31	52	31

1997-8 DIVISION 2	P	W	D	L	F	A	PTS
STRANRAER	36	18	7	11	62	44	61
CLYDEBANK	36	16	12	8	48	31	60
LIVINGSTON	36	16	11	9	56	40	59
QUEEN OF THE SOUTH	36	15	9	12	57	51	54
INVERNESS CALEDONIAN THISTLE	36	13	10	13	65	51	49
EAST FIFE	36	14	6	16	51	59	48
FORFAR ATHLETIC	36	12	10	14	51	61	46
CLYDE	36	10	12	14	40	53	42
STENHOUSEMUIR	36	10	10	16	44	53	40
BRECHIN CITY	36	7	11	18	42	73	32

1998-9 DIVISION 2	P	W	D	L	F	A	PTS
LIVINGSTON	36	22	11	3	66	35	77
INVERNESS CALEDONIAN THISTLE	36	21	9	6	80	48	72
CLYDE	36	15	8	13	46	42	53
QUEEN OF THE SOUTH	36	13	9	14	50	45	48
ALLOA ATHLETIC	36	13	7	16	65	56	46
STIRLING ALBION	36	12	8	16	50	63	44
ARBROATH	36	12	8	16	37	52	44
PARTICK THISTLE	36	12	7	17	36	45	43
EAST FIFE	36	12	6	18	42	64	42
FORFAR ATHLETIC	36	8	7	21	48	70	31

1999-2000 DIVISION 1	P	W	D	L	F	A	PTS
ST MIRREN	36	23	7	6	75	39	76
DUNFERMLINE	36	20	11	5	66	33	71
FALKIRK	36	20	8	8	67	40	68
LIVINGSTON	36	19	7	10	60	45	64
RAITH ROVERS	36	17	8	11	55	40	59
INVERNESS CALEDONIAN THISTLE	36	13	10	13	60	55	49
AYR UNITED	36	10	8	18	42	52	38
GREENOCK MORTON	36	10	6	20	45	61	36
AIRDRIE	36	7	8	21	29	69	29
CLYDEBANK	36	1	7	28	17	82	10

230

LEAGUE TABLES

2000-1 DIVISION 1	P	W	D	L	F	A	PTS
LIVINGSTON	36	23	7	6	72	31	76
AYR UNITED	36	19	12	5	73	41	69
FALKIRK	36	16	8	12	57	59	56
INVERNESS CALEDONIAN THISTLE	*36*	*14*	*12*	*10*	*71*	*54*	*54*
CLYDE	36	11	14	11	44	46	47
ROSS COUNTY	36	11	10	15	48	52	43
RAITH ROVERS	36	10	8	18	41	55	38
AIRDRIE	36	8	14	14	49	67	38
GREENOCK MORTON	36	9	8	19	34	61	35
ALLOA ATHLETIC	36	7	11	18	38	61	32

2001-2 DIVISION 1	P	W	D	L	F	A	PTS
PARTICK THISTLE	36	19	9	8	61	38	66
AIRDRIE	36	15	11	10	59	40	56
AYR UNITED	36	13	13	10	53	44	52
ROSS COUNTY	36	14	10	12	51	43	52
CLYDE	36	13	10	13	51	56	49
INVERNESS CALEDONIAN THISTLE	*36*	*13*	*9*	*14*	*60*	*51*	*48*
ARBROATH	36	14	6	16	42	59	48
ST MIRREN	36	11	12	13	43	53	45
FALKIRK	36	10	9	17	49	73	39
RAITH ROVERS	36	8	11	17	50	62	35

2002-3 DIVISION 1	P	W	D	L	F	A	PTS
FALKIRK	36	25	6	5	80	32	81
CLYDE	36	21	9	6	66	37	72
ST JOHNSTONE	36	20	7	9	49	29	67
INVERNESS CALEDONIAN THISTLE	*36*	*20*	*5*	*11*	*74*	*45*	*65*
QUEEN OF THE SOUTH	36	12	12	12	45	48	48
AYR UNITED	36	12	9	15	34	44	45
ST MIRREN	36	9	10	17	42	71	37
ROSS COUNTY	36	9	8	19	42	46	35
ALLOA ATHLETIC	36	9	8	19	39	72	35
ARBROATH	36	3	6	27	30	77	15

2003-4 DIVISION 1	P	W	D	L	F	A	PTS
INVERNESS CALEDONIAN THISTLE	*36*	*21*	*7*	*8*	*67*	*33*	*70*
CLYDE	36	20	9	7	64	40	69
ST JOHNSTONE	36	15	12	9	59	45	57
FALKIRK	36	15	10	11	43	37	55
QUEEN OF THE SOUTH	36	15	9	12	46	48	54
ROSS COUNTY	36	12	13	11	49	41	49
ST MIRREN	36	9	14	13	39	46	41
RAITH ROVERS	36	8	10	18	37	57	34
AYR UNITED	36	6	13	17	37	58	31
BRECHIN CITY	36	6	9	21	37	73	27

APPENDIX D
LEAGUE OPPOSITION RECORD

	1994-5 Home	1994-5 Away	1995-6 Home	1995-6 Away	1996-7 Home	1996-7 Away	1997-8 Home	1997-8 Away	1998-9 Home	1998-9 Away
		Division 3		Division 3		Division 3		Division 2		Division 2
Albion Rovers	2-1,0-2	1-0,2-1	6-1,1-1	2-2,2-0	1-1,4-1	0-0,3-0				
Alloa Athletic	2-2,0-1	1-1,0-1	1-1,0-0	5-0,2-0	1-0,3-1	2-0,0-1			3-2,1-1	1-1,4-1
Arbroath	5-2,1-1	2-1,0-2	5-1,1-1	1-2,2-1	2-0,4-1	4-1,0-0			2-1,2-0	1-0,1-3
Brechin City			1-2,0-1	0-0,1-0			0-0,2-1	2-2,1-3		
Clyde							1-2,5-1	3-4,6-1	1-1,3-0	1-4,1-1
Clydebank							0-0,3-2	1-1,0-1		
Cowdenbeath	0-3,3-1	1-1,3-1	3-2,2-0	0-0,1-2	1-3,2-1	4-3,1-2				
East Fife							0-1,4-0	5-1,1-0	4-2,4-0	5-1,2-3
East Stirling	3-3,3-3	0-2,0-1	1-1,0-3	5-0,5-1	2-0,3-2	0-0,3-0				
Forfar Athletic	3-1,1-1	1-2,1-4			1-1,0-4	1-3,0-2	2-2,0-0	1-2,2-1	2-2,2-0	2-2,3-0
Livingston			0-3,1-2	2-0,2-2			1-1,2-2	2-2,2-1	2-1,3-1	1-2,3-4
Montrose	0-4,0-3	1-3,1-0			2-0,3-2	2-2,2-0				
Partick Thistle									3-2,3-2	1-0,1-2
Queen of the South							2-1,0-2	1-2,0-1	3-2,1-0	2-2,1-1
Queen's Park	0-4,1-1	2-0,1-4	3-1,1-1	3-0,2-1	2-2,1-0	3-2,2-1				
Ross County	0-0,3-0	3-1,1-3	1-1,1-1	0-2,1-2	2-0,3-0	3-1,3-0				
Stenhousemuir							4-1,2-1	2-3,3-0		
Stirling Albion									3-1,2-2	1-0,5-1
Stranraer							2-2,1-2	1-2,1-3		

	1999-2000 Home	1999-2000 Away	2000-1 Home	2000-1 Away	2001-2 Home	2001-2 Away	2002-3 Home	2002-3 Away	2003-4 Home	2003-4 Away
		Division 1		Division 1		Division 1		Division 1		Division 1
Airdrie	2-0,1-5	1-1,4-1	2-0,4-0	2-1,1-1	1-2,1-0	0-6,0-3				
Alloa Athletic			2-1,2-0	4-1,1-1			0-0,1-1	6-0,5-1		
Arbroath					5-1,3-2	2-3,0-1	5-0,2-0	2-1,3-1		
Ayr United	1-1,1-1	0-1,3-1	7-3,1-0	3-3,1-1	3-1,1-1	0-3,0-1	2-0,0-1	3-3,0-1	1-0,2-1	3-0,1-1
Brechin City									5-0,1-0	2-0,4-2
Clyde			1-2,2-2	1-1,2-2	5-1,1-1	1-1,0-1	1-0,1-2	0-3,1-4	0-0,3-1	0-1,2-1
Clydebank	1-0,4-1	3-0,1-0								
Dunfermline	1-1,1-2	0-4,0-1								
Falkirk	2-3,0-3	2-0,2-2	2-3,1-1	2-2,1-2	1-2,3-2	2-1,0-0	1-2,3-4	1-1,3-2	1-2,0-0	1-2,1-2
Greenock Morton	1-1,6-2	1-5,2-0	4-0,4-2	0-2,3-0						
Livingston	2-0,4-1	2-2,1-1	2-2,2-3	1-3,1-4						
Partick Thistle					1-2,3-0	0-1,1-4				
Queen of the South							5-3,1-0	3-1,0-0	4-1,4-1	2-3,1-2
Raith Rovers	0-2,1-1	2-4,0-2	1-2,2-0	1-4,1-1	5-2,5-0	5-1,0-0			2-1,3-0	3-1,1-0
Ross County			0-1,3-3	3-0,1-0	3-0,1-1	1-2,0-0	2-0,1-5	2-0,2-0	3-3,1-0	1-1,0-1
St Johnstone							2-1,1-2	0-1,0-2	1-0,3-1	2-1,2-3
St Mirren	1-1,5-0	2-3,0-2			1-2,4-2	1-1,0-0	4-1,3-1	4-0,4-1	2-0,1-1	4-0,0-0

	94-5 Home	94-5 Away	95-6 Home	95-6 Away	96-7 Home	96-7 Away	97-8 Home	97-8 Away	98-9 Home	98-9 Away	99-0 Home	99-0 Away	00-1 Home	00-1 Away	01-2 Home	01-2 Away	02-3 Home	02-3 Away	03-4 Home	03-4 Away
Aberdeen											1-1	0-1								
Annan Athletic							8-1													
Arbroath													4-3			2-0				
Ayr United																				
Brechin City																			5-1	
Celtic												3-1					1-0			
Dunfermline																		0-1**	1-1^	2-3*
Dundee																				
Dundee United			1-1	1-1 x			2-3 aet	1-1												
East Fife																				
Hamilton					1-3												6-1			
Hearts														3-1						
Kilmarnock											1-1	1-2								
Livingston			3-2						1-2											
Motherwell																				1-0
Partick Thistle															0-1	2-2				
Q of the South	1-2																			
Queen's Park							2-0													
Raith Rovers																	2-0			
Rangers			0-3 >																	
Stenhousemuir				1-0																
St Mirren																				
Stranraer					0-0 ^	1-1														
Whitehill Welfare							3-1													

x 3-1 penalties aet

> played at Tannadice

^ 4-3 penalties aet

** Semi-final at Hampden

^ Semi-final at Hampden

* Semi-final replay at Pittodrie

APPENDIX F LEAGUE CUP OPPOSITION RECORD

Coca-Cola Cup — 1994-5 to 1997-8
League Cup — 1998-9
CIS Insurance Cup — From 1999-2000

	94-95 Home	94-5 Away	95-6 Home	95-6 Away	96-7 Home	96-7 Away	97-8 Home	97-8 Away	98-9 Home	98-9 Away	99-00 Home	99-00 Away	00-1 Home	00-1 Away	01-2 Home	01-2 Away	02-3 Home	02-3 Away	03-4 Home	03-4 Away
Aberdeen									0-3											
Airdrie													0-2							
Albion Rovers																2-0				
Ayr United																1-5				
Berwick Rangers				1-1 @																
Celtic																		2-4		
Clyde						0-1 aet														
Dumbarton																	2-0			
Dundee		0-3																		
Dunfermline																1-1 aet¬				
East Stirling		2-0																		
Motherwell								2-2 ~			0-1									
Partick Thistle															3-3 aet»					
Peterhead														3-2						
Q of the South										4-1										
Queen's Park																			1-2	
St Mirren											2-0 aet						3-1			
Stenhousemuir							5-1					3-1								

@ 3-5 penalties aet
~ 1-4 penalties aet
» 4-2 penalties aet
¬ 4-1 penalties aet

234

B&Q Cup — 1994-5
League Challenge Cup — 1995-6 to 1997-8
Not played — 1998-9
Bell's Challenge Cup — 1999-2000 to 2001-2
Bell's Cup — From 2002-03

	94-5 Home	94-5 Away	95-6 Home	95-6 Away	96-7 Home	96-7 Away	97-8 Home	97-8 Away	98-9 Home	98-9 Away	99-00 Home	99-00 Away	00-1 Home	00-1 Away	01-2 Home	01-2 Away	02-3 Home	02-3 Away	03-4 Home	03-4 Away
Airdrie United																				2-0+
Alloa Athletic			1-2									4-4^		3-2		2-3 aet				
Berwick Rangers																		0-1		
Clydebank											2-0									
Dundee	1-1 *																			
Forfar Athletic															3-2 aet					5-0
Gretna																				
Hamilton Academicals												3-0								
Livingston						2-1					1-0									
Peterhead																				2-1
Q of the South							0-2													
Raith Rovers																				4-0
Ross County											1-0								1-0	
St Mirren																				
Stirling Albion						1-3							1-2							
Stranraer																				

* 3-4 penalties aet   ^ Final at Airdrie. 4-5 penalties aet   +Final at Perth

REF	PLAYER	LEAGUE					CUP					TOTAL		
		APP	SUB ON	ALL APP	SUB	GLS	APP	SUB ON	ALL APP	SUB	GLS	ALL APP	ALL SUB	ALL GLS
1	Mark McRitchie	31		31	4		6		6			37	4	
2	Dave Brennan	36	4	40	2	2	5		5	1		45	3	2
3	Mark McAllister	50	5	55	4	4	5	1	6	1	1	61	5	5
4	Alan Hercher	53	14	67	6	20	9	3	12	1	3	79	7	23
5	John Scott	49	4	53		6	8		8	1		61	1	6
6	Mike Andrew	19		19	1	3	4		4			23	1	3
7	Danny MacDonald	7	1	8			2	1	3		1	11		1
8	Paul McKenzie	20	6	26	1	4	3	1	4			30	1	4
9	Mike Noble	93	2	95	5	3	17	1	18			113	5	3
10	Graeme Bennett	48	9	57	9	3	8	5	13	1		70	10	3
11	Wilson Robertson	23	4	27		5	4		4		1	31		6
12	Allan Smart	2	2	4	1		1	2	3			7	1	
13	Jim Calder	166	1	167	50		28		28	13		195	63	
14	Martin Lisle	29	11	40	8	1	2	1	3	1		43	9	1
15	Sergei Baltacha	9		9			1		1	1		10	1	
16	Richard Hastings	177	3	180	4	2	37	1	38			218	4	2
17	Norman MacMillan	26	9	35	4	5	3		3		1	38	4	6
18	Robin Gray				10								10	
19	Charlie Christie	222	35	257	4	32	46	11	57		2	314	4	34
20	Colin Mitchell	38	11	49	10	4	1	3	4	3		53	13	4
21	Colin Sinclair	10		10	4		1		1			11	4	
22	Bruce McCraw	7	8	15	1	2						15	1	2
23	Steven MacDonald	10	1	11	1		1		1			12	1	
24	Gary Watt	1	1	2	1							2	1	
25	Kevin Sweeney	6	1	7								7		
26	John MacDonald	2		2		1						2		1
27	Angus MacRae				1								1	
28	David Buchanan	5	1	6	1							6	1	
29	Mike Sanderson	3	4	7								7		
30	Billy Urquhart	2	1	3								3		
31	Mark Holmes	1		1								1		
32	Dave McGinlay	9	13	22	5		1	2	3	4		25	9	
33	Robbie Benson	3		3	6		2		2	1		5	7	
34	Davie Ross	66	22	88	6	9	11	6	17	4	1	105	10	10
35	Iain Stewart	100	17	117	2	70	25	2	27		12	144	2	82
36	Dougie Green	4	7	11		1	2		2			13		1
37	Iain MacArthur	79	4	83	4		14	1	15			98	4	

APPEARANCES AND GOALS

38	Mike Teasdale	163	19	182	7	16	39		39	2	3	221	9	19
39	Brian Thomson	66	11	77	2	25	16		16		9	93	2	34
40	Paul Cherry	85	4	89	1	12	15		15		2	104	1	14
41	Ross Tokely	206	22	228	15	18	48	7	55	1	2	283	16	20
42	Barry Wilson	142	17	159		49	29	2	31		10	190		59
43	Neal Sinclair		3	3	3					1		3	4	
44	Marco De-Barros	4	19	23	5	1		2	2			25	5	1
45	Scott McLean	60	11	71	5	30	11		11	1	5	82	6	35
46	Wayne Addicoat	14	32	46	7	3		7	7	1	1	53	8	4
47	Don McMillan	1		1								1		
48	Les Fridge	63		63	29		15		15	5		78	34	
49	Vetle Andersen	30	2	32			8		8			40		
50	Neil McCuish				2					1		3		
51	James Glass				1							1		
52	Mark McCulloch	99	1	100		8	19		19		1	119		9
53	Duncan Shearer	38	17	55	9	17	5	3	8	2	2	63	11	19
54	Barry Robson	102	33	135	14	17	24	8	32	3	10	167	17	27
55	Sandy Robertson	16		16		1	4		4			20		1
56	Paul Sheerin	117	2	119		36	22	1	23		9	142		45
57	Gregg Hood	3		3								3		
58	Martin Bavidge	59	41	100	18	15	12	10	22	6	4	122	24	19
59	Gary Farquhar	9	3	12	3		1	1	2			14	3	
60	Grant Munro	63	10	73	43	2	11	4	15	11		88	54	2
61	Andrew Allan	13	5	18	12		1		1	1		19	13	
62	Jordan MacDonald				2							2		
63	David Hind	2	3	5	12		1	1	2	1		7	13	
64	Hugh Robertson	12		12		1						12		1
65	David Craig	6	4	10	3			1	1			11	3	
66	Martin Glancy	15	16	31	8	6	2	5	7	2	1	38	10	7
67	Bobby Mann	171		171	1	14	43		43		3	214	1	17
68	Gary Nicol	1	3	4								4		
69	Stuart Golabek	118	12	130	28	3	35	1	36	10		166	38	3
70	Kevin Byers	25	18	43	13	1	3	9	12	1	1	55	14	2
71	Davide Xausa	35	6	41		17	6	1	7		3	48		20
72	Dennis Wyness	119	10	129	5	67	26	4	30	1	13	159	6	80
73	Neil MacDonald	1	16	17	6	2		3	3	2		20	8	2
74	Graeme Stewart	7	24	31	24	2	1	2	3	11		34	35	2
75	David Bagan	42	22	64	12	10	7	3	10	4	1	74	16	11
76	Roy McBain	127	5	132	4	8	31	3	34		1	166	4	9

No	Name													
77	Ally Ridgers				37					11		48		
78	Stuart McCaffrey	118	1	119	12	4	28		28	1	1	147	13	5
79	Brian Gilfillan		2	2	6					4		2	10	
80	Tony Low	2	14	16	13	1		3	3	3		19	16	1
81	David Graham		2	2				2	2			4		
82	Paul Bradshaw	2		2	1		2		2			4	1	
83	Paul Ritchie	80	23	103	3	46	26	3	29		17	132	3	63
84	Russell Duncan	82	8	90	3	2	24	2	26	1		116	4	2
85	Nicky Walker	27		27	2		7		7			34	2	
86	David MacRae		2	2	6			1	1	2		3	8	
87	Niall Calder				1							1		
88	Richie Hart	43	8	51	3	9	13		13	1	3	64	4	12
89	Liam Keogh	24	29	53	8	3	6	5	11	2		64	10	3
90	Mark Brown	72		72			19		19			91		
91	Chris Miller		1	1	4					1		1	5	
92	Mike Fraser				46					11		57		
93	Steve Hislop	23	17	40	2	11	5	3	8		5	48	2	16
94	David Bingham	31	2	33		13	9		9		4	42		17
95	Darran Thomson	7	14	21	14	1	2	9	11		1	32	14	2
96	David Proctor	4	7	11	6		1	6	7	1		18	7	
97	Lewis MacKinnon		1	1						2		1	2	
98	Craig MacMillan		10	10	8			1	1	2		11	10	
99	Darren Mackie	5	1	6			1	1	2			8		
100	Jonathon Smith				1							1		

APPENDIX I
PLAYER PROFILES

Players listed in order of first squad appearance

1. Mark McRitchie (1994-5 to 1995-6)
Goalkeeper – born Clydebank 7.7.70 – debut 9.8.94, last game 26.8.95.
37 appearances (31 league, 6 cup). 6 shut-outs, 3 penalty saves (plus 1 in shoot-out).
Debut for Caledonian in 1988-9 then to Lossiemouth on loan. Back to Caledonian 1990-1 First choice goalkeeper when the unified club entered the Scottish League and only missed seven games in 1994-5. Lost his place to Jim Calder in September 1995. Second Team Player of the Year 1995-6. Signed for Lossiemouth July 1996 and to Forres March 1999.

2. Dave Brennan (1994-5 to 1995-6)
Defender – born Bellshill 2.1.71 – debut 9.8.94, last game 6.4.96.
45 appearances (40 league, 5 cup). 2 league goals.
Signed for Caledonian from Shotts Bon Accord and played one season in the Highland League. First choice for the number 2 shirt in 1994-5 but the signing of Iain MacArthur marked the end of his hold on the position. Signed for Forres September 1996 then to Clach November 1996.

3. Mark McAllister (1994-5 to 1996-7)
Defender – born Inverness 13.2.71 – debut 9.8.94, last game 10.8.96.
61 appearances (55 league, 6 cup). 5 goals (4 league, 1 cup).
Defender who played six seasons for Caledonian before joining the unified club. Missed one game in 1994-5 and on 20 January 1996 became the first player to reach 50 appearances. Moved to London in August 1996 and joined Dulwich Hamlet. Players' Player and Supporters' Player of the Year 1994-5.

4. Alan Hercher (1994-5 to 1996-7)
Midfield/Forward – born Dingwall 11.8.65 – debut 9.8.94, last game 1.2.97.
79 appearances (67 league, 12 cup). 23 goals (20 league, 3 cup).
Signed for Caledonian in 1986 and after three seasons went to Stirling Macedonia in Australia. Returned to Telford Street in 1990-1. Became an instant Caley Thistle hero with a hat-trick against Arbroath in the first ever league match. First club captain and top scorer 1994-5 with seven goals. Third Division Championship medal 1996-7. Testimonial match against St Johnstone on 28 July 1997. Later to Clach and Brora.

5. John Scott (1994-5 to 1995-6)
Midfield – born Aberdeen 9.3.75 – debut 9.8.94, last game 4.5.96.
61 appearances (53 league, 8 cup). 6 league goals.
Scottish schoolboy Under-15 and Under-16 internationalist. Spent three seasons with Liverpool then signed for Caley Thistle in time to play in the first competitive match on 9 August 1994. Left to take up a soccer scholarship in the USA. Back to Deveronvale, Fraserburgh then Buckie.

6. Mike Andrew (1994-5)
Defender – born Lenzie 19.4.59 – debut 9.8.94, last game 8.4.95.
23 appearances (19 league, 4 cup). 3 league goals.
Played for both Inverness Thistle (7 years) and Caledonian (6 years). Captained Caledonian to success in the 1991-2 North Qualifying Cup and the 1993-4 North of Scotland Cup. Left for Fort William in July 1995. Later to Clach.

7. Danny MacDonald (1994-5)
Midfield – born Inverness 29.8.66 – debut 9.8.94, last game 15.10.94.
11 appearances (8 league, 3 cup appearances). 1 cup goal.
Started in the Caledonian youth programme then moved to Clach, Thistle and back to Caley in 1989-0. Combined playing for Caley Thistle with post as first team coach before sustaining a cruciate ligament injury. This resulted in a long spell on the sidelines and prevented a return to first team football. Player/manager of reserve side from March 1996 then Youth Development Coach. Later to Ross County in a coaching role. Returned in July 2003 as Community and Football Development Manager.

8. Paul McKenzie (1994-5 to 1995-6)
Forward – born Aberdeen 4.8.69 – debut 9.8.94, last game 20.4.96.
30 appearances (26 league, 4 cup). 4 league goals.
Came to the club from Burnley after spells with Peterhead, Wycombe Wanderers, Leyton Orient, Sunderland and Preston. A cruciate ligament injury kept him out of action from March 1995 to March 1996 and he never regained a regular first team place. To Peterhead in June 1996. Later to Fraserburgh.

9. Mike Noble (1994-5 to 1998-9)
Defender – born Inverness 18.5.66 – debut 9.8.94, last game 20.9.97.
113 appearances (95 league, 18 cup). 3 league goals.
Product of the Caledonian youth programme then to Clach, Thistle, Elgin and back to Caledonian. Captain 1995-6 and 1996-7 (Third Division championship winning season). Players' Player of the Year 1995-6. Made the most appearances in 1995-6 when he played in all 43 matches. First to reach 100 Appearances on 11 March 1997 away to Alloa and scored in that match. Third Division Championship medal 1996-7. Testimonial against St Johnstone on 4 April 2000. To Forres in October 1998.

10. Graeme Bennett (1994-5 to 1996-7)
Midfield/Defender – born Inverness 7.5.65 – debut 9.8.94, last game 10.5.97.
70 appearances (57 league, 13 cup). 3 league goals.
Started with Caledonian youth then to Thistle, Nairn, Clach, Elgin and back to Clach. Signed from Clach in August 1994. Third Division Championship medal 1996-7. After the club's Third Division championshif and became vice-chairman in May 2002.

11. Wilson Robertson (1994-5)
Forward – born Aberdeen 27.1.63 – debut 9.8.94, last game 13.5.95.
31 appearances (27 league, 4 cup). 6 goals (5 league, 1 cup).
Left winger who was a great servant and prolific goalscorer for Caledonian. Scored the first ever Caley Thistle goal in the cup win at East Stirling on 9 August 1994. To Buckie Thistle July 1995. Later to Bon Accord Juniors.

12. Allan Smart (1994-5)
Forward – born Perth 8.7.74 – debut 9.8.94, last game 12.11.94.
7 appearances (4 league, 3 cup).
Forward who joined Caledonian from Brechin in 1993-4 and scored 13 goals that season. Signed for Preston in November 1994 then moved to Carlisle, Northampton (loan), Watford. Part of the Watford team that won promotion to the Premiership in 1998-9. Scored the winning goal in the play-offs. Later to Hibernian (loan), Stoke (loan), Oldham, Dundee United and Crewe Alexandra.

APPENDIX I

13. Jim Calder (1994-5 to 2001-2)
Goalkeeper – born Grantown-on-Spey 29.7.60 – debut 14.1.95, last game 27.4.02.
195 appearances (167 league, 28 cup). 48 shut-outs, 14 penalty saves (plus 5 in shoot-outs).
Former Inverness Thistle striker and goalkeeper. Started his Caley Thistle career as understudy to Mark McRitchie but took over in September 1995. The arrival of Les Fridge in the summer of 1997 led to fierce competition but Calder was first choice for most of 1997-8 and 1998-9. Fridge had the edge in 1999-2000 but the following season Calder regained possession. Final season spent mostly as understudy to Nicky Walker. 63 consecutive games from 2 September 1995 to 18 January 1997. Testimonial match against Hibernian 9 March 1999. Supporters' Player of the Year 1995-6 & 1997-8. Matchday Programme Player of the Year 1995-6. Third Division Championship medal 1996-7. Played his final game on 27 April 2002 against Partick Thistle and was captain for the day. Oldest club player so far at 41 years 272 days. To Strathspey Thistle in July 2002. To Nairn County July 2004.

14. Martin Lisle (1994-5 to 1995-6)
Midfield – born Inverness 9.1.63 – debut 13.8.94, last game 4.5.96.
43 appearances (40 league, 3 cup). 1 league goal.
Former Caledonian player who played in excess of 500 times for Caledonian over 15 years. Played in Caley Thistle's first ever league game on 13 August 1994. To Elgin City at the end of 1995-6 but only played once and returned to the ICT reserve side in February 1997.

15. Sergei Baltacha (1994-5)
Defender – born Mariupol, Ukraine 17.2.58 – debut 22.10.94, last game 14.1.95.
10 appearances (9 league, 1 cup).
Caledonian player/manager 1993-4 and Caledonian Thistle player/manager 1994-5. Playing appearances for the unified club restricted by injury. Played for Dynamo Kiev, Ipswich and St Johnstone before coming to Inverness. 47 full USSR international caps. Resigned in May 1995 for family reasons. Later a coaching role at St Mirren, manager of CSKA (Ukraine) then Football Development Officer for Dumfries and Galloway.

16. Richard Hastings (1994-5 to 2000-1)
Defender – born Prince George, BC, Canada 18.5.77 – debut 20.8.94, last game 14.4.01.
218 appearances (180 league appearances, 38 cup). 2 league goals.
Signed from Nairn County then came into the first team in 1994-5 from the youth side. Eventually took over the number three shirt from Mark McAllister. Scottish Under-18 internationalist before his reputation crossed the Atlantic to the land of his birth Played for Canadian Under-20 side in 1995-6 and 1996-7. First full cap on his 21st birthday on 18 May 1998 against Macedonia. Part of the Canadian Gold Cup winning side in February 2000 – scored quarter final golden goal. 36 caps by November 2003. Youngest player for club on debut 20 August 1994 at 17 years 94 days Under-18 Player of the Year 1994/95. Third Division Championship medal 1996-7. Most appearances 1997-8 – 43 out of 44. To Ross County August 2001, Grazer AK (Austria) July 2002 and MV Maastricht (Holland) August 2003. Re-signed for ICT July 2004.

17. Norman MacMillan (1994-5 to 1995-6)
Midfield/forward – born Portree 9.12.74 – debut 20.8.94, last game 4.11.95.
38 appearances (35 league, 3 cup). 6 goals (5 league, 1 cup).
Signed from Nairn County in August 1994 and made 29 appearances in 1994-5. Found it hard to compete with Steve Paterson's new signings in 1995-6. To Clach then later to Brora and Fort William.

18. Robin Gray (1994-5)
Goalkeeper – born Inverness 3.4.65 –10 sub appearances but not used.
Former Caledonian goalkeeper who was back-up to Mark McRitchie and Jim Calder in 1994-5. Played in the reserves for part of 1994-5 and signed for Forres in September 1995.

19. Charlie Christie (1994-5 to 2003-4)
Midfield/forward – born Inverness 30.3.66 – debut 3.9.94, last game 7.2.04.
314 appearances (257 league, 57 cup). 34 goals (32 league, 2 cup).
The only player to appear for the unified club in all of its first ten seasons. First to reach 150, 200, 250 and 300 Appearances. Debut for Caledonian in October 1983, to Thistle February 1985, to Celtic September 1987 (25 goals in 56 reserve appearances) and back to Caledonian May 1989 as player and commercial manager. Missed the start of 1994-5 through injury but went on to become the club's most consistent and influential player. Started in a striking role but moved to midfield. Combines playing with coaching and running the fund-raising Centenary Club. Third Division Championship medal 1996-7. Testimonial match against Celtic on 7 April 1998. Matchday Programme Player of the Year 1998-9. Man of the Match in the Celtic cup win 8 February 2000. Most appearances in 2000-1 – 42 out of maximum 43. First Division Championship medal 2003-4. Retired from playing at the end of 2003-4.

20. Colin Mitchell (1994-5 to 1995-6)
Midfield/forward – born Glasgow 24.3.71 – debut 1.10.94, last game 20.4.96.
53 appearances (49 league, 4 cup). 4 league goals.
Previously with Caledonian, Inverness Thistle and Reading. Entertaining and skilful player who was unlucky to be competing with Iain Stewart and Charlie Christie. Transfer listed at the end of 1994-5 but stayed for one more season. To Forres then Clach.

21. Colin Sinclair (1994-5)
Defender – born in Inverness 3.3.70 – debut 28.9.94, last game 13.5.95.
11 appearances (10 league, 1 cup).
Started in the Caledonian youth side, moved to Nairn County and returned to Caledonian 1992-3. Fell victim to Steve Paterson's rebuilding programme and left for Clach July 1995.

22. Bruce McCraw (1994-5)
Forward – born Keith 19.9.72 – debut 22.10.94, last game 13.5.95.
15 league appearances, 2 league goals.
Former Nairn County player. Scored two goals on his debut against Arbroath. Left at the end of 1994-5 on loan to Clach. Released April 1996 and signed for Clach.

23. Steven MacDonald (1994-5)
Defender – born Inverness 7.12.75 – debut 29.10.94, last game 29.4.95.
12 appearances (11 league, 1 cup).
One of the few former Inverness Thistle players to play for the Caley Thistle first team. Appearances curtailed by bad leg injury sustained against Montrose on 14 February 1995 To Elgin on loan in July 1995 then to Maitland City (Australia), Forres, Elgin City and Clach.

24. Gary Watt (1994-5)

Midfield/forward – born Inverness 1.1.75 – debut 26.12.94, last game 14.1.95.
2 league appearances.
Ex-Inverness Thistle player who also had a spell at Dundee United. Mainly a reserve player. Later to Elgin City then Forres.

25. Kevin Sweeney (1994-5)
Defender – born Inverness 3.8.67 – debut 21.1.95, last game 11.4.95.
7 league appearances.
Former Caledonian, Inverness Thistle, Nairn and Brora defender who played for the unified club as an amateur. Knee injury stopped him going to Forres after release. Came back 1997-8 as assistant to second team coach John Docherty.

26. John MacDonald (1994-5)
Forward – born Glasgow 15.4.61 – debut 21.1.95, last game 4.2.95.
2 league appearances. 1 league goal.
Former Rangers player who came on trial in January 1995. Scored on his debut. After two appearances he was offered terms but declined for travel reasons. Later coached at Partick Thistle.

27. Angus MacRae (1994-5)
Goalkeeper – born Inverness 11.4.75 – 1 sub appearance but not used.
Reserve goalkeeper. Substitute for the first team on 11 February 1995 against Albion Rovers.

28. David Buchanan (1994-5)
Defender – born Cardiff 7.4.76 – debut 4.3.95, last game 6.5.95.
6 league appearances.
One of the youngsters introduced by Sergei Baltacha towards the close of 1994-5. Not retained by Steve Paterson and left for Ross County. Later to Elgin, Nairn and Brora Rangers.

29. Mike Sanderson (1994-5)
Forward – born Inverness 24.11.77 – debut 4.3.95, last game 29.4.95.
7 league appearances.
Youngster introduced towards the close of 1994-5. To Nairn County on loan for 1995-6 then released. Later to Forres, Elgin and Clach.

30. Billy Urquhart (1994-5)
Forward – born Inverness 22.11.56 – debut 1.4.95, last game 13.5.95.
3 league appearances.
One of the all time Caledonian greats. Made his Caledonian debut in August 1972, signed for Rangers in July 1978, moved to Wigan in November 1980 and returned to Caledonian in August 1981. Retired officially in May 1993 but made a nostalgic return for the final Caledonian/Thistle derby on 11 May 1994. Came out of retirement in January 1995 to play for the unified club's reserve side and turned out for the first team near the end of 1994-5.

31. Mark Holmes (1994-5)
Forward – born Inverness 21.7.75 - debut/last game 13.5.95.
1 league appearance.
Named Man of the Match on his only league outing. To Clach on loan August 1995 then released April 1996. Signed for Clach then to Capalaba, Newmarket and Brisbane Strikers (all Australia) before returning to play for Forres, Buckie then Nairn.

32. Dave McGinlay (1995-6)
Defender – born Fort William 9.2.69 – debut 5.8.95, last game 4.5.96.
25 appearances (22 league, 3 cup).

Signed by Steve Paterson from Huntly and previously played for Fort William, Elgin, North Shore United (North Shore United) and Kitchee United (Hong Kong). First team regular in 1995-6. Later to Lossiemouth, Deveronvale, Turriff United (player/manager), Cove Rangers and Huntly.

33. Robbie Benson (1995-6 to 1996-7)
Defender – born Inverness 9.4.68 – debut 5.8.95, last game 2.9.95.
5 appearances (3 league, 2 cup).
Former Clach player whose first team Caley Thistle career was cut drastically short by a cruciate ligament injury. Second Team Player of the Year 1996-7. To Clach in summer 1997.

34. Davie Ross (1995-6 to 1997-8)
Midfield/Forward – born Inverness 30.6.70 – debut 5.8.95, last game 28.3.98
105 appearances (88 league, 17 cup). 10 goals (9 league, 1 cup).
One of Steve Paterson's first signings in June 1995 from Brora Rangers. His flying runs and 100% effort made 'Daisy' a firm favourite with the Inverness fans. A fixture in the team in 1995-6 and 1996-7 but in 1997-8 faced stiff competition for the number eleven shirt from Paul Sheerin and Barry Robson. Third Division Championship medal 1996-7. To Ross County 31 March 1998 on loan then signed. Later to Elgin then Clach.

35. Iain Stewart (1995-6 to 2000-1)
Forward – born Dundee 23.10.69 – debut 5.8.95, last game 16.9.00.
144 appearances (117 league, 27 cup). 82 goals (70 league, 12 cup).
Prolific goalscorer who started at Dundee before being released and signing for Lossiemouth. Sergei Baltacha tried to bring him to Inverness in 1994-5 but failed. Steve Paterson succeeded the following season and it proved an inspired signing. Fee of £30000 set by SFA tribunal. Three very successful seasons before appearances restricted by injury. Top club goalscorer of the first decade with a total of 82 including four hat-tricks. Division 3 Player of the Year nominee 1995-6 – won title 1996-7. Played in all 42 matches 1996-7. Third Division Championship medal 1996-7. Players' Player of the Year 1997-8. 88 consecutive games 13 January 1996 to 31 January 1998. Top Club/Division scorer 1995-6 (24), 1996-7 (29) and 1997-8 (20 – joint). To Peterhead October 2000. Appointed Peterhead player/manager in January 2004.

36. Dougie Green (1995-6)
Forward – born Elgin 3.1.73 – debut 5.8.95, last game 18.11.95.
13 appearances (11 league, 2 cup). 1 league goal.
Came highly recommended from New Elgin Juniors but never settled at the club. To Elgin City June 1996 then spent time in the junior ranks before joining Lossiemouth in July 2003.

37. Iain MacArthur (1995-6 to 1998-9)
Defender – born Elgin 18.10.67 – debut 9.9.95, last game 26.9.98.
98 appearances (83 league, 15 cup).
Signed from Elgin City. Previously played for North Shore United in New Zealand. High quality defender whose career was curtailed by a knee injury. Players' Player and Supporters' Player of the Year 1996-7. Third Division Championship medal 1996-7. Shared captaincy with Paul Cherry 1997-8. Retired through injury December 1999.

38. Mike Teasdale (1995-6 to 2001-2)
Defender – born Elgin 28.7.69 – debut 16.12.95, last game 15.12.01.
221 appearances (182 league, 39 cup). 19 goals (16 league, 3 cup).
Former Elgin City and Dundee defender who signed in December 1995 just in time to win an Inverness Cup winner's medal. His grit and determination made him a great favourite with fans. Played in

all games 1996-7 and 1998-9. Matchday Programme Player of the Year 1996-7 and Supporters' Player of the Year 1998-9. Third Division Championship medal 1996-7. Joined Elgin City March 2002 to combine playing with running the commercial department.

39. Brian Thomson (1995-6 to 1997-8)

Forward – born Fraserburgh 19.6.66 – debut 16.12.95, last game 2.5.98.

93 appearances (77 league, 16 cup). 34 goals (25 league, 9 cup).

Hard-hitting striker who signed from Huntly the day before the December 1995 Inverness Cup win. Previously with Fraserburgh, Motherwell, Peterhead and Arbroath. Joint top Second Division scorer 1997-8 (20). Hat trick, 2 August 1997. Missed part of 1996-7 with trapped nerve in back. Most valuable goal was the winner against Stenhousemuir on 17 February 1996 which earned the Scottish Cup Quarter Final tie against Rangers. Third Division Championship medal 1996-7. To Fraserburgh then Buckie Thistle.

40. Paul Cherry (1996-7 to 1998-9)

Defender/Midfield – born Derby 14.10.64 – debut 3.8.96, last game 24.4.99.

104 appearances (89 league, 15 cup). 14 goals (12 league, 2 cup).

Came to Inverness after a highly successful career with Cowdenbeath, Hearts and St Johnstone. Shared captaincy with Iain MacArthur 1997-8. Third Division Championship medal 1996-7. Part of the 1998-9 team that won promotion to the First Division. Retired December 1999 after hernia operation.

41. Ross Tokely (From 1996-7)

Defender/Midfield – born Aberdeen 8.3.79 – debut 3.8.96.

283 appearances (228 league, 55 cup). 20 goals (18 league, 2 cup).

Signed from Huntly at age 17 and second-longest serving player at the club. Scored the first goal in the cup win against Hearts January 2002. 250 appearance milestone reached 4 October 2003. Scotland Under-16, -17 and -18 International. Third Division Championship medal 1996-7. Bell's Cup winner's medal 2003. Supporters' Club Player of the Year 2003-4. First Division Championship medal 2003-4.

42. Barry Wilson (1996-7 to 1999-2000) (From 2003-4)

Forward – born Kirkcaldy 16.2.72 – two spells at the club.

1996-7 to 1999-2000 - debut 3.8.96, last game 6.5.00. From 2003-4 - debut 2.9.03.

1996-7 to 1999-2000 - 156 appearances (130 league, 26 cup). 45 goals (38 league, 7 cup).

2003-4 - 34 appearances (29 league, 5 cup). 14 goals (11 league, 3 cup).

Total – 190 appearances (159 league, 31 cup). 59 goals (49 league, 10 cup).

A major player at the club as a goalscorer and creator. Moved from Ross County to Raith Rovers then came to Inverness for the first time in the summer of 1996. Third Division Championship medal 1996-7. Played in all 39 matches 1998-9. Into the history books as the scorer of the last Scottish League or Cup goal of the old millennium on 27 December 1999 and the first of the new on 3 January 2000. Players' Player of the Year 1998-9. To Livingston May 2000 but returned to the club in August 2003. Bell's Cup winner's medal 2003. First Division Championship medal 2003-4.

43. Neal Sinclair (1996-7)

Forward – born Dingwall 1.3.77 – debut 31.8.96, last game 10.5.97.

3 league appearances.

Signed from Nairn County but previously with Caledonian. Although his competitive debut was not until August 1996, he played for the first team in a friendly against Celtic on 17 September 1994. Scotland Under-18 International. Back to club July 1996 after loan to Nairn County for 1995-6. Later to Wick Academy and Nairn.

44. Marco De-Barros (1996-7 to 1997-8)

Forward – born London 18.8.71 – debut 14.9.96, last game 9.8.97.

25 appearances (23 league, 2 cup). 1 league goal.

Gifted player who never realised his full potential. Signed from Huntly and previously with Elgin and Lossiemouth. Scored a 32-second goal in a friendly at Wick on 19 July 1997, then the fastest goal but record since beaten. Third Division Championship medal 1996-7. Returned to Huntly then to Brechin City before playing briefly for several Highland League sides.

45. Scott McLean (1996-7 to 1999-2000)

Forward – born East Kilbride 17.6.76 – debut 21.9.96, last game 6.11.99.

82 appearances (71 league, 11 cup). 35 goals (30 league, 5 cup).

Signed from St Johnstone. Prolific goalscorer but lost a year from March 1997 due to a cruciate ligament injury. Third Division Championship medal 1996-7. To Clach on loan February 1998 to regain fitness. Runner up Division 2 top goalscorer and top club goalscorer 1998-9 (20). To Queen of the South on loan then to Partick Thistle, St Mirren and Stirling.

46. Wayne Addicoat (1996-7 to 1998-9)

Forward – born Middlesbrough 17.6.79 – debut 16.11.96, last game 30.1.99.

53 appearances (46 league, 7 cup). 4 goals (3 league, 1 cup).

Signed from Deveronside. Most appearances were as a substitute – just 14 starts. Third Division Championship medal 1996-7. To Ross County on loan March to October 1998. To Huntly on loan February 1999 then signed.

47. Don MacMillan (1996-7)

Goalkeeper – born Helmsdale 12.12.73 - debut/last game 22.1.97.

1 league appearance (shut-out).

Started with Brora then to Ross County. Signed as cover for Jim Calder. Played mainly in the reserve side but made one first team appearance against Queen's Park. Left for Brora in the summer of 1997. Later to Wick.

48. Les Fridge (1997-8 to 2001-2)

Goalkeeper – born Inverness 27.8.68 – debut 2.8.97, last game 27.1.01.

78 appearances (63 league, 15 cup). 21 shut-outs and 6 penalty saves (plus 1 in shoot-out).

Played in the Inverness Thistle first team at age 15 before signing for Chelsea. Moved on to St Mirren, Clyde, Raith Rovers and Irish club Dundalk. Signed in May 1997 and vied with Jim Calder for the number one shirt over his first four seasons at Caledonian Stadium. Dropped to third in the pecking order when Nicky Walker arrived in the summer of 2001. To Ross County March 2002 and appointed manager of Nairn County in late May 2004.

49. Vetle Andersen (1997-8)

Defender – born Kristiansand, Norway 20.4.64 – debut 2.8.97, last game 9.5.98.

40 appearances (32 league, 8 cup).

Played for many European clubs before spells with Raith Rovers and Dunfermline. Transfer listed November 1997 but stayed until the end of the season before going to Sweden.

PLAYER PROFILES

50. Neil McCuish (1997-8)
Midfield – born Inverness 28.8.80
3 sub appearances, not used.
Originally signed on schoolboy 'S' form. To Clach.

51. James Glass (1997-8)
Midfield – born Inverness 1.8.78
1 sub appearance, not used.
Made just one bench appearance on 16 August 1997. To Clach on loan early 1998 then released.

52. Mark McCulloch (1997-8 to 1999-2000)
Defender – born Inverness 19.5.75 – debut 23.8.97, last game 6.5.00.
119 appearances (100 league, 19 cup). 9 goals (8 league, 1 cup).
Signed from Dunfermline Athletic in August 1997. Formerly with Nairn and Clach. Matchday Programme Player of the Year 1997-8. Captain from 1998-9 to 1999-2000. Most appearances in 1999-2000 – 46 out of a maximum 47. Signed for Livingston in July 2000. After a season with Livingston he joined Partick Thistle then Ross County. Played for all three clubs against Caley Thistle in successive seasons.

53. Duncan Shearer (1997-8 to 2001-2)
Forward – born Fort William 28.8.62 – debut 13.9.97, last game 14.9.99.
63 appearances (55 league, 8 cup). 19 goals (17 league, 2 cup).
Scottish international striker who came to Inverness in September 1997 after a high-profile career at Aberdeen, Chelsea, Huddersfield, Swindon and Blackburn. Combined playing with the role of community coach until appointed first team coach in May 1998. By the summer of 1999 his first team appearances were restricted to that of substitute. When Alex Caldwell left in February 2000 Shearer became assistant manager. Three bench appearances 2001-2 in a trialist role. Steve Paterson left for Aberdeen in December 2002 and Shearer went as his assistant.

54. Barry Robson (1997-8 to 2002-3)
Midfield/Forward – born Aberdeen 7.11.78 – debut 4.10.97, last game 10.5.03.
167 appearances (135 league, 32 cup). 27 goals (17 league goals, 10 cup).
Came from Rangers youth set-up. Loan to Forfar October 1999 to April 2000. In 2001-2 he became an automatic first team choice. 2002-3 was his finest season with 13 goals. Bid from Dundee United rejected by the club in January 2003 but deal concluded at the end of 2002-3. Internet Player of the Year 2001-2. Bell's Player of the Month November 2002. Record fastest competitive goal – 40 seconds against Ross County on 9 November 2002.

55. Sandy Robertson (1997-8)
Midfield – born Edinburgh 26.4.71 – debut 29.11.97, last game 28.3.98.
20 appearances (16 league, 4 cup). 1 league goal.
Former Rangers, Coventry and Dundee United player who came on a short-term contract from November 1997 to March 1998. To Livingston then Clydebank.

56. Paul Sheerin (1997-8 to 2000-1)
Midfield – born Edinburgh 28.8.74 – debut 17.1.98, last game 5.5.01.
142 appearances (119 league, 23 cup). 45 goals (36 league, 9 cup).
Formerly with Alloa, Southampton and Ostersund (Sweden). Scored crucial third goal in cup win over Celtic in February 2000. Players' Player of the Year 1999-2000. Tennent's Scottish Cup Player of Round 3 in January 2001. First Division Player of the Year nominee 2000-

1. Played in all 42 matches 1996-7 and all 39 matches 1998-9. 98 consecutive appearances from 31 January 1998 to 18 March 2000. Top scorer 1999-2000 with 17 goals. To Ayr United June 2001 then to Aberdeen January 2003.

57. Gregg Hood (1997-8)
Defender – born Bellshill 29.5.74 – debut 28.3.98, last game 11.4.98.
3 league appearances.
Former Ayr United defender and captain who came on loan for a short period. Scotland Under-21 international.

58. Martin Bavidge (1998-9 to 2001-2)
Forward – born Aberdeen 30.4.80 – debut 1.8.98, last game 27.4.02.
122 appearances (100 league, 22 cup). 19 goals (15 league, 4 cup).
Signed in the summer of 1998 from Lewis United. Spent most of 1998-9 on loan to Forres Mechanics. Appearances in 1999-2000 were mostly from the bench but made 29 starts in both 2000-1 and 2001-2. At the end of 2001-2 he decided to revert to part-time football and use his geology degree to give him a career outside football. Signed for Forfar Athletic on a part-time basis in May 2002.

59. Gary Farquhar (1998-9 to 2000-1)
Midfield – born Wick 23.2.71 – debut 1.8.98, last game 17.4.99.
14 appearances (12 league, 2 cup).
From St Johnstone in the summer of 1998. Loan to Clach for part of 1998-9. Loan to Wick in October 2000 and left for Nairn County in June 2001.

60. Grant Munro (From 1998-9)
Defender – born Inverness 15.9.80 – debut 2.1.99.
88 appearances (73 league, 15 cup). 2 league goals.
Former 'S' form signing who made the breakthrough to become a regular first team player. Strong, dependable player who has been forced to watch patiently from the bench on many occasions. Always gives 100% when called into action. Loan to Fort William for part of 1998-9 and to Elgin City for part of 2000-1. Bell's Cup winner's medal 2003. First Division Championship medal 2003-4.

61. Andrew Allan (1998-9 to 1999/2000)
Defender – born Inverness 5.11.80 – debut 29.8.98, last game 15.4.00.
19 appearances (18 league, 1 cup).
Signed for club on schoolboy 'S' form. Loan to Clach October 2000 then transfer made permanent in March 2001. Joined the Royal Navy in 2002.

62. Jordan MacDonald (1998-9 to 1999/2000)
Midfield – born Inverness 7.9.82
2 sub appearances, not used.
Loan to Fort William for part of 1998-9. To Elgin, Clach then on loan to Brora.

63. David Hind (1998-9 to 2000-1)
Defender/midfield – born Inverness 15.9.82 – debut 8.1.00, last game 2.9.00.
7 appearances (5 league, 2 cup).
'S' form signing. Loan to Fort William from November 2000 to March 2001. To Elgin March 2001.

64. Hugh Robertson (1998-9)
Defender – born Aberdeen 19.3.75 – debut 3.10.98, last game 27.12.98.
12 league appearances, 1 league goal.

From Dundee on loan because of long-term injury to Richard Hastings. Loan period ended when he was offered a new contract at Dundee. Later to Ayr United, Ross County and Hartlepool United.

65. David Craig (1998-9 to 1999/2000)
Forward – born Inverness 22.1.80 – debut 2.1.99, last game 6.5.00.
11 appearances (10 league, 1 cup).
Product of the ICT youth team. Loan to Wick October 2000. Signed for Elgin City February 2001. Joined the RAF in 2003.

66. Martin Glancy (1998-9 to 1999/2000)
Forward – born Glasgow 24.3.76 – debut 9.1.99, last game 26.2.00.
38 appearances (31 league, 7 cup). 7 goals (6 league, 1 cup).
Came on loan from Dumbarton in January 1999 then signed. To Clydebank November 2000 and Airdrie United 2002-3.

67. Bobby Mann (1998-9 to 2003-4)
Defender – born Dundee 11.1.74 – debut 6.2.99, last game 15.5.04.
214 appearances (171 league, 43 cup). 17 goals (14 league, 3 cup).
Signed from Forfar in February 1999, previously played for St Johnstone. Strong defender with excellent timing and a regular goalscorer from set-pieces. Captain from 2000-1 to 2003-4. His solid performances at the heart of the defence made him a firm favourite with the fans. Matchday Programme Player of the Year for three seasons from 1999-2000 to 2001-2. Supporters' Player of the Year 1999-2000 and 2000-1. Internet Player of the Year 2000-1. Bell's Cup winner's medal 2003. First Division Championship medal 2003-4. To Dundee at the end of 2003-4.

68. Gary Nicol (1998-9)
Forward – born Inverness 7.9.80 – debut 3.4.99, last game 24.4.99.
4 league appearances.
Released by Celtic and came to Inverness for a trial period. To Ross County April 1999. Later to Huntly and Deveronvale.

69. Stuart Golabek (From 1999-2000)
Defender – born Inverness 5.11.74 – debut 31.1.99.
166 appearances (130 league, 36 cup). 3 league goals.
Strong-tackling defender formerly with Clach and Ross County. Very dependable and enthusiastic player whose wholehearted performances always impress. Swept the board in 2002-3 – Player's Player, Supporters' Club Player and Internet Player of the Year. Bell's Cup winner's medal 2003. First Division Championship medal 2003-4.

70. Kevin Byers (1999-2000 to 2000-1)
Midfield – born Kirkcaldy 23.8.79 – debut 17.8.99, last game 5.5.01.
55 appearances (43 league, 12 cup). 2 goals (1 league, 1 cup).
Came from his home club Raith Rovers and scored on his debut. Loan to Montrose from December 2000 to March 2001. To Forfar July 2001.

71. Davide Xausa (1999-2000 to 2000-1)
Midfield/forward – born Vancouver, Canada 10.3.76 – debut 11.9.99, last game 13.3.01.
48 appearances (41 league, 7 cup). 20 goals (17 league, 3 cup).
Canadian international player who joined from Dutch side Dordrecht 90 in September 1999. Formerly Stoke City and St Johnstone. In Canadian Gold Cup winning squad February 2000 but missed the final through injury. 32 international caps. Hat-trick 18 March 2000. To Livingston March 2001, to Falkirk August 2003 and returned to Canada February 2004.

72. Dennis Wyness (1999-2000 to 2002-3)
Forward – born Aberdeen 22.3.77 – debut 28.9.99, last game 10.5.03.
159 appearances (129 league, 30 cup). 80 goals (67 league, 13 cup).
To Inverness on loan from Aberdeen in September 1999 and signed in January 2000. Eventually became a major player and a prolific goalscorer. Top goalscorer from 2000-1 to 2002-3. Players' Player of the Year 2000/01, Supporters' Player of the Year 2002/03, Bell's First Division Player of the Month four times. Bell's First Division Player of the Year and top goalscorer 2002-3. Record 119 games in a row from 21 October 2000 to 10 May 2003 – including every game in seasons 2001-2 and 2002-3. Scored the winner against Celtic on 23 March 2003. To Hearts May 2003.

73. Neil MacDonald (1999-2000 to 2001-2)
Forward – born Isle of Lewis 8.1.83 – debut 15.4.00, last game 27.4.02.
20 appearances (17 league, 3 cup). 2 league goals.
Most appearances from the bench – one start. Loan to Fort William from October 2000 to March 2001. Spectacular first goal against Morton 7 April 2001. To Clach June 2002.

74. Graeme Stewart (1999-2000 to 2002-3)
Midfield – born Aberdeen 2.4.82 – debut 6.5.00, last game 29.4.03.
34 appearances (31 league, 2 cup). 2 league goals.
Signed from Lewis United. Loan to Clach October 2000. To Peterhead at end of 2002-3.

75. David Bagan (2000-1 to 2002-3)
Midfield – born Kilmarnock 26.4.77 – debut 5.8.00, last game 10.5.03.
74 appearances (64 league, 10 cup). 11 goals (10 league, 1 cup).
Won a Scottish Cup winner's medal in 1996/97 with Kilmarnock. 40 appearances in 2000-1 but injured for part of the next two seasons. Scored a classic goal in the Scottish Cup victory against Hearts in January 2002 – voted the 'goal of the day' on BBC Sportscene. To Queen of the South at the end of 2002-3.

76. Roy McBain (From 2000-1)
Defender/midfield – born Aberdeen 7.11.74 – debut 8.8.00.
166 appearances (132 league, 34 cup). 9 goals (8 league, 1 cup).
Came to the club after four seasons with local rivals Ross County. Formerly with Dundee. His stirring forward runs and 100% effort have made him very popular with the fans. Players' Player of the Year and Supporters' Club Player of the Year 2001-2. Bell's Cup winner's medal 2003. First Division Championship medal 2003-4.

77. Ally Ridgers (1999-2000 to 2003-4)
Goalkeeper – born Inverness 30.6.82 – 48 sub appearances but not used.
Progressed through the club's youth system to the first team squad. Loan to Strathspey Thistle for part of 2000-1 and loan to Forres for part of 2001-2. From 2002-3 vied with Mike Fraser for the goalkeeping spot on the bench. The form of Mark Brown halted progress and he left for Clach in January 2004.

78. Stuart McCaffrey (From 2000-1)
Defender – born Glasgow 30.5.79 – debut 9.9.00.
147 appearances (119 league, 28 cup). 5 goals (4 league, 1 cup).
Came on loan from Aberdeen in September 2000 then signed in December 2000. Formerly with Hibernian and Duntocher Boys' Club. Very solid defender who never lets the side down and whose timely

PLAYER PROFILES

tackles have saved the day on many occasions. Supporters' Club Player of the Year 2000-1. Supporters' Player of the Year 2001-2. Bell's Cup winner's medal 2003. Joint Matchday Programme Player of the Year 2003-4. First Division Championship medal 2003-4.

79. Bryan Gilfillan (2000-1 to 2002-3)
Defender/midfield – born Kirkcaldy 14.9.84 – debut 24.8.02, last game 21.9.02.
2 league appearances. Former 'S' form signing who made two league appearances from the bench. To Cowdenbeath July 2003 and Gretna August 2004.

80. Tony Low (2000-1 to 2003-4)
Midfield/forward – born Glasgow 18.8.83 – debut 6.8.02.
19 appearances (16 league, 3 cup). 1 league goal.
Progressed through from the ICT youth system to the fringes of the first team. Loan to Brora for part of 2001-2. Loan to Albion Rovers January 2004. To Clach July 2004.

81. David Graham (2000-1)
Forward – born Edinburgh 6.10.78 – debut 13.1.01, last game 17.2.01.
4 appearances (2 league, 2 cup). Loan from Dunfermline. All appearances from the bench. To Torquay United later in 2000-1. £215,000 transfer to Wigan June 2004.

82. Paul Bradshaw (2001-2)
Defender/Midfield – born Inverness 25.9.79 – debut 4.8.01, last game 14.8.01.
4 appearances (2 league, 2 cup). Formerly Ross County and Brora Rangers. Never settled at the club and left to join Forres Mechanics in September 2001.

83. Paul Ritchie (2001-2 to 2003-4)
Forward – born St Andrews 25.1.69 – debut 4.8.01, last game 15.5.04.
132 appearances (103 league, 29 cup). 63 goals (46 league, 17 cup).
Prolific goalscorer over three seasons. Formerly with Dundee, Hamilton, Brechin, Happy Valley (Hong Kong), Yee Hope (Hong Kong) and Derry City. Bell's Player of the Month April 2003 and April 2004. Six hat-tricks including four in 2002-3. Bell's Cup winner's medal 2003. Nominated for SPFA First Division Player of the Year 2003-4. Bell's Player of the Year 2003-4. First Division Championship medal 2003-4. Reverted to part-time with Brechin City at the end of 2003-4 to concentrate on a career in accountancy.

84. Russell Duncan (From 2001-2)
Midfield – born Aberdeen 15.9.80 – debut 4.8.01.
116 appearances (90 league, 26 cup). 2 league goals.
From Aberdeen in the summer of 2001. Midfield player formerly of Hall Russells and Forfar. First played at Caledonian Stadium 6 March 1997 as captain of the Scottish Under-16 team which beat England 5-1. Has developed into a vital member of the team with his stylish play and accurate passing. Bell's Cup winner's medal 2003. First Division Championship medal 2003-4.

85. Nicky Walker (2001-2)
Goalkeeper – born Aberdeen 29.9.62 – debut 25.8.01, last game 13.4.02.
34 appearances (27 league, 7 cup). 6 shut-outs and 4 penalty saves in shoot-outs.
Much-travelled Scottish internationalist who started his career with

the Caledonian youth team and came to ICT from Ross County. Former clubs – Aberdeen, Partick, Dunfermline, Hearts, Rangers, Leicester and Elgin. First choice for most of 2001-2 then retired.

86. David MacRae (From 2001-2)
Midfield – born Drumnadrochit 25.10.84 – debut 10.1.04.
3 appearances (2 league, 1 cup). Product of the ICT youth set-up. Part of the first team squad in 2003-4. First Division Championship medal 2003-4. Loan to Nairn County July 2004.

87. Niall Calder (2001-2 to 2002-3)
Midfield – born Inverness 3.9.84 - One bench appearance.
Former 'S' form. Scotland Under-16 international player 2000-1. To Ross County March 2003 and later to Brora.

88. Richie Hart (From 2002-3)
Midfield – born Inverness 30.3.78 – debut 3.8.02.
64 appearances (51 league, 13 cup). 12 goals (9 league, 3 cup).
From Ross County via Brora Rangers. Outstanding midfield player and has won many Man of the Match awards. Matchday Programme Player of the Year 2002-3. Bell's Cup winner's medal 2003. Injury restricted appearances in 2003-4. First Division Championship medal 2003-4.

89. Liam Keogh (From 2002-3)
Forward – born Aberdeen 6.9.81 – debut 3.8.02.
64 appearances (53 league, 11 cup). 3 league goals.
Former Celtic youth player – loan periods from Celtic at Forfar and St Mirren. Most appearances in 2002-3 were from the bench but played regularly in 2003-4. Bell's Cup winner's medal 2003. Internet Player of the Year 2003-4. First Division Championship medal 2003-4.

90. Mark Brown (From 2002-3)
Goalkeeper – born Motherwell 28.2.81 – debut 3.8.02.
91 appearances (72 league, 19 cup). 35 shut-outs and 1 penalty save.
Former Rangers goalkeeper who left Motherwell in the summer of 2002 as a result of the club's financial difficulties. Ever-present 2002-3 and 2003-4. Player of Round 5 in the Scottish Cup March 2003. First played at Caledonian Stadium in the Scotland Under-15 team against Wales on 20 March 1997. Fine young goalkeeper with an ever-growing reputation. Bell's Cup winner's medal 2003. Bell's Player of the Month April 2003. Supporters'& Players' Player of the Year 2003-4. Joint Matchday Programme Player of the Year 2003-4. First Division Championship medal 2003-4.

91. Chris Miller (2002-3)
Midfield – born Paisley 19.11.82 - debut/last game 31.8.02. 1 league appearance.
Signed from Barnsley in August 2002. Left for East Fife in January 2003.

92. Mike Fraser (From 2002-3)
Goalkeeper – born Inverness 8.10.83 - 57 sub appearances but not used.
Progressed through to the first team squad from the club's youth system. From 2002-3 he competed with Ally Ridgers for the goalkeeping bench spot. Mark Brown's form prevented a first-team appearance. Bell's Cup winner's medal 2003. First Division Championship medal 2003-4.

93. Steve Hislop (From 2002-3)
Forward – born Edinburgh 14.6.78 – debut 8.2.03.
48 appearances (40 league, 8 cup). 16 goals (11 league, 5 cup).

Signed in the January 2003 transfer window from Ross County. Striker who formerly played for East Stirling. Goal in 56 seconds against Brechin 29 November 2003. Broke through into the starting eleven in 2003-4 but appearances restricted by a knee injury. Bell's Cup winner's medal 2003. First Division Championship medal 2003-4.

94. David Bingham (2003-4)
Forward – born Dunfermline 3.9.70 – debut 2.8.03, last game 15.5.04.
42 appearances (33 league, 9 cup). 17 goals (13 league, 4 cup).
Prolific goalscorer throughout a long career with Livingston, Dunfermline, Forfar Athletic and St Johnstone. Signed in June 2003 to replace Dennis Wyness and proved to be an excellent goalscorer and provider. Goal in 29 seconds at Forfar 26 July 2003. Nominated for SPFA First Division Player of the Year 2003-4. Bell's Cup winner's medal 2003. First Division Championship medal 2003-4. To Gretna June 2004.

95. Darran Thomson (From 2003-4)
Midfield – born Edinburgh 31.1.84 – debut 2.8.03.
32 appearances (21 league appearances, 11 cup). 2 goals (1 league, 1 cup).
Signed in summer 2003 from Hibs. Bell's Cup winner's medal 2003. Scored a dramatic late winner against St Mirren in the fourth round of the Scottish Cup on 7 February 2004. First Division Championship medal 2003-4.

96. David Proctor (From 2003-4)
Midfield/forward – born East Kilbride 4.5.84 – debut 2.8.03.

18 appearances (11 league, 7 cup).
Signed in summer 2003 from Hibs. After a good start he was sidelined with a shoulder injury for an extended period but came back into the first team squad in March 2004. First Division Championship medal 2003-4.

97. Lewis MacKinnon (From 2003-4)
Forward/defender – born Inverness 11.7.83 – debut 14.2.04.
1 league appearance. ICT youth player who had a spell with Dufftown Juniors. Loan to Nairn County July 2004.

98. Craig MacMillan (From 2003-4)
Forward – born Inverness 25.6.84 – debut 18.10.03.
11 appearances (10 league, 1 cup).
Highly-rated ICT youth player who had a spell at Clachnacuddin. Part of first team squad 2003-4. First Division Championship medal 2003-4.

99. Darren Mackie (2003-4)
Forward – born Inverurie 5.1.82 – debut 10.1.04, last game 24.4.04.
8 appearances (6 league, 2 cup).
Came on loan from Aberdeen in January 2004. Bright start but hospitalised with an appendicitis on 7 February 2004 just before St Mirren cup tie. Returned to the squad in April 2004 but loan period cut short by a further injury.

100. Jonathon Smith (From 2003-4)
Goalkeeper - born Inverness 26.11.87 – 1 squad appearance.
Bench appearance on 20 March 2004 at Ayr.

APPENDIX J

20 May 1993	Inverness and Nairn Enterprise announce the start of talks with Clach, Thistle and Caledonian regarding a possible merger
27 May 1993	Scottish League AGM vote to add two clubs and expand to four leagues of ten
12 August 1993	Clach withdraw from merger discussions
9 September 1993	Agreement reached by Caledonian and Thistle on submission to Scottish League
1 October 1993	Closing date for applications to join the Scottish League
30 November 1993	Potential sites for stadium identified – Stratton Farm, West Seafield, Inshes and East Longman
13 December 1993	Peace between rival factions of Caledonian and Thistle supporters brokered by INE chairman Norman Cordiner
16 December 1993	Caledonian Thistle presentation to Scottish League
12 January 1994	Caledonian Thistle (68 votes) and Ross County (57 votes) elected to the league
24 February 1994	First Caledonian Thistle board meeting in Balnain House
24 February 1994	John 'Jock' McDonald elected chairman by the Board
10 March 1994	Sergei Baltacha appointed manager
11 May 1994	Highland League match at Telford Street – Caledonian 1 Thistle 0 Final Caledonian/Thistle local derby match
14 May 1994	Last Caledonian and Inverness Thistle matches in Highland League
	Huntly 1 Caledonian 1 and Thistle 0 Lossiemouth 2
1 June 1994	Start of trading by Inverness Thistle and Caledonian FC Ltd.
9 June 1994	Inverness District Council's Policy and Resources Committee invite the club to consider the let of 9 to 10 acres at East Longman for the new stadium
7 July 1994	Inverness Thistle Special General Meeting concerning terms of merger
20 July 1994	First Caledonian Thistle match – friendly at RAF Kinloss (2-0)
27 July 1994	Inverness District Council approve lease of Longman site in principle
30 July 1994	First official game – 3-0 defeat by St Mirren at Telford Street
9 August 1994	First competitive match Coca-Cola Cup Round 1 against East Stirling at Firs Park (2-0)
11 August 1994	Inverness Thistle Special General Meeting concerning terms of merger

MILESTONES

13 August 1994	Scottish League debut – Division 3 match against Arbroath at Telford Street (5-2)
27 August 1994	First league derby match against Ross County (3-1 at Victoria Park, Dingwall)
28 September 1994	Debut in B&Q Cup at home against Dundee (lost on penalties)
7 November 1994	Secretary Scott Byrnes announces his resignation, replaced by Jim Falconer
1 December 1994	Caledonian members' meeting and vote regarding asset transfer
8 December 1994	Thistle members' meeting and vote regarding asset transfer
17 December 1994	Debut in Tennent's Scottish Cup at home to Queen of the South (lose 2-1)
28 March 1995	Hearing by Sheriff James Fraser regarding interdict preventing transfer of Thistle's assets
3 May 1995	Sergei Baltacha announces resignation as player/manager
4 May 1995	Decision by Sheriff James Fraser in favour of Thistle Committee allowing transfer of Thistle's assets to the unified club
13 May 1995	Sergei Baltacha's last game in charge (1-1 at home to Queen's Park)
24 May 1995	Steve 'Pele' Paterson appointed manager
24 May 1995	Highland Regional Council planning committee approve new stadium
29 May 1995	Dougie McGilvray succeeds Jock McDonald as chairman
9 June 1995	Alex Caldwell appointed assistant manager
29 June 1995	First AGM of Members' Club
30 July 1995	Stand at Kingsmills Park destroyed by fire
5 August 1995	Steve Paterson's first competitive game, Coca-Cola Cup first-round tie away to Berwick Rangers (lose on penalties)
18 August 1995	SFA Tribunal awards £30000 to Lossiemouth for transfer of Iain Stewart
3 October 1995	First ceremonial turf cut for new stadium by Provost William Fraser
9 December 1995	Beat Ross County 5-2 to win the Inverness Cup (Grant Street Park)
18 December 1995	Inverness District Council agreement to pay £900,000 towards stadium, subject to Objective One and INE funding being payable
20 January 1996	Mark McAllister is first player to make 50 appearances (5-1 away to East Stirling)
23 January 1996	Stadium contract awarded to McGregor Construction with infrastructure by Morrison Construction.
15 February 1996	EGM of Members' Club approves change of name to incorporate 'Inverness'.
9 March 1996	Quarter final of Tennent's Scottish Cup, CT 0 Rangers 3 (home match switched to Tannadice by SFA)
1 April 1996	Members of Highland Council (at their first ever meeting) agree to honour former Council's commitment to pay £900,000 towards stadium and infrastructure costs
1 June 1996	Bruce Graham becomes the club's first general manager
30 July 1996	Meeting to form Official Supporters' Club
1 August 1996	Danny MacDonald becomes full time community and development Officer
3 August 1996	First competitive match as Inverness Caledonian Thistle (0-1 away to Clyde)
12 August 1996	Ann Nicoll appointed to chair the Supporters' Club
16 September 1996	Share issue launched
5 October 1996	Last competitive game at Telford Street – league game against Arbroath (2-0)
20 October 1996	Last game at Telford Street – against Highland League Select (0-3)
21 October 1996	Demolition of Telford Street Park started
6 November 1996	First game at Caledonian Stadium – against Inverness & District Select (6-2)
9 November 1996	Official opening & first competitive match at Caledonian Stadium, league game against Albion Rovers (1-1)
9 November 1996	Close of share issue – £564,370 raised
11 March 1997	Mike Noble is first player to make 100 appearances (2-0 away to Alloa)
15 March 1997	Third Division record league crowd 5525 at home derby match (3-0)
5 April 1997	Promotion to Second Division achieved – home 3-2 win against Montrose
12 April 1997	Third Division championship secured – home 4-1 win against Albion Rovers
3 May 1997	Presentation of Third Division trophy
3 May 1997	Steve Paterson confirmed as having accepted a four-year, full-time contract
6 May 1997	Richard Hastings is first player to go full time
4 June 1997	John Docherty appointed reserve team coach
1 July 1997	Pre-season training starts for first season as full-time team
2 August 1997	Highland Council Civic Reception for winning of Third Division championship
6 August 1997	Debut in Second Division (1-1 at home to Livingston)
23 August 1997	Publication of Charles Bannerman's book - Against All Odds – the Birth of Inverness Caledonian Thistle F.C.
14 October 1997	1996/97 Inverness Cup won – Ross County defeated 2-0 at home
6 January 1998	Beat Clach 2-1 in final of Inverness Cup (Caledonian Stadium)
24 January 1998	Scottish Cup round 3 match at home against Annan Athletic – record 8-1 win
14 February 1998	Scottish Cup round 4 match – draw 1-1 away to Dundee United
18 February 1998	Scottish Cup replay against Dundee United – narrowly lose 3-2 after extra time
31 March 1998	General manager Bruce Graham resigns
9 May 1998	Reserve side clinches North Caledonian League championship (3-0 at Golspie)
13 March 1999	Charlie Christie is first player to make 150 appearances (4-0 home to East Fife)
26 March 1999	Ross County beaten 1-0 in final of Inverness Cup (Caledonian Stadium)

3 April 1999	Promotion to First Division secured (3-0 home win against Clyde)
1 May 1999	Championship decider away to Livingston – narrow 4-3 loss in classic match
7 August 1999	Debut in First Division (lose 4-0 away to Dunfermline)
12 September 1999	Win North Cup at Forres – beat Lossiemouth 3-0
21 November 1999	Bell's Challenge Cup final at Airdrie – lose to Alloa after extra time and penalties
24 November 1999	Beat Forres Mechanics 6-0 in final of Inverness Cup (at Forres)
27 December 1999	Barry Wilson scores the last Scottish League or Cup goal of the 1900s 87th minute goal on Monday 27 December against Clydebank (3.30pm kick off).
3 January 2000	Barry Wilson scores the first Scottish League or Cup goal of the 2000s 72nd minute goal against Livingston on 3 January 2000 (1pm kick off)
10 January 2000	David Sutherland takes over as chairman
29 January 2000	Scottish Cup third-round tie at Celtic Park postponed due to stand damage
8 February 2000	SuperCaleyGoBallistic – Celtic beaten 3-1 in Round 3 of Scottish Cup at Celtic Park
15 February 2000	Duncan Shearer takes over as assistant manager to replace Alex Caldwell
20 February 2000	Scottish Cup Round 4 match at home against Aberdeen live on Sky TV (1-1)
29 February 2000	Scottish Cup Round 4 replay at Aberdeen – lost 1-0
4 March 2000	Lowest crowd – 168 at league match against Clydebank at Cappielow, Greenock
15 August 2000	Charlie Christie is first player to make 200 appearances (3-2 away to Alloa)
2 December 2000	Record 7-3 home league win against Ayr United
17 February 2001	Scottish Cup Round 4 match at home against Kilmarnock – drew 1-1
28 February 2001	Scottish Cup replay at Kilmarnock abandoned after 27 minutes – frozen pitch
6 March 2001	Kilmarnock Scottish Cup replay finally completed – lose 2-1
22 September 2001	Highest league defeat – 6-0 at Airdrie
9 October 2001	CIS Cup Round 3 tie at Dunfermline – win 4-1 on penalties after 1-1 draw
9 October 2001	Charlie Christie is first player to make 250 appearances (at Dunfermline)
11 December 2001	Ross County beaten 3-2 in final of Inverness Cup (Caledonian Stadium)
12 January 2002	Opening of Kevin Bisset enclosure (5-0 against Raith Rovers)
26 January 2002	Scottish Cup Round 4 match away to Hearts – win 3-1
23 February 2002	Scottish Cup quarter-final tie away to Partick Thistle – draw 2-2
5 March 2002	Scottish Cup quarter-final replay at home to Partick Thistle – lose 1-0
17 May 2002	New chairman Ken Mackie takes office
19 October 2002	Highest league win – 6-0 at Alloa
23 October 2002	CIS Insurance Cup Round 3 match away to Celtic – lose 4-2 Record away crowd - 34592
9 November 2002	Barry Robson scores fastest competitive goal – 40 secs at home v Ross County
7 December 2002	Steve Paterson and Duncan Shearer's last game in charge – 3-3 draw at Ayr
11 December 2002	Steve Paterson and Duncan Shearer resign to join Aberdeen
26 December 2002	John Robertson appointed manager
28 December 2002	John Robertson's first game in charge – away to St Mirren in league (won 4-1)
3 January 2003	Donald Park named head coach
15 February 2003	Charlie Christie is first player to make 300 appearances (0-2 at St Johnstone)
23 March 2003	Scottish Cup quarter final home win against Celtic (1-0)
20 April 2003	Scottish Cup semi-final at Hampden (lose 1-0 to Dundee)
26 July 2003	David Bingham scores fastest goal for the club – 29 seconds in friendly at Forfar
26 October 2003	Bell's Cup Final victory over Airdrie United (2-0 at McDiarmid Park, Perth)
10 April 2004	Scottish Cup semi-final at Hampden (1-1 draw with Dunfermline)
20 April 2004	Scottish Cup semi-final replay at Pittodrie (lose 3-2 to Dunfermline)
8 May 2004	2-1 away win against Clyde in the league sets up a dramatic finale to the season
15 May 2004	Final game of the season and the first decade. 3-1 win at home to St Johnstone clinches the First Division championship
27 May 2004	Groundshare agreement reached with Aberdeen
28 May 2004	Groundshare details submitted to SPL
1 June 2004	SPL members vote 7-3 (2 abstentions) to refuse ICT promotion – ICT appeal
7 June 2004	SPL agree to hold second ballot after Hibs/Hearts proposal
16 June 2004	Highland Council Budget Working Group agrees to lend £400,000 towards ground improvements – Tulloch to invest £400,000 and ICT £200,000
22 June 2004	ICT admitted to SPL after second ballot – this time 10-2 in favour
24 June 2004	SPL fixture list issued with ICT included. Partick Thistle announce intention to appeal against 22 June decision
29 June 2004	Partick Thistle appeal lodged with SFA
8 July 2004	SFA Appeals Committee rejects Partick's appeal
9 July 2004	SPL admission ensured after Partick decide against further legal action

APPENDIX K
TROPHIES, ACHIEVEMENTS AND AWARDS

TEAM TROPHIES AND ACHIEVEMENTS
Scottish Football League Division 1 Championship and promotion to SPL – 2003-4
Scottish Football League Division 3 Championship and promotion to Division 2 – 1996-7
Scottish Cup Semi-Finalists – 2002-3 and 2003-4
Promotion to Division 1 – 1998-9
Bell's Cup Winners – 2003-4
Bell's Challenge Cup runners up – 1999-2000
Inverness Courier Challenge Cup winners – 1994-5, 1995-6
Inverness Cup winners – 1995-6, 1996-7, 1997-8, 1998-9, 1999-2000, 2001-2
North Cup winners – 1999-2000
North Caledonian League Championship – 1994-5, 1997-8
Football Times Cup winners – 1998-9
Chic Allan Cup winners – 1994-5, 1998-9
PCT Cup winners – 1998-9
Tennent's Scottish Cup Team of the Round – Third Round v Celtic, February 2000

BELL'S FIRST DIVISION PLAYER OF THE MONTH
December 2000 – Dennis Wyness
February 2002 – Dennis Wyness
September 2002 – Dennis Wyness
October 2002 – Dennis Wyness
November 2002 – Barry Robson
April 2003 – Paul Ritchie
September 2003 – Mark Brown

BELL'S PLAYER OF THE YEAR
2003-4 – Paul Ritchie

SCOTTISH PROFESSIONAL FOOTBALLERS' PLAYER OF THE YEAR
Division 3, 1996-7 – Iain Stewart
Division 1, 2002-3 – Dennis Wyness

TENNENT'S SCOTTISH CUP PLAYER OF THE ROUND
Third Round – January 2001 – Paul Sheerin
Fifth Round – March 2003 – Mark Brown

BELL'S MANAGER AWARDS
Sergei Baltacha, Manager of the Month – September 1994
Steve Paterson , Manager of the Month – October 1995, January 1996, February 1996, November 1996, December 1996, February 1997, February 1998, September 1999, October 1999, December 2000, January 2001, January 2002, September 2002, October 2002, November 2002
Steve Paterson, SFL Third Division Manager of the Year – 1996-7
John Robertson, Manager of the Month – September 2003, December 2003, April 2004
John Robertson, SFL First Division Manager of the Year – 2003-4

APPENDIX L
RECORD APPEARANCES AND GOALS

TOP APPEARANCES:

314 – Charlie Christie
283 – Ross Tokely
221 – Mike Teasdale
218 – Richard Hastings
214 – Bobby Mann
195 – Jim Calder
190 – Barry Wilson
167 – Barry Robson
166 – Stuart Golabek and Roy McBain
159 – Dennis Wyness

TOP GOALSCORERS:

82 – Iain Stewart
80 – Dennis Wyness
63 – Paul Ritchie
59 – Barry Wilson
45 – Paul Sheerin
35 – Scott McLean
34 – Brian Thomson
34 – Charlie Christie
27 – Barry Robson
23 – Alan Hercher

APPEARANCE MILESTONES

50 – Mark McAllister v East Stirling 20.1.96
100 – Mike Noble v Alloa 11.3.97
150 – Charlie Christie v East Fife 13.3.99
200 – Charlie Christie v Alloa 15.8.00
250 – Charlie Christie v Dunfermline 9.10.01
300 – Charlie Christie v St Johnstone 15.2.03

MOST APPEARANCES BY SEASON

1994-5:	39 – Mark McAllister (max 40)	
1995-6:	43 – Mike Noble (max 43)	
1996-7:	42 – Mike Teasdale and Iain Stewart (max 42)	
1997-8:	43 – Richard Hastings (max 44)	
1998-9:	39 – Mike Teasdale, Barry Wilson and Paul Sheerin (max 39)	
19992000:	46 – Mark McCulloch (max 47)	
2000-1:	42 – Charlie Christie (max 43)	
2001-2:	46 – Dennis Wyness (max 46)	
2002-3:	44 – Mark Brown and Dennis Wyness (max 44)	
2003-4:	47 – Mark Brown (max 47)	

MOST GOALS BY SEASON

1994-5:	7 – Alan Hercher	
1995-6:	24 – Iain Stewart	
1996-7:	29 – Iain Stewart	
1997-8:	20 – Iain Stewart & Brian Thomson	
1998-9:	20 – Scott McLean	
1999-2000:	17 – Paul Sheerin	
2000-1:	26 – Dennis Wyness	
2001-2:	22 – Dennis Wyness	
2002-3:	27 – Dennis Wyness	
2003-4:	23 – Paul Ritchie	

CONSECUTIVE APPEARANCES

119 – Dennis Wyness (21.10.00 to 10.5.03)

MOST GOALS IN ONE MATCH

4 – Dennis Wyness - League v Raith Rovers (Home) 19.9.01

FASTEST GOAL FOR

29 seconds – David Bingham, Friendly v Forfar Athletic (Away) 26.7.03
40 seconds – Barry Robson, League v Ross County (Away) 9.11.02

FASTEST GOAL AGAINST

16 seconds – Steve McConologue (Clyde), League v Clyde (away) 18.3.03

FASTEST HAT-TRICK

Alan Hercher , League v Arbroath (Home) 13.8.94 (13, 31 & 33 mins)

APPENDIX M
FACTS AND STATISTICS

CHAIRMEN
1994-5 – John McDonald; 1995-6 to January 2000 – Dugald McGilvray; Jan 2000 to April 2002 – David Sutherland; from May 2002 – Ken Mackie.

CAPTAINS
1994-5 – Alan Hercher; 1995-6 & 1996-7 – Mike Noble; 1997-8 – Paul Cherry and Iain MacArthur; 1998-9 and 1999-2000 – Mark McCulloch; 2000-1 to 2003-4 – Bobby Mann.

YOUNGEST PLAYER
17 years 94 days – Richard Hastings v Queen's Park, 20.8.94.

OLDEST PLAYER
41 years 272 days – Jim Calder v Partick, 27.4.02.

RECORD SCORES AND GOALS
Highest League Win (Home):	5-0 v St Mirren, 6.5.00 (plus three others and one 6-1)
Highest League Win (Away):	6-0 v Alloa ,19.10.02
Highest League Defeat (Home):	0-4 v Queen's Park, 20.8.94 (plus three others and two 1-5)
Highest League Defeat (Away):	0-6 v Airdrie, 22.9.01
Highest Cup Win (Home):	8-1 v Annan Athletic, 24.1.98
Highest Cup Win (Away):	3-0 v Hamilton, 24.8.99
Highest Cup Defeat (Home):	0-3 v Rangers, 9.3.96 (Tannadice) & 0-3 v Aberdeen 8.8.98
Highest Cup Defeat (Away):	1-5 v Ayr United, 28.11.01
Most League Goals For:	7 v Ayr United, 2.12.00 (home)
Most League Goals Against:	6 v Airdrie,22.9.01 (away)
Most Cup Goals For:	8 v Annan, 24.1.98 (home)
Most Cup Goals Against:	5 v Ayr, 28.11.01 (away)
Highest Aggregate Goals:	7-3 v Ayr United, 2.12.00 (League, home)

RECORD CROWDS
Largest Crowd – Home League Match:	6092 v St Johnstone, 15.5.04
Largest Crowd – Away League Match:	7300 v Falkirk, 10.5.03 (Brockville's last match)
Largest Crowd – Home Cup Match:	6290 v Aberdeen, 20.2.00 (Tennent's Scottish Cup), (11296 v Rangers, 9.3.96, Home Tennent's Scottish Cup match played at Tannadice)
Largest Crowd – Away Cup Match:	34389 v Celtic, 08.02.00 (Scottish Cup, Celtic Park)
Smallest Crowd – Home League Match:	491 v Albion Rovers, 11.4.95 (Telford Street)
Smallest Crowd – Away League Match:	168 v Clydebank, 4.3.00 (Cappielow, Greenock)
Smallest Crowd – Home Cup Match:	635 v Clydebank, 14.9.99 (Bell's Challenge Cup)
Smallest Crowd – Away Cup Match:	298 v Hamilton, 24.8.99 (Bell's Challenge Cup, Firhill)

MANAGERS' RECORDS

Sergei Baltacha (10 March 1994 to 13 May 1995)
League record -	played 36, won 12, drew 9, lost 15 (goals for 48, goals against 61)
Cup record -	played 4, won 1, lost 3 (goals for 4, goals against 6)
All matches -	played 40, won 13, drew 9, lost 18 (goals for 52, goals against 67)

Steve Paterson (24 May 1995 to 11 December 2002)
League record -	played 269, won 124, drew 71, lost 74 (goals for 512, goals against 350)
Cup record -	played 56, won 28, drew 6, lost 22 (goals for 100, against 83)
All matches -	played 325, won 152, drew 77, lost 96 (goals for 612, against 433)

Graeme Bennett (interim manager 14 and 21 December 2002)
League matches only -	played 2, drew 2 (goals for 2, goals against 2)

John Robertson (26 December 2002 to 15 May 2004)
League record -	played 53, won 29, drew 8, lost 16 (goals for 97, against 60)
Cup record -	played 15, won 11, drew 1, lost 3 (goals for 34, against 10)
All matches -	played 68, won 40, drew 9, lost 19 (goals for 131, against 70)

*Page references in **bold type** refer to photographs. All names beginning with 'Mc' or 'Mac' are filed together as if spelt 'Mac', so 'McRitchie' precedes 'Madej'. Names beginning with 'St' are filed as if spelt 'Saint', so 'St Mirren' precedes 'Scott'.*